DECISIONS AT
SHILOH

OTHER BOOKS IN THE COMMAND DECISIONS IN AMERICA'S CIVIL WAR SERIES

DECISIONS
AT
SHILOH

The Twenty-Two Critical Decisions
That Defined the Battle

Dave Powell
Maps by David Friedrichs

COMMAND DECISIONS
IN AMERICA'S CIVIL WAR
Matt Spruill and Larry Peterson,
Series Editors

The University of Tennessee Press / Knoxville

Library of Congress Cataloging-in-Publication Data

Names: Powell, David A. (David Alan), 1961- author. |
Friedrichs, David A., contributor.

Title: Decisions at Shiloh : the twenty-two critical decisions that defined
the battle / Dave Powell ; maps by David Friedrichs.

Description: Knoxville : The University of Tennessee Press, [2023] | Series:
Command decisions in America's Civil War | Includes bibliographical refer-
ences and index. | Summary: "The Battle of Shiloh took place April 6–7, 1862,
between the Union Army of the Tennessee under General Ulysses S. Grant
and the Confederate Army of Mississippi under General Albert Sidney Johnston. Johnston launched a surprise attack on Grant but was mortally wounded
during the battle. General Beauregard, taking over command, chose not to
press the attack through the night, and Grant, reinforced with troops from the
Army of the Ohio, counterattacked the morning of April 7th and turned the
tide of the battle. Intended for a general readership, *Decisions at Shiloh* intro-
duces readers to critical decisions made by Federal and Confederate commanders who attempted to achieve strategic and tactical victories under considerable
duress. Like previous volumes in this series, this book contains maps, photo-
graphs, and a guided tour of the battlefield"—Provided by publisher.

Identifiers: LCCN 2022042501 (print) | LCCN 2022042502 (ebook) |
ISBN 9781621907527 (paperback) | ISBN 9781621907534 (Kindle edition) |
ISBN 9781621907541 (pdf)

Subjects: LCSH: Shiloh, Battle of, Tenn., 1862. | Command of troops—
Case studies.

Classification: LCC E473.54 .P694 2023 (print) | LCC E473.54 (ebook) |
DDC 973.7/31—dc23/eng/20220913

LC record available at https://lccn.loc.gov/2022042501
LC ebook record available at https://lccn.loc.gov/2022042502

CONTENTS

ILLUSTRATIONS

Photographs

Maps

PREFACE

Is the study of military affairs a science or an art? College and university cata-logues all over the United States list the courses they provide students within the framework of their R.O.T.C. program (Reserve officer Training Corps—the source of up to a third of all active-duty military officers in the American armed forces) as classes in Military Science. Conversely, we have texts both ancient and modern that offer a different interpretation: as evidenced by Sun Tzu's famous classic treatise, *The Art of War*. War as science implies a set of certainties than can be learned, like formulae, used as a civil engineer might use math to calculate the carrying capacity of a bridge. War as art implies the "application of human creative skill and imagination," as the Oxford English dictionary phrases it.

Of course, mastering warfare requires both skill sets. Much about war can be quantified. Indeed, it must be quantified, or chaos will result. Moving, feeding, arming, orchestrating, and coordinating many thousands of men onto a battlefield requires men of science: mathematicians and engineers. Much else of war, however, cannot be reduced to numbers. Both sides seek to conceal their plans and intentions from the other, meaning that critical variables will not be known when battle looms. Some of what is known will be turn out to be false, mistakenly interpreted or deceits actively sown by one's opponent to strew confusion. This means that no military decision can ever be made without some risk, some leap of intuition that transcends the known facts and moves into the murky world of probabilities and likelihoods.

It also means that sometimes the decision-maker will make the wrong guess, or follow the wrong assumption.

Decisions have consequences. No soldier spends much time in uniform without learning that lesson, in combat most quickly of all. The burden of command lies in making those decisions, even in the face of incomplete information, and even at the expense of lives. An author who writes military history soon comes to understand this hard lesson as well, if only by association, as we delve into the letters and diaries of so many young men whose lives are cut short by those decisions. Many volumes are written each year devoted to analyzing decisions and their repercussions. Field training exercises and terrain walks seek to achieve similar results.

In 1906, Major Eben Swift imported the concept of the staff ride to the United States, when he led a contingent of twelve officers from the General Service and Staff School to the newly preserved and well-monumented battlefield of Chickamauga. The concept originated in Prussia, under the fabled chief of the German General Staff, Helmut Von Moltke, and used as a training tool by armies all over the world. The purpose of the staff ride is to impart what "German military theorist Karl von Clausewitz in *On War* defined as critical analysis: determine the facts, establish cause and effect, and analyze the results."[1] In short, they explore both the reasons underlying and effects of military decision-making. Staff rides are different from battlefield tours, because they involve the audience in the process of examining those decisions. Nor are staff rides useful only for the military. Many of the leadership lessons found in the staff ride process are also applicable in civilian fields of endeavor.

My study of the Civil War began while I was in high school, as I became fascinated with military history in general. That interest intensified and became more specific to our sectional conflict when I attended the Virginia Military Institute, graduating with a history degree in 1983. While at V.M.I., I had ample opportunity to study the battlefields of Virginia, Maryland, and Pennsylvania. My reading also focused on the eastern theater.

My connection with Shiloh began in 1979, when I visited the park one spring weekend of my senior year in high school. Four of us drove down from suburban Chicago on a lark, just looking for a road trip. I was already interested in military history and headed to V.M.I. the next fall; a trip to a battlefield seemed like just the thing.

College furthered my interest in the Civil War. As I have noted elsewhere, I played historical boardgames, including titles on the battles of Gettysburg and Shiloh; I also became involved with the hobby of Civil War reenacting, spending many weekends portraying Civil War soldiers in living history encampments and at battle reenactments. Since V.M.I. was so closely aligned with the Civil War Battlefield of New Market, Virginia—where V.M.I.'s corps of cadets were engaged in the real thing in 1864—I became very familiar with that engagement. I was also deeply interested in the battles of Gettysburg and Chickamauga. I visited Shiloh a couple more times, including attending the 125th battle reenactment in 1987, but Shiloh was not my primary focus.

My writing career began in 2010, when my first book, *The Maps of Chickamauga,* was published. When I began the map study project, I soon discovered that I did not know near enough about what happened in North Georgia that September of 1863. My first task, then, was to learn all I could. I walked the field many times, alone and with friends, and at least once had the privilege of accompanying Dr. William G. Robertson as he led his Command and General Staff class on a staff ride of Chickamauga. This experience taught me how unique the resource of the battlefield really was: time and again clues of topography made sense of the accounts I read and re-read. To date, I have published five volumes directly concerned with Chickamauga; the map study, a cavalry monograph entitled *Failure in the Saddle: Nathan Bedford Forrest, Joe Wheeler, and the Confederate Cavalry in the Chickamauga Campaign,* and a three-volume narrative entitled: *The Chickamauga Campaign.* The last of these was published in 2016.

With the completion of my work on Chickamauga, I began to think about what came next. One of those potential projects was a book on Shiloh. As I had done with Chickamauga, I began collecting primary sources relating to Shiloh, with the intention of writing somewhere down the road. In the meantime, I returned to the battlefield more often, to study the most significant primary source of them all: the park and its monuments, tablets, and markers. In this journey I was fortunate enough to befriend Dr. Tim Smith, a former ranger at Shiloh, who has his own deep relationship with the field and who has written extensively on the subject. Tim provided invaluable insights and proved to be a tremendous resource in his own right.

As with Chickamauga, deep exposure to the primary sources often uncovered conflicting viewpoints, but also provided a framework for synthesis, a process that often only happened after I walked the pertinent part of the field repeatedly. Again, the physical resource was invaluable. I also fell back on the concept of the staff ride, applying the rigorous scrutiny of Clausewitz's *critical analysis,* which provided yet another unique lens through which to view Shiloh.

This book is not a narrative history of the battle or campaign. Instead, I assume readers will have a basic working knowledge of the course of the events described. Admittedly, that can be a tall order, for Shiloh can also be a very confusing action. It was fought in heavily wooded terrain, with the Federals surprised nearly in their camps early on a Sunday morning. The attacking commander's plans did not survive contact with the enemy: The defending commander cannot be said to have any plans at all prior to the beginning of the fight.

In keeping with previous works in this series, I focus on those decisions that chart the course of the battle. Some of those decisions are strategic in nature, made by the commanders, others are tactical, made in the heat of battle by subordinates far removed from any army command tent. Each of them, however, changed the battle in a critical way. Collectively, they determined the outcome of the historical event we now call the battle of Shiloh.

Winnowing the countless decisions made by the participants down to a subset of those that rise to the standard of being "critical to the outcome" is no simple matter. I have settled on just twenty-two. Discussion of the following twenty-two decisions will follow the same blueprint: I lay out the choices, discuss the information available to the decision-maker at the time, and explore the consequences. I try not to pass judgment on whether a particular decision was good or bad. Instead, I try and focus on the consequences of that choice, and how it affected the battle going forward. Readers hopefully will come to their own conclusions about good and bad, right and wrong. Remember, however, that each decision was made with incomplete information, under intense stress, and often with little time to ponder consequences. The 'art' of military leadership revolves around this most difficult aspect of command, and if you judge, don't judge too harshly.

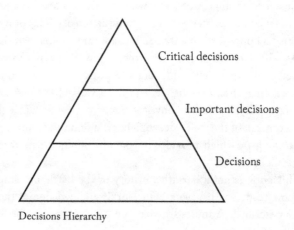

Decisions Hierarchy

Most of all, I hope that this work will spur readers to pursue a greater understanding of Shiloh. It was the conflict's first really large bloodbath, shocking both sides, and it was among the nation's first five national military parks. Shiloh is also among the most pristine of our parks, remote from urban sprawl, and is the most nearly complete of those parks in terms of preserving the field: something like 90% of Shiloh's battleground is preserved. As stated in the enabling legislation, these parks exist "for the purpose of preserving and suitably marking for historical and professional military study the fields of some of the most remarkable maneuvers and most brilliant fighting in the war of the rebellion."

***

I wish to acknowledge and thank the many people who have made this work possible. Firstly, I wish to thank Colonel Matt Spruill for thinking of me for this project, and for his guidance along the way. Secondly, I must thank Tim Smith for his encouragement, his willingness to serve as a sounding board, and for his limitless knowledge of the subject matter. Tim's own contributions to the historiography of Shiloh are foundational; they will be considered important works on the subject for decades to come. Thank you for sharing your time and thoughts with me, Tim.

As ever, archival staffs across the country were helpful in digging out material. Closer to home, the staff of the Algonquin Area Public Library in Illinois provided invaluable help in locating and retrieving many items via interlibrary loan.

Most of all, I wish to thank my wife Anne for her tireless patience and support in all my writing projects. Anne has supported me from day one in pursuing this dream, and is also responsible for introducing me to the world of canine companions. This project has been supervised by our most current cohort of hounds, Cletus, Ellie, and Sassy.

DECISIONS AT
SHILOH

INTRODUCTION

On February 16, 1862, Confederate major general Simon B. Buckner surrendered twelve thousand men to Federal brigadier general Ulysses S. Grant at Fort Donelson, Tennessee, on the Cumberland River. In combination with the surrender of Fort Henry on the Tennessee River, Donelson's capture proved devastating to the Confederacy's defensive scheme in the Western Theater. The previous fall Gen. Albert Sidney Johnston had been given sweeping authority over all Rebel defenses from the Appalachian Mountains to Arkansas and Missouri, and he was tasked with guarding the new nation's exposed northern border. Since Kentucky had opted for neutrality in 1861, Johnston was never able to base his defenses along the Ohio River; instead, he was forced to cover the Tennessee-Kentucky border, roughly three hundred miles in length and bereft of any significant defensible geographical feature.[1]

Subsequent events forced Johnston to move into Kentucky. After one of his subordinates, Maj. Gen. Leonidas Polk, forced his hand by unilaterally occupying the strategic town of Columbus, Kentucky, on the Mississippi River, Johnston scrambled to make the best of a bad situation ordering the forces at Nashville northward. However, the Confederates were only able to occupy Bowling Green. The Federals seized Paducah, Louisville, Frankfort, and Lexington—nearly the whole of the state. Since construction on Forts Henry and Donelson had already commenced, Johnston continued that work despite—in Fort Henry's case—the existence of a much better site farther north. Even worse, Johnston's Department No. 2 lacked troops. At the end of 1861,

Johnston's entire force numbered only about fifty-four thousand present for duty, with an aggregate strength of about sixty-eight thousand. It was not nearly enough manpower to match the growing Federal strength in the region.[2]

No one understood Johnston's weakness better than the general himself. Back on September 16, 1861, Johnston had informed Pres. Jefferson Davis, "We have not half the armed forces that are now likely to be required for our security against disaster." Even though those numbers grew over the following months, they never increased as rapidly as did Federal strength, leaving Johnston to rely instead on bluff and exaggeration to keep the Yankees at bay. His ruse was destined to backfire if put to the test. That test came in February 1862.[3]

In 1861, the Federals were divided into two commands: the Department of the Missouri, led by Maj. Gen. Henry W. Halleck, and the Department of the Ohio, headed by Maj. Gen. Don C. Buell. Both men had graduated from West Point—Halleck in 1839, and Buell in 1841. Now they were rivals leading competing armies. Halleck's duties embraced both defending the state of Missouri, which contained many pro-Confederate citizens, and opening the Mississippi River. Buell was intent on securing Kentucky, which also contained a significant pro-secession minority, and he was also tasked with the capture of Nashville and occupying East Tennessee. This last objective ranked especially high on President Lincoln's list of priorities.[4]

Alone, Buell's Department of the Ohio matched Johnston's entire force. On January 23, 1862, Buell reported that his command numbered nearly forty-four thousand troops "present for duty and fit for the field," as well as another twenty-six thousand "present, [but] raw or not organized." Halleck's soldiers were more widely dispersed, with a large number spread across Missouri. Even so, by February Halleck had forty thousand men positioned to strike south along the Mississippi or, as Grant would soon demonstrate, via the Cumberland and Tennessee Rivers. Moreover, the Union numbers swelled daily as new regiments were organized, outfitted, and shipped south.[5]

When Albert Sidney Johnston took command of Department No. 2 he was well aware of the odds he faced. A capable soldier, Johnston was one of the most experienced officers of the prewar army. He was also a West Pointer, class of 1826; Confederate president Jefferson Davis was two years behind him. In addition, the two had known each other at Transylvania University, which they both attended before enrolling in the US Military Academy. Johnston left the army in 1834 to care for his sick wife. She died in 1836, so he subsequently traveled to Texas to join the revolution against Mexico. He arrived too late for any of the fighting against Santa Anna, but he did rise to become the commander of the Texian Army and, later, the Texas secretary of war.

In 1840 Johnston returned to civilian life, settling back in Kentucky. When the annexation of Texas in 1845 led to war between Mexico and the United States in 1848, Johnston led a regiment of Texas volunteers and reentered the United States Regular Army at the conclusion of the conflict. His most notable commands prior to secession were in leading the Utah Expedition against rebellious Mormons in 1857, and serving as colonel of the Second United States Cavalry. Though the Mormon campaign was resolved peacefully, it still provided him with a fund of invaluable command and logistical experience. When the Civil War broke out, Johnston was in California, and he had to travel cross-country to join this newest revolution. Davis had the utmost faith in his old friend and immediately appointed him to command the forces in the West.[6]

Though Johnston knew he needed more men, the new Confederacy had many competing priorities that year. The main seat of war was in Virginia, where Washington, DC, and the new Confederate capital of Richmond were a mere one hundred miles apart. Fears of Federal incursions along the Confederate seacoast also required substantial garrisons in North Carolina; Charleston, South Carolina; Mobile, Alabama; and New Orleans, Louisiana. Thus, Johnston's pleas for reinforcements went largely unanswered: there were too few available troops for the South to be strong everywhere. The Rebels were also short of weapons. Some regiments were armed with antiquated flintlocks, and other newly mustering units were sent home when no weapons could be had at all. The rush to war created shortages in every category of military equipage.

Johnston at least had unity of command. The Federals, while gaining in strength, remained divided. Though Halleck's primary concern remained Missouri, he was also assembling sufficient forces to defend Cairo, Illinois, at the confluence of the Ohio and Mississippi Rivers; and Paducah, Kentucky, where the Tennessee met the Ohio. Meanwhile, Buell was tasked with advancing on Bowling Green, Nashville, and, eventually, Chattanooga, Tennessee. Control of that last locale would not only grant entry into East Tennessee, but also open the door to the heartland of the Deep South beyond the Appalachian Mountain chain.

If Johnston was the old army's most experienced field officer, Henry Wager Halleck was its leading intellectual. A talented protégé of West Point's most famous professor, Dennis Hart Mahan, Halleck taught at the military academy after graduation, traveled to Europe to study the French military, and published a book in 1846 that became required reading for rising young officers. *Elements of Military Art and Science*, derived from a series of lectures Halleck gave at the Lowell Institute of Boston, was a summation of leading

European military thought of the day. Principally, these ideas came from Antoine-Henri, the Baron Jomini, a famous Napoleonic staff officer and military theorist whose own writings catapulted him into fame across Europe. Halleck drew heavily from Jomini while writing *Elements*, and the American even translated the French officer's monumental four-volume biography of Napoleon Bonaparte into English while on a months-long voyage from New York to California. The translation was eventually published in 1864.[7]

Halleck experienced the conflict with Mexico on the Pacific coast, far from the main theater of war. Nevertheless, his efforts claimed the Mexican provinces of Alta and Baja California for the United States, though Baja California was returned to Mexico at the war's end. With peace, however, Halleck wearied of garrison life and resigned from the military to practice law and pursue business opportunities in the newly formed state of California, then booming with the gold rush. When war came again, however, he was not forgotten; Mahan and General-in-Chief Winfield Scott both believed that Halleck's talents were indispensable, and he was immediately offered a major general's commission. Like A. S. Johnston, Halleck returned east too late to play a leading role in the Eastern Theater and was instead dispatched to St. Louis.[8]

In strategy and temperament, both Buell and Halleck were careful, cautious commanders. Ulysses S. Grant, by contrast, soon demonstrated that he was confident, audacious, and aggressive. Grant took command of the Union post at Cairo, Illinois, in the summer of 1861. He quickly occupied Paducah that September, immediately after Leonidas Polk's rash seizure of Columbus. In November, Grant attacked Confederates at Belmont, Missouri, just across the Mississippi from Columbus, bringing on a fight that did little more than season some of the raw recruits on both sides. In mid-January 1862, Grant visited Halleck in St. Louis to propose a new movement: traveling up the Tennessee and Cumberland Rivers and capturing the Confederate forts defending those waterways. To his chagrin, Grant later recollected that "Halleck cut [me] off, 'as if my plan was preposterous.'"[9]

The plan was not what worried Halleck; it was the man. In fact, both Halleck and Buell had very recently proposed similar movements against the Confederate center. The strategic advantages of such a move were clear. It would outflank the Confederate forces defending both Columbus and Bowling Green, and it would also offer a rapid method of penetrating as far as northern Alabama (in the case of the Tennessee River) and threatening Nashville (along the Cumberland). Best of all, such a move would place the main US Army between the now-divided Confederate forces—the classic strategic recipe for defeating foes in detail. Halleck's problems with Grant's proposal were twofold. First, he viewed Grant as unprofessional and unprepared, just the kind of slovenly soldier he expected to fail, and not a man to be trusted with this responsibility. Second, Halleck also seemed unable to work with Buell. In fact, neither Halleck nor Buell willingly cooperated with the other, despite constant prodding from Washington, DC. Each had his own significantly divergent ideas of what to do after the forts were taken, and neither was willing to voluntarily subordinate his forces to the other man's.[10]

Despite Halleck's refusal, Grant persisted, recruiting Capt. Andrew Hull Foote of the US Navy to help sell the idea. In early February, with Foote on board, Halleck finally agreed. "Old Brains" (Halleck's prewar army nickname) still felt all was not ready, but another factor proved decisive. Fed up with inaction on all fronts, on January 27 President Lincoln issued General Orders No. 1 instructing all the Federal armies to move no later than the anniversary of George Washington's birthday, February 22.[11]

Grant set off and succeeded brilliantly, much to Halleck's bemusement. Fort Henry was already swamped due to spring flooding, and it fell after a short naval bombardment. Fort Donelson was subsequently encircled and succumbed after a hard fight. Grant's dizzying success only seemed to increase the friction with Halleck, who thought him lax in reporting his army's status and actions. When Grant subsequently traveled to Nashville to meet with General Buell, he technically left the bounds of his own department without authorization. On March 2 Halleck reprimanded Grant and, more importantly, complained about the officer to his superior back in Virginia, Gen. George McClellan. Halleck accused Grant of "neglect and inefficiency," and further hinted that Grant had "resumed his former bad habits"—i.e., drink. None of these charges were accurate. Grant had been reporting regularly, but a treacherous telegraph operator proved to be the cause of the lack of communication. As for the drinking, it proved exceedingly hard to tar the newly minted hero of Fort Donelson, "Unconditional Surrender" Grant, with that innuendo. Still, for nearly two weeks in March, Grant was effectively sidelined. When McClellan called Halleck's bluff and authorized him to relieve Grant if necessary, Halleck demurred.[12]

Despite this contretemps, Grant's success secured Halleck's position in Washington's eyes. Just a day after Donelson's capitulation, Halleck boldly wired the following: "Make Buell, Grant and Pope major generals of volunteers, and give me command in the West. I ask this in return for Forts Henry and Donelson." Heartened by success, Lincoln agreed. On March 11, 1862, Halleck was assigned to lead the newly created Department of the Mississippi, with control over everything between Colorado and Knoxville. He now had the complete authority he had craved. What would he do with it?[13]

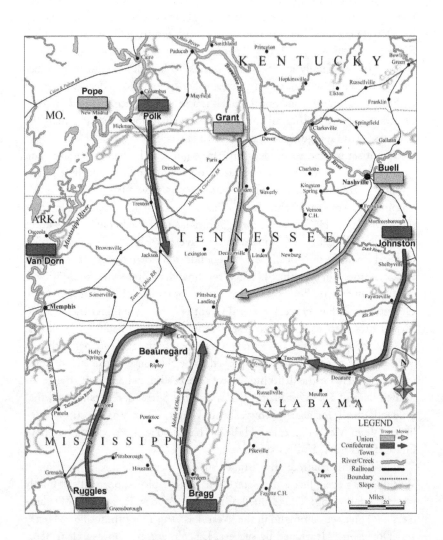

CHAPTER 1

BEFORE THE BATTLE

*Henry W. Halleck Concentrates His Forces
along the Tennessee River*

Situation

The capture of Fort Henry achieved the results Halleck had hoped for and more. On February 7 Albert Sidney Johnston, after consultation with Confederate generals William J. Hardee and Pierre Gustave Toutant Beauregard, recognized that Bowling Green would have to be abandoned. He ordered Hardee—the immediate commander of the Bowling Green garrison—to retreat to Nashville. Beauregard, already westward bound to take charge of Leonidas Polk's forces at Columbus, Kentucky, received further instructions on February 12 to withdraw Polk's Command southward into West Tennessee. Then came the disaster at Fort Donelson on February 16. The most significant Confederate withdrawal soon followed: after discovering the lack of proper defenses at Nashville, Johnston evacuated the Tennessee capital on February 23.[1]

Every professional military man on both sides of the conflict understood the importance of the opening of the Tennessee River. Federal gunboats could now travel as far upstream as Florence, Alabama. These vessels could threaten the strategic Memphis & Charleston Railroad bridge over Bear Creek, on the Tennessee-Mississippi state line. Further, where gunboats could steam,

Major General Henry W. Halleck
in 1861.

transports could follow, bringing US troops with them as they journeyed deep
into the heart of the nascent Confederacy.

Various Union leaders now saw a host of vulnerable objectives beckoning
them southward but lacked the forces to exploit every opportunity simultaneously. In southwestern Missouri, Maj. Gen. Samuel R. Curtis led twenty
thousand Federals to oppose a Confederate army of similar numbers assembled in northwest Arkansas. Curtis's mission was to protect Union-controlled
Missouri, moving southward into Arkansas when practicable. In southeast
Missouri, Brig. Gen. John Pope commanded another twenty-five thousand
Federals; these troops were positioned to advance down the Mississippi River's western bank against the secessionists garrisoning New Madrid. Grant's
force, now grown to forty thousand, stretched between Fort Henry, on the
Tennessee, and Clarksville, halfway to Nashville. Buell's fifty-thousand-man
command occupied Nashville, the first rebellious state capital returned to
government control. Grant's missions were to maintain contact with Buell
and provide the needed strength to thrust due south up the Tennessee River
into Mississippi. But Buell's orders directed him southeast toward Chattanooga and East Tennessee. Liberating East Tennessee, which opposed secession and was still largely pro-Union, was something President Lincoln
greatly desired.[2]

Taken together, these missions pulled the Federals into four different
axes of advance, spreading out in an arc across hundreds of miles. They could

not all be pursued concurrently—especially with the security of Missouri still in doubt. Maj. Gen. William T. Sherman summed up Halleck's dilemma in a letter to his brother John, a US senator: "As soon as Halleck 'moves a man from the interior [of Missouri] to go to Cairo [Confederate general Sterling] Price will return. That is his game. And in that way with a comparatively small force he holds in check five times his number.'"[3]

Two important incidents in early March greatly simplified the task at hand. The first occurred over March 7 and 8, 1862, when Curtis and his ten thousand troops defeated a larger Confederate force of sixteen thousand under Maj. Gen. Earl Van Dorn at the Battle of Pea Ridge in northwestern Arkansas. Van Dorn, who had assembled a collection of troops from Arkansas, Sterling Price's Missourians, some Texans, a few Louisianians, and even a combined Indian force recruited from modern-day eastern Oklahoma, threatened to reinvade Missouri. Curtis's victory crushed that hope and eased Halleck's fears over the security of St. Louis.[4]

The second event was Halleck's own promotion on March 11 to command the entire Western Theater. Now, instead of independent commanders (Halleck and Buell) with differing priorities pulling in opposite directions, Halleck would decide on the future conduct of all Federal operations. At the same time, Maj. Gen. George B. McClellan was relieved of overall command of the Federal war effort since, as Lincoln reasoned, he had "personally taken the field as the head of the Army of the Potomac." Not only had Halleck been granted all the authority he sought, he now answered only to the president.[5]

Options

Halleck's choices narrowed to three: The first was a thrust directly down the Mississippi from Cairo. The second lay with Grant, who could advance south along the corridor of the Tennessee. The third was to support Buell's drive to the southeast toward Chattanooga and Knoxville.

Option 1

A direct advance down the Mississippi would be the simplest maneuver, especially logistically. Even in shallow water the lower Mississippi was fully navigable. Troops and supplies could be shuttled south with relative ease. Further, Halleck would enjoy the best communications with the expedition, via telegraph as far as Cairo and then by dispatch boat the rest of the way. A move down the Mississippi would also allow Halleck to recall troops quickly if needed to counter a surprise Confederate reinvasion of Missouri. Though this threat was unlikely after Van Dorn's defeat, it could never be dismissed entirely. Since the Mississippi ran all the way to New Orleans and the Gulf of Mexico, controlling it would sever the Confederacy in two, isolating Texas, Arkansas, and much of Louisiana from the rest of the South.

However, the biggest disadvantage lay in the fact that any Federal drive down the Mississippi would encounter a series of Confederate strongholds, each of which would have to be isolated and destroyed in turn. Nor was there any direct rail connection between Cairo and points farther south. The Mobile & Ohio line had not yet reached the Ohio River; it ran only as far as Columbus, Kentucky, on the Mississippi.[6] Further, it diverged from the river line to connect to Jackson, Tennessee, then extended to Corinth and Columbus in Mississippi. A smaller line, the Memphis & Ohio, diverged back to the river to terminate at Memphis but farther south, only the Mississippi Central line ran to New Orleans. Moreover, the rails, unlike America's great river, were vulnerable to sabotage, especially the bridges. As a result, every significant structure would have to be guarded.[7]

Option 2

An advance up the Tennessee River offered more interesting possibilities. First and foremost, it turned the rail vulnerability on its head; by using the Tennessee to plunge into northern Mississippi, the Federals could threaten the Confederate rails. If US troops could take Corinth, they would immediately sever Memphis's most important rail connection, the Memphis & Charleston line that ran across Tennessee, Mississippi, and Alabama to connect near Chattanooga. From there, another direct line ran through East Tennessee and into Virginia. This linkage was the only direct rail connection between the eastern and western Confederacy in the entire South. Further, by placing a Federal army between the scattered Southern forces, Halleck would force his opponent to concentrate to meet him or risk defeat in detail. It was the best way to force a classic Napoleonic "decisive battle," and to Halleck, the quintessential Napoleonic scholar of the antebellum army, this was a deeply desirable outcome.

There were two significant drawbacks to the Tennessee River line of advance. The first was that any such approach did not sever the Trans-Mississippi from the rest of the Confederacy. For example, there was nothing to stop Earl Van Dorn's army from transiting the river and moving to join the forces concentrating against Halleck. Nor would the Confederacy be isolated from the food and livestock that regularly moved across the great river to feed the growing Rebel field armies. The second disadvantage was that once at Corinth, the Federals could pursue no other immediately obvious strategic objective. It was another 150 miles from Corinth to Jackson, Mississippi's capital, and no river offered another secure route of advance. Eventually, any Union column driving south to the Gulf of Mexico would have to return to the line of the Mississippi. Nor could the Tennessee be used to sustain a drive across northern Alabama toward that other strategic objective—Chattanooga. The impassable shallows of Muscle Shoals, near Florence, prevented boats from ascending the Tennessee any farther. While other vessels could ply the river as far as Knoxville (and beyond, in high water), direct navigation between Knoxville and the Ohio River was not possible.

Option 3

If controlling the Mississippi carved off a large hunk of Southern territory, Chattanooga offered the only accessible means of doing the same east of the Mississippi. Though the city numbered barely 2,500 souls in 1860, Chattanooga, not Corinth, was the true Crossroads of the Confederacy. As already discussed, the Mobile & Ohio connecting to the Georgia & East Tennessee, and then the Virginia Central, offered the only continuous east–west rail line in the Confederacy. Similarly, various railroad companies linked Louisville, Nashville, Chattanooga, Atlanta, Macon, and Savannah (these last in Georgia) to form one direct link from the Ohio River to the Atlantic coast; from Atlanta other lines linked Montgomery and Mobile to the Gulf Coast. Even more important was Chattanooga's natural geography, which is also why so many rail lines converged there. The city sat in the only water-level passage of the Appalachian mountain chain between Alabama and Maryland, where the Baltimore & Ohio Railroad ran west along the upper Potomac River to link Washington, DC, with the Northern heartland. Logistically, any large-scale Federal invasion of the Deep South would have to come either down the Atlantic coast or through Chattanooga.

But, thanks to Muscle Shoals, the Tennessee River could not provide a secure invasion route to Chattanooga. The Cumberland, which ran to Nashville, was even less reliable; for at least half the year it was unnavigable as far as the Tennessee state capital. Any advance on Chattanooga, then, would have to rely on rails. And, as noted above in discussing an advance into Mississippi from Corinth, those rails would have to be guarded. Such a move would require vast numbers of troops to secure the army's supply line and would be ever vulnerable to raids and guerrilla action. Chattanooga might offer even greater rewards than the line of the Mississippi, but it also came with greater liabilities.

Decision

Even before he was given authority over Buell, Halleck favored the Tennessee ascent. As early as March 1 Halleck informed Grant, "Transports will be sent to you as soon as possible to move your column up the Tennessee River. The main object of this expedition will be to destroy the railroad bridge over Bear Creek, near Eastport, Miss., and also the connections at Corinth [Mississippi], Jackson [Tennessee], and Humboldt [Tennessee]." Halleck further warned Grant to "avoid any general engagement with strong forces," declaring, "It will be better to retreat than risk a general battle." Wary of giving Grant another chance to slip the leash, Halleck also specified that "General C. F. Smith, or some very discreet officer, should be selected for such command." He continued, "having accomplished these objects, or such of them as may be practicable, you will return to Danville and move on Paris [Tennessee]." In this latter instruction, Halleck was still focused on flanking the Confederate fortress at Columbus. However, the situation was rapidly evolving, and on March 5, he revised that point of concentration for this gathering force: "If successful, the expedition will not return to Paris [Tennessee], but will camp at Savannah, unless threatened by superior numbers."[8]

In addition, Halleck began sending as many troops to Savannah as he could spare. On March 6 he authorized William T. Sherman, at Paducah, to "join General Smith's column." Four days later, on March 10, Halleck informed McClellan in Washington (who was still his boss at the time, though for just one more day), "Reserves intended to support Curtis will now be . . . sent to the Tennessee. . . . That is now the strategic line of the Western Campaign."[9]

Halleck acted equally swiftly with Buell. On March 13, while reassuring him that "the new arrangement . . . will not interfere with [Buell's] command," Halleck asked Buell for a summary of his own strength and deployments. Then on March 16, despite the other general's stated desire to launch a two-pronged advance toward Decatur, Alabama, and toward Chattanooga, Halleck instead ordered him, "Move your forces by land to the Tennessee as rapidly as possible." Within a week, then, Halleck was implementing his grand concentration against the Confederate center.[10]

Results/Impact

Unquestionably, Halleck had set in motion a brand-new, unified Federal western strategy. He intended to mass overwhelming Union combat power at what he regarded as the decisive point and use that power to render success inevitable—at least at Corinth. What was lacking, however, was any sense of urgency on the tactical level. All of his communications to Grant, Buell, C. F.

Smith, and even Sherman emphasized caution. No one was to attack the enemy. Nor did Halleck want the Rebels to attack him. His entire concept was to achieve success *without* a battle and by dint of brilliant maneuver. In that thinking he was mistaken, for Albert Sidney Johnston could not surrender so much Confederate territory without fighting.

One further point needs to be considered. After Donelson, the Confederacy was vulnerable in several strategically significant places: Memphis and Corinth, to be sure, but also Chattanooga and East Tennessee. Moreover, Johnston had far fewer troops than did Halleck and Buell with which to defend those places. Arguably, the single most important geographic point in the western Confederacy was not Corinth but Chattanooga, whose vital rail connections offered a gateway through the Appalachian Mountains. Pulling Buell's army westward to combine with Grant's force meant concentrating overwhelming combat power in southwest Tennessee, but it also meant forgoing any effort towards Chattanooga when that city was most vulnerable. Given that the Federals would spend much of the following year and many thousands of soldiers' lives trying to capture Chattanooga, the city's rapid loss in 1862 could have shortened the war considerably.

Halleck's desire to concentrate devastating force along the Tennessee clearly changed the nature of the war in the West that spring. The next theater of action had been defined, and it would be located along the Tennessee and Mississippi River valleys.

Albert Sidney Johnston Concentrates the Confederates at Corinth

Situation

The first harbinger of the Confederate disaster to come was not Fort Donelson's surrender, but rather a defeat at the Battle of Mill Springs (also known as Fishing Creek or Logan's Crossroads) in eastern Kentucky. Fought on January 19, six thousand Confederates under Maj. Gen. George B. Crittenden attacked forty-five hundred Federals commanded by Brig. Gen. George Thomas. The battle went badly for the Rebels, though losses were not heavy. However, a tactical reverse soon deteriorated into a panicked rout, with Crittenden, later accused of drunkenness on the field, unable to control his men. The small Rebel force abandoned their artillery and retreated to Carthage, Tennessee, fifty miles east of Nashville, arriving as little more than a disorderly mob. On the face of it, Mill Springs need not have been anything more than a minor Confederate setback—except for the ensuing panic.[11]

General Albert Sidney Johnston.

The week following the surrender at Fort Donelson was a bad one for Johnston. His shell of a defensive line proved easily shattered. Worse yet, between the battle casualties and prisoners taken at Donelson, amounting to some 15,000 men, Johnston lost more than a quarter of his total force at a stroke. He ordered the evacuation of Columbus and Bowling Green, then Nashville, beginning a headlong retreat south of the Cumberland River. The South was stunned and distraught. Johnston was excoriated in the Confederate Congress, and newspapers across the new Confederacy clamored for his removal. Of course, much of the criticism was profoundly unfair, since Johnston had never been assigned anything like the resources needed to defend his department successfully. But his decision to reinforce Donelson with only part of his Bowling Green troops helped make the disaster much worse. For his part, President Davis maintained full public support for the general. When the Tennessee congressional caucus demanded Johnston's removal, insisting he was unfit for the job, "Davis replied, 'If he is not a general, we had better give up the war, for we have no general.'" In a private communication to Johnston, however, Davis wrote, "It would be worse than useless to point out to you how much depends on you."[12]

As February closed, Johnston's forces were badly scattered. Polk commanded about eighteen thousand effectives (twenty-two thousand aggregate present) now in West Tennessee, mainly at Jackson. Hardee's force amounted to about the same, having lost virtually all those troops committed to Donelson but incorporating Crittenden's remnants from Mill Springs. Three other major sources of manpower were available. Earl Van Dorn's roughly twenty thousand soldiers were in Arkansas, recovering from the fight at Pea Ridge and subject to Johnston's authority. Meanwhile, Confederate major general Braxton Bragg commanded thirteen thousand men at Mobile and Pensacola, while Maj. Gen. Mansfield Lovell headed up seventy-five hundred effectives defending New Orleans. Both of those commands lay outside Johnston's authority, and they would require President Davis's approval to come to Johnston's aid.[13]

Johnston initially considered defending Nashville, a decision that was soon overtaken by events. February 23 found Johnston at Murfreesboro, thirty miles southeast of Nashville along the Nashville & Chattanooga Railway. There, he reorganized Hardee's wing into a "central army" of three divisions and a reserve brigade, integrating George Crittenden's Mill Springs force and then formally taking command. From this location, Johnston intended to retreat farther southeast to Stevenson, Alabama.[14]

By the next day, however, further importuning from Beauregard, who anticipated the Federal buildup along the Tennessee, convinced Johnston to change his destination from Stevenson to Decatur, Alabama, straight south along the Nashville & Decatur Railroad. At Decatur, Johnston would be seventy miles west of Stevenson and one hundred miles east of Corinth. Beauregard, at Jackson, was fifty miles north of Corinth. Only a handful of troops were sent to hold Chattanooga. If all these forces did unite, however, Johnston could field an army of nearly sixty thousand troops. But could he chance a concentration without risking a new strategic disaster in one of the places left vulnerable?[15]

Options

Johnston also faced three basic options. He could concentrate all his forces at one place, risking everything else to achieve decisive effect. Or he could order his forces to retreat deep into the Confederacy, trading space for time, in hopes that sufficient reinforcements could eventually be assembled. Finally, Johnston could order Beauregard and Polk to unite with the Trans-Mississippi forces in a more limited concentration while he fell back toward Chattanooga.

Option 1

The textbook solution to Johnston's problem was to assemble a concentration of force and attack. By doing so, even though the overall numbers were against him, Johnston could achieve a local tactical superiority of force in one area, defeat one of the invading columns, then turn to deal with each of the others. Even if forced to give up some ground in the process—or so the theory went—those territorial losses would be temporary, to be regained as Johnston dealt with the other invading columns in turn.

Two key questions underlay this strategy of concentration. First, where should the point of the concentration be? Second, would the enemy move slowly enough to surrender the initiative and give Johnston time to achieve it?

Option 2

If concentrating contained risks, Johnston's second option was no less perilous. He could surrender considerable tracts of land—Kentucky and much of Tennessee—in order to retreat into the interior of the Confederacy until new regiments could be raised and rushed to the front.

Johnston's most obvious fallback was to a position south of Murfreesboro along the Nashville & Chattanooga Railroad. He could post his force behind the Highland Rim, a line of hills where the lowlands of the Nashville geographic basin transitioned to the uplands of Middle Tennessee, rising eventually to the Cumberland Plateau, a forbidding mountain mass south of the Elk River. From here, Johnston could defend Chattanooga's northern approaches. Two factors, however, rendered that position untenable. The first was the existence of the Nashville & Decatur Railway, which ran due south into northern Alabama, where it joined the Memphis & Charleston tracks at Decatur, also on the Tennessee River. A Federal force could track due east from Decatur toward Chattanooga, completely outflanking Johnston's Highland Rim position. In early 1862, with Federals already ranging up the Tennessee as far as Florence, the combination of available rails and river access made this a very likely avenue of attack—especially if the Federals captured Corinth, where the Mobile & Ohio and the Memphis & Charleston Railroads intersected. Johnston had far too few troops to defend Chattanooga from both the north and the west.

The better fallback was to Chattanooga. There, the combination of mountains and the Tennessee River would make for a set of formidable obstacles, imposing enormous logistical challenges on the Federals and multiplying Johnston's limited combat strength through fortification. By holding Chattanooga directly, Johnston also negated the flanking threat from Alabama. The Memphis & Charleston joined the Nashville & Chattanooga rails just east of Stevenson, Alabama, reducing enemy options to a single avenue of advance.

Similarly, Polk's force could retreat deep into Mississippi, where the delta would offer a useful buffer against any speedy US advance. The territory ceded to the enemy would still be subject to partisan operations and cavalry raids, meaning it would be no easy task for the Federals to secure their newly won geography.

Such a strategy bought time for more Confederate troops to be raised and equipped, increasing Johnston's overall numbers. Equally useful was the fact that the Federals would have to divide their forces if they wished to pursue multiple objectives. Perhaps most importantly, the Federal commanders would have to both repair the rail lines supporting their advances against Johnston's chosen strongholds and garrison those lines as they progressed. Occupying and controlling Middle and West Tennessee would require thousands of Union troops, so many that the tip of Halleck's spear would be greatly weakened.

But there was no guarantee that Johnston could reclaim those ceded regions. And in the meantime, at the very least Memphis and Nashville would be lost to the Confederate war effort. Tennessee's agricultural produce would also be denied to the Confederacy. The state was a vital source of horses and mules, animals without which the Rebel armies would be immobilized. For these reasons, the idea of such a strategic retreat was nearly unthinkable.

Option 3

P. G. T. Beauregard proposed what amounted to a third option, though seemingly without discussing it with Johnston. On February 21, Beauregard was at Jackson, Tennessee, assuming command of Polk's Corps and other sundry

General P.G.T. Beauregard.

forces along the Mississippi. Beauregard's plan also called for a concentration, though not with Hardee's Bowling Green troops. Writing to Van Dorn, Beauregard explained that his forces were "entirely cut off from those under General A. S. Johnston, and must now depend on themselves alone for the defense of the Mississippi River." Writing to the governors of Tennessee, Mississippi, Louisiana, and Alabama, Beauregard called on them to provide five thousand new troops each. He explained what these twenty thousand reinforcements, united with his own fifteen thousand men and ten thousand from Van Dorn, could do: "We could thus take the field with 40,000 men; take Cairo, Paducah, the mouths of the Tennessee and Cumberland Rivers, and most probably be able to take Saint Louis by the river." Looking past the bombast and overly grandiose objectives, Beauregard's plan did have real merit, but it was suggested before Van Dorn fought and lost the Battle of Pea Ridge. Van Dorn's move to northwest Arkansas and subsequent defeat made Beauregard's scheme increasingly impractical, and hence less appealing to Johnston.[16]

Decision

Some troops were already gathering at Corinth. In reaction to the crisis, on February 8 President Davis ordered Mansfield Lovell to send five thousand men to Columbus from New Orleans. Over the next few days, they were first halted at Memphis and then diverted to Corinth. By February 27 Lovell reported dispatching a total of "eight regiments and two batteries" northward. For his part, Braxton Bragg, who had sent a staff officer to confer with Johnston just after the fall of Fort Henry, on February 10 sent "a regiment to Decatur . . . to save [the] railroad bridge." Another proponent of concentration, Bragg had already been urging Davis to forsake point defense and assemble a large field army. This force would be drawn from the New Orleans garrison and Bragg's own command at Pensacola and Mobile. On February 18 Davis agreed, directing Confederate secretary of war Judah P. Benjamin to inform Bragg, "Proceed as promptly as possible . . . and hasten to the defense of the Tennessee line." Small garrisons would be left to man the forts defending Mobile. "But," Benjamin acknowledged, "the risk of [Mobile]'s capture must be run." As for destination, Richmond proved vague: "By the time you can reach the Memphis & Charleston Railroad we will be able to determine towards what point [you] are to move." Bragg personally departed Mobile on February 28 with ten thousand of "the finest and best disciplined body of troops the Confederacy ever had."[17]

Corinth was an obvious place for a gathering. It was far enough south that it could not be outflanked by water, since the great bend in the Tennessee

River at Eastport and the shoals at Decatur rendered the upper Tennessee much less vulnerable to the US Navy's riverine expeditions. Corinth was also roughly parallel with Memphis to the west, meaning that for a time, at least, that important Tennessee city would remain in Confederate hands. The intersection of the Memphis & Charleston and the Mobile & Ohio tracks further ensured that most, if not all, these new reinforcements would head there initially. But it was not yet the decisive point as Jomini or Clauswitz might have defined it.

In later years, Beauregard would claim that it was he who first selected Corinth, sending various aides and confidants to Johnston at Murfreesboro to urge that movement on February 26 or 27. In 1880, Tennessee governor Isham G. Harris confirmed that he was one of those messengers, noting that "Beauregard requested me to urge General A. S. Johnston to concentrate, as speedily as possible . . . at Corinth. . . . I informed him [Johnston] fully as to . . . [Beauregard's] suggestion . . . when General Johnston promptly answered that he was [already] preparing . . . to move the army . . . to or near Corinth." Johnston's biographer (and son) William Preston Johnston suggested that the general had decided on Corinth even before he left Bowling Green, with Beauregard adopting Johnston's views wholeheartedly. According to Johnston biographer Charles Roland, "Probably both Johnston and Beauregard independently selected Corinth as the point of junction." After all, the city was the obvious spot. Beauregard, however, could only suggest; it fell to Johnston to make the final call.[18]

Johnston made that decision on February 27 at Murfreesboro, as outlined in a dispatch to Secretary of War Judah P. Benjamin: "Considering the peculiar geography of this State, and the great power which the enemy's means afford them upon the Tennessee and Cumberland [Rivers], . . . the force under my command cannot successfully cover the whole line against the advance of the enemy. I am compelled to elect whether he shall be permitted to occupy Middle Tennessee, or turn Columbus, take Memphis, and open the valley of the Mississippi. To me the defense of the valley seems of paramount importance, and consequently I will move this corps . . . [across] the river near Decatur, in order . . . to cooperate or unite with General Beauregard."[19]

Results/Impact

On February 28, the same day Braxton Bragg left Mobile, Albert Sidney Johnston marched out of Murfreesboro with seventeen thousand men. He first moved due south to Decatur as planned, damaging the Nashville & Decatur line as he went. Johnston informed locals that he was retreating to

General Braxton Bragg.

Stevenson and Chattanooga, hoping they would in turn pass that information to the advancing Yankees. Cavalry screened the retreat, and the general's movements were deliberate, not panicked; the sick and wounded were evacuated safely, and many tons of munitions and stores were shuttled south. Not all supplies were safely evacuated, of course. Large quantities had been lost at Donelson and Nashville, but Johnston retained enough supplies and ammunition to be able to risk battle.[20]

Throughout March, troops marched into Corinth. On March 10, the Tenth Mississippi Infantry, one of Bragg's regiments from Mobile, arrived after a convoluted journey: men traveled by rail via Montgomery, Atlanta, and Chattanooga, then embarked on more rail travel via Huntsville to Eastport, then made the last leg of the journey to Corinth by foot. The Third Mississippi Battalion, one of the first of Johnston's Command to reach the city, only arrived on March 20, with the last of Hardee's Corps tramping into town on the twenty-fourth.

Johnston, like Beauregard, also thought of Van Dorn. On March 17, under orders from Johnston, Van Dorn departed Van Buren, Arkansas, for Memphis and ultimately Corinth. Lacking rail or steamboat transport, he had to march across Arkansas amid the spring rains, which turned roads to quagmires and made every watercourse a raging torrent. Even though Van Dorn himself reached Corinth briefly at the end of March to confer with Johnston, his army of roughly eighteen thousand men was weeks behind him. One regiment arrived in time to fight in the coming battle, but the bulk of these soldiers only traveled as far as Memphis by April 18, eleven days after the Battle of Shiloh ended.[21]

Johnston's decision to concentrate at Corinth led directly to a battle at Shiloh. Had Johnston fallen back toward Chattanooga, Beauregard's army, even when combined with Van Dorn's in mid-April, would have been too weak to contemplate an offensive without Hardee's wing of the army. And even though Van Dorn's force (roughly one-third of the whole force Johnston sought to bring to bear) did not arrive in time, Johnston still managed to gather forty thousand men at Corinth while Grant's and Buell's forces were still separated. Johnston just barely won the race to mass his forces first. Now he had parity of numbers, if not a decided numerical advantage, and was willing to fight.

Arguably, Van Dorn's force was better used in doing exactly what he did—trying to threaten Missouri, or perhaps deal with the Federal force thrusting down the Mississippi toward Island No. 10 and Memphis—rather than heading to Corinth. One of Halleck's greatest fears was the security of southern Missouri, as well as Cairo and St. Louis. However, to pose a threat Van Dorn had to win. The Confederate defeat at Pea Ridge greatly lessened Halleck's concerns, freeing the Federals to ship more men up the Tennessee. Van Dorn would belatedly reach Corinth, but not in time to help Albert Sidney Johnston win the Battle of Shiloh.

And the Confederacy did pay a steep price for reinforcing Johnston. Both Mobile and New Orleans were left exposed to the Union's combined naval and army operations along the Gulf Coast due to being stripped of troops. When Bragg departed Mobile, he expected it to be attacked and probably captured. Instead, US Navy flag officer David G. Farragut targeted New Orleans, which was defended by Confederate brigadier general Mansfield Lovell. Denuded of most of his troops, Lovell placed his remaining hopes in the defense of Forts Jackson and St. Philip, which protected both banks of the Mississippi below the city. Farragut successfully passed them on April 18, seizing New Orleans on April 29, 1862. The bulk of Lovell's manpower, of course, was sent to Johnston. New Orleans would remain in Federal hands for the rest of the war.

Charles F. Smith Chooses Pittsburg Landing as the Federal Campsite

Situation

The arrival of the Federal army at Savannah proved to be a haphazard affair. On March 6, William Sherman reported to the newly promoted Maj. Gen.

C. F. Smith at Fort Henry, leading a flotilla of eighty-two vessels containing most of his division from Paducah. According to Sherman, Smith ordered him to halt his fleet by the "burned railroad bridge, to await the rendezvous of the rest of the army." This was the Danville bridge, which spanned the Tennessee about fifteen miles upriver from Fort Henry.[22]

Sherman complied, waiting to join his command to several other divisions being assembled to strike for Savannah. However, the general noted, "Among my colonels I had a strange character—Thomas Worthington, colonel of the 46th Ohio. He was a graduate of West Point, of the class of 1827; was therefore, older than General Halleck, General Grant, or myself, and claimed to know more of war than all of us put together." The contentious Worthington had already proved to be a burr under Sherman's metaphorical saddle back in Paducah, and he was trending toward rashness. While in Paducah, Worthington had heard reports "of mistreatment of Union sympathizers" in Savannah, and he was therefore determined to press on immediately. Later, the colonel justified his action when he wrote, "[Being] one of five regiments ordered to report to Gen. C. F. Smith at Savannah, Tennessee, the 46th Ohio was the only regiment that promptly executed the order."[23]

Worthington reached the landing at Savannah on the evening of March 8, finding that part of the Fortieth Illinois Infantry preceded him. He immediately placed himself in command of the town, taking charge of both his own regiment and the Illinoisans. When Sherman arrived the next day, Worthington was holding a dress parade. The general recalled, "I found that Worthington . . . was flying about giving orders, as though he were commander in chief. I made him get back to his boat, and gave him to understand that thereafter he must keep his place." Four days later C. F. Smith arrived, heading up a much larger flotilla transporting three more divisions.[24]

These four divisions of troops numbered thirty thousand men. In contrast, Savannah was a town of about four hundred souls. Across the river and several miles upstream was Crump's Landing, and about eight miles farther upstream was Pittsburg Landing, also on the west bank of the Tennessee. The river was high and would likely go higher, since the spring flood stage would arrive shortly, so finding enough space to debark and set up camps for these men was difficult. Bottomland along both banks was either swampy or likely to be completely flooded soon. Similarly, many of the smaller landing places along the river would quickly be unusable. Smith and Sherman needed to find a place with plenty of high, dry ground and a landing big enough to accommodate dozens of boats at once, given the size of their combined flotillas. Further, the officers had to decide whether to set up camp on the eastern bank, the better to wait for Buell, who was marching overland from

Nashville. Alternatively, they could establish a bridgehead on the western bank, closer to Corinth and the Confederates. It would not do to assemble the entire army and then have troops fight their way across the river in an opposed crossing.

Options

The Federals could decide to remain on the east bank, effectively secure from any attack. They could also establish limited defensible bridgeheads on the west bank, or they could place the entire army west of the Tennessee to facilitate a later advance.

Option 1

The safest option was to establish the army's base camp on the east side of the river at Savannah. Though the small town's structures could not begin to accommodate all of Smith's army (let alone Buell's men), local dwellings could serve as comfortable headquarters for the senior officers. Moving inland a short distance, soldiers could find high ground aplenty for their needed campsites. Establishing communications with Buell once his army arrived would also be far simpler.

Conversely, Smith and Sherman were loath to surrender the west bank entirely to the Rebels. If the Confederates occupied the few viable landings in force, US troops would have to fight their way across the river. Even with massive gunboat support, this was sure to be no easy feat.

Option 2

A second choice would be camping the main force on the east bank around Savannah while placing troops on the west bank at one or more of the better landings to ensure a Federal foothold there. Once all was ready, the main army could be ferried across the Tennessee using the prodigious Federal steamboat fleet. Troops could then begin the expected advance against the railroads at Corinth, as well as against the smaller towns of Burnsville and Iuka, Mississippi. At Burnsville, the Memphis & Charleston established a repair depot, making that otherwise unimportant hamlet a strategic objective of Halleck's intended campaign.

An army on the offensive had sound reasons for straddling the river or at least establishing forward outposts on the western bank. Defensively, however, such a posture violated several military precepts. If attacked, those Federals on the western bank would have to fight with their backs to a major river that was both unfordable and unbridgeable, and they would also be dealing with the swampy bottomland near every landing. While such terrain reduced enemy options to little more than a frontal assault, there was no safe line of retreat if things went badly. Further, with the army divided by the river, the force's western half could potentially be badly outnumbered by Albert Sidney Johnston's gathering Army of the West, effectively negating Halleck's decision to concentrate his own forces.

<u>Option 3</u>

The third option, then, was an obvious answer to the dilemma posed by the choice above: Instead of dividing the army, Smith and Sherman could camp the whole force on the west bank of the Tennessee and leave only a small force to hold Savannah. The modest number of soldiers at Savannah would present only a small risk since the Rebels could not cross the Tennessee in force while opposed by the US Navy, and since Buell's army of about thirty thousand men was expected to arrive soon.

This alternative still had the same drawbacks, all of which flew in the face of military orthodoxy: defending with one's back to the river, navigating the bottomlands, and having Buell on the eastern shore. However, by concentrating the bulk of the army at one location, the Federals were much less likely to be overwhelmed by an attacker's greater numbers—assuming proper outposts and pickets were maintained. Cavalry could keep a close eye on the Rebels at Corinth, alerting Sherman, Smith, or Grant (or Halleck, when he eventually came to command the assembled legions) to a potential attack well before that blow could land.

Decision

When General Smith arrived in Savannah, he conferred with Sherman. Smith, said Sherman, was "quite unwell, and was suffering from his leg, which was swollen and very sore, from a mere abrasion in stepping into a small boat." This "mere abrasion" was actually a serious injury. On the evening of March 12, after conferring with Lew Wallace, Smith "lost his balance, . . . fell forward, and scraped his leg on the sharp edge of a seat" in the boat. "It was a deep laceration on the shin of his right leg from the ankle to the knee." Two weeks later, on March 27, Smith described the extent of his incapacitation in a letter to his wife: "The injury is deep seated in the bone, which the surgeons fear may exfoliate. I shall have to ride to the battlefield in an ambulance; for although I can limp about the cabin of the steamer, in which I make my headquarters, I cannot stand up for more than a few minutes without great pain and damage to the aggrieved part. Of course sitting on a horse is the same thing."[25]

Unable to undertake active operations himself, Smith established his headquarters aboard the steamboat *Continental* at Savannah and ordered Sherman to steam upriver, "land at some point below Eastport, and make a break of the Memphis & Charleston." Sherman set out immediately. Along the way, he passed Pittsburg Landing. Capt. William Gwin, commander of the gunboat *Lexington*, informed Sherman that on a previous excursion the landing had been defended by "a rebel regiment of cavalry . . . and that it was the usual landing-place for the people about Corinth." Sherman sent word back down the river, suggesting to Smith that "he ought to post some troops at Pittsburg Landing."[26]

Sherman's expedition failed to reach the railroad, let alone damage it. Torrential rains swelled every creek and made the roads impassable. After a floundering effort to reach Burnsville, Sherman abandoned the mission as hopeless and steamed back to Pittsburg Landing on the night of March 14, hoping "to make the attempt from there." When he arrived, he "found [Brig. Gen. Stephen A.] Hurlbut's division in boats." Ordering his own command to tie up alongside Hurlbut's men, Sherman steamed back to Savannah to report to Smith, who digested the news of the failure to cut the rails. Seeing "in the flooded Tennessee the full truth of my report," recalled Sherman, Smith "then instructed me to disembark my own division, and that of General Hurlbut, at Pittsburg Landing; to make positions well back, and to leave room for his whole army; telling me that he would soon come up in person, and move out in force to make the lodgment on the railroad, contemplated by General Halleck's orders." This exchange marked the first decision to occupy the west bank, and to do so in force.[27]

Results/Impact

Unquestionably, Smith's decision to establish the army at Crump's and Pittsburg Landings, both on the west bank of the Tennessee, made the Battle of Shiloh possible. Albert Sidney Johnston was determined to strike a redemptive blow against the Federals, but he could only do so if he could reach the Union army. Had Smith established camps for his troops around Savannah to await Buell, Johnston would have had no way to cross the river in the face of the US Navy, let alone risk battle with that same navy behind him preventing any chance of retreat. All the Confederate determination in the world could not overcome the hard reality of the gunboats.

But Smith's mind-set was offensive, not defensive, despite Halleck's counterintuitive instructions to avoid battle. The best way to strike that offensive blow was to establish secure bridgeheads on the west bank. Smith wasted no time in doing so, or in attempting to strike inland. Here the weather came to Johnston's aid, preventing either US expedition from cutting the rail lines to Corinth, and buying more time for Johnston to gather strength. As a result, both armies spent the next three weeks preparing for that climactic struggle.

Simultaneously, Smith ordered Maj. Gen. Lew Wallace's division to debark at Crump's Landing, also on the west bank of the Tennessee, perhaps five miles upstream from Savannah and approximately seven miles by road from Pittsburg Landing. Wallace's orders were to cut the Mobile & Ohio Railroad north of Corinth at Bethel Station. Smith's strategy, as he explained to Halleck, was simple: Corinth, strongly garrisoned and reputedly well entrenched, was too strong to assail directly. Smith elaborated on this point: "That [a direct attack] would lead inevitably to a collision in numbers that I am ordered to avoid. Hence my efforts north of Purdy [Bethel Station] and east of Corinth [Burnsville]." Wallace debarked on March 12 and headed inland, hampered by the same drenching rains that foiled Sherman. Eventually Wallace's three brigades halted and established camps at Crump's Landing; Adamsville, five miles west; and Stoney Lonesome, halfway between. All three brigades sat astride side roads that led south to the main army at Pittsburg Landing.[28]

Ulysses S. Grant Establishes His Headquarters at Savannah

Situation

Writing from Savannah on March 15, C. F. Smith reported the following: "[Maj. Gen. John A.] *McLernand's* division . . . occupies this place and its surroundings. . . . I have now *Wallas's* [Wallace's] division with its transportation at Crump's landing, about 3 1/2 miles up; *Hurlbut's* division with its transportation at Pittsburgh, some 9 miles up—watching [Confederate Brig. [G]eneral [Benjamin F.] *Chetam* [at Purdy and Bethel Springs] and to prevent his moving against Genl *Sherman*; and *Sherman's* division with its transportation at *Cook's* Landing still farther up." Most of the troops were still on transports. "Am I to disembark more troops? Or keep them in hand for expeditions?" Smith asked.[29]

The answer came soon; he was to disembark and send the boats back north to bring up additional forces. Smith complied, dispatching Sherman on his return to Pittsburg Landing, which became the army's main encampment. Wallace remained at Crump's Landing. Within a few days, McClernand's men also shifted upriver to Pittsburg Landing, taking up campsites behind Sherman's forward line of brigades. C. F. Smith, however, remained aboard the *Continental*, apparently at Savannah, crippled by his worsening leg.

General Ulysses S. Grant and his staff, 1861.

Between March 1 and March 13, Grant remained at Fort Henry, leading a rear area garrison and wondering about his fate. On March 13, Halleck restored him to command, disingenuously informing Grant that "accounts of [Grant's] misbehavior had reached Washington and directed him to investigate and report the facts." "He forwarded also a copy of a detailed dispatch from himself . . . entirely exonerating me"; added Grant wryly, "but he did not inform me that it was his own reports that had created all the trouble." Believing that Halleck had saved his reputation and career, Grant was grateful; he would not discover the truth until after the war. On March 17 he was happy to be traveling to Savannah, where he immediately resumed command of what was becoming a sizable army.[30]

The Federal force now consisted of five divisions: McClernand's First, C. F. Smith's Second, Lew Wallace's Third, Hurlbut's Fourth, and Sherman's Fifth. A sixth division was being organized out of new arrivals and placed under the command of Brig. Gen. Benjamin M. Prentiss, but as of early April it had yet to fully organize. By the end of March, all these troops except Lew Wallace's were concentrated at Pittsburg Landing. When Buell arrived, Grant planned to have his men occupy camps at Hamburg Landing, four miles upstream from Pittsburg Landing, south of Lick Creek.[31]

As the army coalesced at Pittsburg Landing, General Smith intended to establish his headquarters there as soon as he was well enough to do so. His increasingly serious leg injury prevented that from happening. Grant, however, had no such worry. He could have moved headquarters to the new site anytime in the days after his arrival on March 17. Yet he remained in Savannah. Why?

Options

Grant could locate his headquarters to be with the army at Pittsburg Landing, which would be the textbook decision. Alternatively, he could remain at Savannah, where army headquarters was already situated.

<u>Option 1</u>

There were multiple reasons why Grant would be expected to set up a field headquarters at Pittsburg Landing. The first and perhaps best reason was because army regulations specified as much: "Generals take post at the center of their commands, on the main channels of communication. If troops bivouac in the presence of the enemy, the Generals bivouac with them." Further, Grant's own "orders mandated that 'encampments will conform as near as possible to Army Regulations.'" With Confederates present in strength at Corinth and Selmer, and with their patrols observing the growing Federal encampment daily, it was hard to argue that Grant's men were not "in the presence of the enemy." A commander's place is always with his troops, especially when combat is possible. Grant's full-time presence at the landing would better allow him to familiarize himself with the terrain, another critical factor in favor of this option.[32]

The second reason concerned morale. No soldier in any army likes suffering the privations of living rough while his leaders enjoy the creature comforts of houses and beds. Accordingly, Robert E. Lee insisted on living in his tent, even when better quarters were available. Grant's force was brand-new, an army just assembling and in need of a firm, inspiring hand. While he was present at the landing most days, since it was a short boat ride from Savannah, he was not in the field the same way his thousands of untested soldiers were.

The third reason for establishing headquarters at Pittsburg Landing was due to command issues. Nominally, Charles Smith commanded the force at the landing. He was senior to all the other divisional commanders present (though McClernand had some question about that ranking), and as such he was clearly in charge. But Smith was ill and not improving. At best, his limited mobility restricted him to brief daytime visits to the main campsite.

Absent Smith, McClernand ranked Sherman, but Sherman had been placed in charge of the camps. This divided command issue was only complicated by that fact that neither Grant nor Sherman (both US Military Academy graduates) held a high opinion of McClernand, an Illinois politician appointed to his rank in 1861. With Grant away, there was no clear line of command on scene at Pittsburg Landing.

Option 2

Conversely, the arguments for keeping headquarters in Savannah were much weaker. First, of course, though there were not anywhere near enough dwellings and commercial buildings to accommodate the whole army and the needed hospitals and supplies, the town's buildings offered some creature comforts that would allow certain headquarters to function more effectively—not to mention to allow senior officers to live in considerably more comfort than the men now under canvas. Beyond that, Savannah would make a good point from which Buell's men could be ferried across the river when they arrived, and so should be garrisoned.

Also, arguably, the city was where Halleck might well establish his headquarters once he arrived from St. Louis at some point soon; hence, by remaining in Savannah, Grant would be more conveniently located to communicate with his superior. This might well have been one of the things that counted the most, for that same lack of effective communication was what conceivably got Grant into trouble with Halleck back in February.

Decision

Grant decided that he and his staff would remain ensconced in William Cherry's comfortable waterfront dwelling. On March 26, nine days after he reached Savannah, Grant issued an order reaffirming Smith's duty as "the senior officer at Pittsburg," and appointing him "to command that post" as long as Grant's own headquarters remained at Savannah. This was a very curious order, since Smith's leg prevented him from leaving his stateroom on the *Continental* without extreme difficulty, and he seemingly rarely visited the landing. On March 31 Grant issued General Orders No. 30, which specified, "The headquarters of the District of West Tennessee is hereby changed to Pittsburg." But the directive quickly added, "An office will be continued at Savannah, where all official communications may be left by troops having easier access with that point than Pittsburg." Grant himself remained in Savannah.[33]

Of course, Grant could commute daily to the landing via his headquarters vessel, the *Tigress*, which was a small, fast side-wheeler of shallow draft.

But daily commuting was no substitute for being continuously on-site, especially given the contrast between living comfortably in Savannah and under canvas in a field.

Results/Impact

Grant's decision to remain at Savannah simultaneously isolated him from both elements of his army, the main body at Pittsburg and Wallace's division at Crump's. This isolation mattered little if the Confederates were content to remain at Corinth, letting Grant dictate the pace of the campaign. So far, that was exactly what had happened since the fall of Donelson, and most senior Federal officers believed that this would continue to be the case. Indeed, Halleck's orders were all about caution, instructing first Smith and subsequently Grant not to bring on a general engagement before Halleck had assembled his full force, including Buell. Underlying those orders was Halleck's assumption that the Rebels would do nothing to disrupt the status quo. For Grant's part, even though he later insisted that "every precaution [was] taken," he also confessed that "I regarded the campaign . . . as an offensive one and had no idea that the enemy would leave strong entrenchments to take the initiative when he knew he would be attacked where he was if he remained."[34]

Sherman shared Grant's complacency. As late as April 3, writing to his wife, Ellen, Sherman noted, "[Even though] we are constantly in the presence of the enemy's pickets . . . I am satisfied they will await our coming at Corinth or at some point of the Charleston [Rail]Road." With the men at the top unworried, most of the rank and file felt the same. Grant's only real concern seemed to be for Lew Wallace's command at Crump's Landing, detached from the main body and hence vulnerable. Grant foresaw what might happen: "[The Rebels could make] a rapid dash upon Crump's and destroy our transports and stores, . . . and then retreat before Wallace could be reinforced."[35]

Accordingly, while Grant chose to visit the army each day, he retired to Savannah every evening. Should his confidence be misplaced and a Confederate strike occur, the army would lack an overall commander until the general learned of the attack and made his way upstream on the *Tigress* to join the battle. Once there, Grant would have to size up the situation before he could decide on a course of action. This process could take several hours, rendering the Federal force bereft of any controlling hand in the meantime. The impact of this decision was evident: Lew Wallace's men at Crump's spent the entire morning of April 6 waiting for orders, and they never played a role in the fighting that day.

Grant Does Not Order the Army to Entrench

Situation

Though sited on what would later prove to be very defensible ground, the Federal camps at Pittsburg Landing were not laid out with an eye toward defense. Instead, they were chosen almost at random. When it landed, Sherman's division simply moved inland far enough to leave room for the other divisions as they arrived. This decision placed the general's four brigades as the southernmost perimeter of Grant's position, the closest to Corinth and Albert Sidney Johnston's Confederate army gathering there. As a result, Sherman's front was exceedingly long, forming an arc along the Hamburg–Purdy Road about three miles long. Col. David Stuart's brigade held a semi-detached position along the Hamburg Road on Sherman's eastern flank. As other divisions came ashore, they established camps behind Sherman that led back to the landing. Then, as Grant's numbers expanded, a new Sixth Division was established under Brig. Gen. Benjamin M. Prentiss, who was assigned new regiments of raw recruits as they arrived. Since the campsites nearer the landing were already filled, the new division was also placed on the outer perimeter of the line on Sherman's left. Prentiss's men were situated between the main body of Sherman's command and Stuart's isolated force near the river.

At first glance, this placement made sense; the gap in Sherman's front between his main body and Stuart was now being filled. However, Sherman's and Prentiss's men were the rawest in the army, placed in the two most recently created commands, and assigned to the first line of Grant's defenses. Experienced commands like McClernand's and Hurlbut's divisions, full of Fort Donelson combat veterans, occupied rear areas. Would Sherman's and Prentiss's novices be as ready if suddenly attacked?

Options

Sherman or Grant could order the army to dig in at Pittsburg Landing. There were arguments for and against such measures. At the very least, the camps could be reoriented to provide a solid defensive frontage for each command.

Option 1

One way to augment the army's defenses and mitigate the inexperience of the troops would be to entrench the camps. Temporary fieldworks have long been a part of warfare: in the ancient era, Roman legions routinely constructed fortified camps when they halted. Moreover, the idea of using fieldworks was a staple of American military thinking that legendary professor of military art and science Dennis Hart Mahan had taught since at least 1832. Mahan espoused the idea of "active defense," teaching his pupils to use temporary earthworks to reduce losses, offset surprise, and stiffen the resolve of raw troops. They paid benefits for armies on the offense, as well. Defensive works preserved the lives of one's own men while allowing defenders to inflict greater losses on any attackers, until it became time to launch a counterblow. Mahan also theorized that "reserves, cavalry, skirmishers, and even pickets" could benefit from entrenching. Given that West Point was first and foremost an engineering school, with the best graduates passing directly into the elite Corps of Engineers, Mahan's ideas on defense saw wide distribution. Additionally, he published two widely read books on military theory that gained great favor among individual state militia establishments. All in all, Mahan was the most influential American military strategist of the antebellum era.[36]

As if that were not enough impetus, one of Mahan's most ardent and influential disciples was Henry Halleck, who had written his 1846 textbook on warfare to include the latest American and European thinking. Halleck, too, advocated for extensive use of entrenchments whenever they could play a role. Had he departed his St. Louis headquarters to take the field before the Battle of Shiloh, he would almost certainly have ordered the army to dig in.[37]

Finally, there was the matter of Fort Donelson. Though the outcome of that campaign was an overwhelming Federal success, the very scope of the triumph partially obscured some alarming elements. Chief among them was the fact that at dawn on February 15 the Confederates launched a surprise attack against McClernand's troops while Grant was off conferring with Flag Officer Foote, the expedition's naval commander. Grant's army first arrived outside the Confederate defenses at Fort Donelson on February 13 and spent two days and nights shivering with cold as snow fell. During this time, little effort was made to erect any defenses. McClernand reported that he constructed an earthwork to protect a battery, but he admitted, "A want of additional implements prevented me from carrying into effect my design to intrench the right of my line."[38]

Undoubtedly, that experience led McClernand to worry about a similar surprise at Shiloh. On March 27, dismayed at the haphazard way in which the camps had sprung up, he "suggested [to Grant] that 'the various camps here should be formed upon some general and connected plan.'" McClernand was apparently the only officer who was concerned about the matter, and since Grant, Sherman, and C. F. Smith all disdained McClernand as a political general who owed his rank to friends in high places rather than any solid military qualifications, he was ignored.[39]

Grant's own Donelson report suggested that he only thought of entrenching there after the failure of the gunboats. He considered conducting a circumvallation as part of a regular siege, but he never got the chance. The Confederates attacked, fumbled away their opportunity to escape, and subsequently surrendered before any such engineering effort got under way. After that, the idea of constructing defenses seemed to fade away, to be completely forgotten two months later. In his memoirs, Grant later dismissed the idea that entrenchments at Shiloh were necessary at all: "The troops were not intrenched, but the nature of the ground was such that they were just as well protected from the fire of the enemy as if rifle-pits had been thrown up. Our line was generally along the crest of ridges. The artillery was protected by being sunk in the ground. The men who were not serving the guns were perfectly covered from fire on taking position a little back from the crest."[40]

Of course, entrenching would require labor and tools. Grant had many thousands of laborers on hand—all the troops in those new regiments coming ashore daily at Pittsburg Landing. But those untried men also had much to learn about basic soldiering. Time spent digging earthworks would not teach them the critical skills of military drill that they would need in combat. Nor had they much familiarity with their weapons. The Eighteenth Wisconsin Infantry "was [only] issued Belgian muskets on March 1st and officially mustered into U.S. military service on March 15th." They were finally given forty rounds of ammunition in early April while passing through Paducah, and the first time they fired their new weapons was while aboard the riverboat bringing them to the army. The new soldiers test-fired random shots at the passing scenery. The drill and evolutions many regiments needed to execute perfectly while under fire on a battlefield were beyond the grasp of much of Grant's burgeoning force. The time required to teach those skills before advancing on Corinth was precious and had to be prioritized.[41]

Then there were the needed tools. By 1864, most regiments in both armies amassed regimental inventories of the necessary picks, spades, and axes. During the Atlanta Campaign, each regiment and brigade in Sherman's army had a wagon devoted to such implements, as did the Confederates. But as General McClernand noted in his Fort Donelson report, tools were in short supply in 1862. In a nation springing to arms overnight, even weapons were in short supply, let alone shovels and axes. The harsh realities of war were already teaching the armies of the need to dig in, but many more lessons lay ahead.

Option 2

There was an option short of digging in: laying out the camps so as to better prepare to meet any attack. The encampments at Shiloh evolved haphazardly, selected with an eye toward space and comfort, not defense. The first troops ashore simply camped on suitable ground close to the landing; as other troops arrived, they followed suit, moving inland just far enough to find suitable sites that were flat, elevated, and well drained. Smith's own division (commanded by W. H. L. Wallace in Smith's absence since April 2) was first, and thus closest to Pittsburg Landing. McClernand's and Hurlbut's men came next, camping in Jones and Woolf Fields (McClernand) and around Cloud Field (Hurlbut). The newest arrivals went still farther out. Three of Sherman's four brigades camped near Shiloh Church between Ben Howell, Rhea, and Lost Fields. David Stuart's brigade, also of Sherman's division, was given the most remote site of all. Stuart's men established their camps in Larkin Bell Field along the Hamburg Road. Last to arrive and still forming, Benjamin Prentiss's division encamped between Stuart and the rest of Sherman's force, though only two of his three brigades had been organized by the time of the battle.

This deployment meant that the very newest troops in the army, including many in Prentiss's division who had barely drilled or fired their weapons, would be Grant's first line of defense if the camps were attacked. Even worse, with Prentiss's division dividing his command, Sherman would be hard pressed to control both sectors of his scattered and divided front. In fact, once the battle began, Sherman made no effort to control, direct, or coordinate with Stuart's brigade on the far left.

Grant could coose to order the army to shift campsites and lay out the lines with a much better eye toward defense. Sherman, who with four brigades had the largest division, could move back into a reserve position; so could Prentiss's command. McClernand and W. H. L. Wallace might occupy the front, their men already seasoned by combat at Donelson. Additionally, each division's camps might form a triangle with two brigades in forward positions and one brigade in the immediate rear. This arrangement would allow each divisional commander to have a brigade he knew and trusted to act as his own tactical reserve. Hurlbut's division could be assigned to guard the Hamburg Road, instead of leaving Stuart's brigade to wage its own isolated fight for much of the day. Such a deployment might go a long way toward mitigating the shock and surprise of those first few hours of combat. While Sherman's and Prentiss's greenhorns mounted a credible defense in the early hours of the fight, by midmorning, the surprise and strain of combat also almost completely dissolved them as effective formations.

Such a wholesale shifting of camps would disrupt much of the army and doubtless produce much grumbling in the ranks. But it would also put the army in much better condition to receive an attack, even without digging in.

Further, the disruption would only be temporary, especially if initiated early in the process of gathering strength, say in late March.

<u>Option 3</u>

The third option was the simplest: do nothing. Grant's army would continue to drill, gain strength, and prepare for what everyone expected to be the real test, the advance to Corinth. As noted, almost everyone in the force was over-confident, even complacent, up to and including the commanding general. Why disrupt the army for no reason? Historian Timothy B. Smith, who has written extensively on Grant's campaigns, notes as much:

> Clear examples abound indicating that Grant, early on, had a real problem with overconfidence. When he routed the Confederates at Belmont, he seemed to disregard any chance of a counterattack, which occurred, and it almost cost him the battle and his life. Obviously, the prime example came a couple of months later when he just could not fathom that the Confederate army at Corinth would march out of their entrenchments and attack him on open ground at his campground around Shiloh Church and Pittsburg Landing.[42]

Decision

Hence, contrary to both his West Point education and his superiors' concerns, Grant issued no orders to entrench the camps at Shiloh. Neither did he reorganize his divisions to place veterans in the forefront, instead leaving Sherman's and Prentiss's raw divisions to bear the initial blow of any Confederate attack. Motivated by a sense of complacency and a desire not to make extra work for the quickly growing army, Grant left things as is. After all, the last thing he expected was an attack. Unlike at Fort Donelson, however, where a decisive victory netted nearly fifteen thousand Rebel prisoners and effectively muted any real criticism of Grant's failure to take defensive steps at that battle, Shiloh would be different.

Results/Impact

Grant, of course, was wrong. The Confederates did attack. The ferocious battle that resulted stunned the home fronts on both sides, producing shockingly unprecedented casualty lists. With the aid of reinforcements, Grant held his own, recapturing lost camps on the second day's action, but this time no Rebel army surrendered, and there was no great triumph to obscure awkward questions.

In their attack on April 6, the Confederates achieved what amounted to operational surprise, catching the Federal army unprepared and largely at rest. Thanks to their own slow start and some early morning Federal patrols, the Rebels achieved less of a tactical surprise. Every Union regiment met the enemy in line and with weapons in hand, though, admittedly some of those lines formed only minutes before being assaulted. Further, many of Sherman's and Prentiss's troops fought in front of or amid their own camps, and, given the circumstances, resisted stubbornly for a considerable time. Had those soldiers been fighting from entrenchments; might things have gone differently for the Federal Fifth and Sixth Divisions?

Of course, there were officers within the Federal ranks that believed the Rebels would attack and advocated for exactly those entrenchments, though most of them (except for McClernand) were not among the more senior commanders. In the lower ranks, one of the most contentious of those men was Col. Thomas Worthington, who had so annoyed Sherman by reaching Savannah ahead of the rest of the army. Worthington was a fellow West Pointer and subject to the pervasive influence of the Mahanian mind-set that influenced so many other graduates. Now Worthington and the Forty-Sixth Ohio were in Sherman's division, stationed on the army's far right. In the days leading up to the battle the colonel made a pest of himself to everyone who would listen, insisting that the Rebels were going to attack and demanding tools to entrench. He was repeatedly rebuffed, which irritated him to no end. In his diary entry of March 29, Worthington complained, "Sherman has refused to sign a requisition for seventy-two axes for my regiment, making it twenty-two, and while a slight abbatis might prevent or avert an attack, there are no axes to make it, nor is there a sledge or crowbar in his division." Worthington would prove to have an inflated sense of his own worth as a soldier, but in this instance, he was not wrong.[43]

Finally, would there have been a battle at all had Grant and Sherman ordered the army to dig in? As will be seen, on the very eve of battle, some Confederate generals despaired of surprising the Federals, and advocated returning to Corinth rather than delivering their assault. On the evening of April 5, Gen. P. G. T. Beauregard believed that all chance of surprise was gone, and that the Rebels would find Grant's men "'intrenched to the eyes,'" assessments with which General "[Braxton] Bragg agreed." And yet, at least one prisoner captured just before the attack, "Major Leroy Crockett of the 72nd Ohio," confirmed "that the Union army was not expecting an attack and had no earthworks for defense." What if Crockett's information actually supported Beauregard's supposition? Would the Confederates have indeed canceled their assault? But Grant was not prepared. After the battle, a torrent of uncomfortable questions would be raised, as multiple reports revealing that unpreparedness made their way into the public sphere.[44]

Johnston Decides to March on April 2

Situation

By the end of March, Johnston had assembled his forces—all at least, but Van Dorn, who was too far away to arrive in a timely manner. It was time to strike. In fact, it was more than time, because the Confederates understood Grant's army at Pittsburg Landing was due to be reinforced by General Buell's ponderous column approaching from Nashville. Should Buell unite with Grant, the Rebels would be outnumbered two to one, eighty thousand men to forty thousand of their own troops. Attacking at those odds was an act of suicidal desperation, not military calculation.

But that was not yet the case. Though they did not know Grant's exact strength, Johnston and his generals did know that Grant's army was deployed at both Crump's Landing (Lew Wallace's division) and Pittsburg Landing, where the main body was assembling. If Johnston attacked either location, he was likely to mass superior numbers, especially if he struck Wallace.

Options

Johnston had three choices: to attack the main Federal army, to strike instead at the detached force at Crump's Landing, or simply to await the enemy's advance in hopes of a better opportunity.

Option 1

Johnston's most aggressive course was to attack the main force at Pittsburg Landing. The Federal camps there were all positioned in what amounted to a triangle bounded by the Tennessee River to the east, with the curving line of Snake and Owl Creeks to the north and west. The result was a rough wedge shape narrowing as one moved from Shiloh Church to Pittsburg Landing. These watercourses were a double-edged sword: while they protected the Confederate right and left flanks as the attack progressed, they also sheltered the flanks of any US force that managed to form a defensive line. However, with their backs and both flanks bounded by those same watercourses, any retreat—let alone a rout—on the Federals' part would be disastrous.

Accordingly, while attacking the main army might lessen Johnston's numerical advantage, that attack also presented him with the best chance for a complete victory in the best Napoleonic tradition. A strike on Pittsburg Landing was the riskiest of Johnston's options, but it was also the most likely to produce a decisive result if his gamble succeeded.

Option 2

Alternatively, Johnston could choose to strike at Lew Wallace's lesser command at Crump's. The Confederates could expect to amass greater odds against Wallace's single division, bringing perhaps 25,000 or 30,000 of their force to bear against Wallace, who numbered only 7,564 officers and men in three brigades. But Wallace was not as vulnerable as the main army. While he also had the Tennessee River to his back and no friendly forces to his north, he could retreat southward toward Sherman's camps at Pittsburg, where presumably he would be reinforced. Wallace's force might be scattered in such an attack, but it would be harder to destroy outright, and the rest of Grant's army would be alerted as a result.

Geographically, attacking Wallace posed one additional risk. Crump's Landing was farther north than Pittsburg Landing, and hence farther from Corinth; Johnston would have to march much of his army past Sherman's camps to strike Wallace. As a result, the bulk of Grant's army would be closer to Johnston's base at Corinth than would Johnston's own forces. If Johnston split his forces to either hold Corinth or mask any Federal lunge toward that place while his own main body was occupied at Crump's, he would only be splitting his own force in the face of the enemy, risking his own piecemeal destruction.

Attacking Crump's Landing, then, offered much less chance of striking a mortal blow at Grant, while potentially exposing Johnston's own supply base to loss in exchange. Even though Wallace and even Grant thought Crump's Landing might be a likelier target than the main position at Pittsburg (though only marginally, as they expected no attack at all), for a variety of reasons, it was not a good trade.

Option 3

Of course, Johnston could choose to sit at Corinth, strengthen his own defenses, and await the inevitable Federal approach. He would continue to gather troops, though not as many or as quickly as would Grant. Johnston's best hope here was that when the Federals did choose to advance, they might blunder, advancing haphazardly or even rushing headlong into his own fixed defenses. He might be presented with an opportunity to strike a part of the enemy force before all of it could close on his position. But if Johnston chose to wait, he surrendered the initiative to the combined enemy armies, something any professionally educated soldier was loath to do.

Decision

Ultimately, Johnston chose to attack Pittsburg Landing. He would not settle for the lesser blow at Crump's, nor would he wait for Grant to make the first move. Indeed, in a teasing letter to his daughter written six years earlier, Johnston had revealed a significant aspect of his military philosophy: "You have some of the high and rare qualities of a good General," he wrote. "You know when to take the initiative. You anticipated my attack by making one."[45]

On April 1, Johnston informed his army that it should be "placed in readiness for a field movement and to meet the enemy within twenty-four hours." The troops did not move on the second, but that evening Johnston received two pieces of intelligence that galvanized him into action. The first was news from Confederate cavalry colonel Nathan Bedford Forrest "that a large force was moving in the direction of . . . Grant," information that heralded Buell's imminent arrival. The second came from Brig. Gen. Benjamin F. Cheatham, commanding a division in Leonidas Polk's newly organized First Corps. Stationed at Bethel, Tennessee, approximately twenty miles north of Corinth along the Mobile & Ohio, and about the same distance west of Crump's Landing, Cheatham reported that a Federal force was advancing in his direction. Polk received this intelligence about 10:00 p.m. and immediately forwarded it to Beauregard. In turn, Beauregard passed it as rapidly on to Johnston with the suggestion that since the Federals were dividing their forces, now was the time to strike. Johnston agreed and issued orders to march on Pittsburg Landing. Those instructions were in the hands of Johnston's generals "by forty minutes past one on morning of the 3rd of April." The march out began in earnest that afternoon.[46]

Results/Impact

Johnston's decision set in motion the Confederate approach to Pittsburg Landing. Polk's, Bragg's, and Hardee's Corps all marched from Corinth (except for Cheatham's Division, which left Bethel to join Polk en route), while Brig. Gen. John C. Breckinridge's Reserve Corps marched from the hamlet of Burnsville, east of Corinth. Forty thousand Rebel troops moved to the attack, but the final decision to strike had yet to be made. One more fateful conference would be held before the Battle of Shiloh could begin.

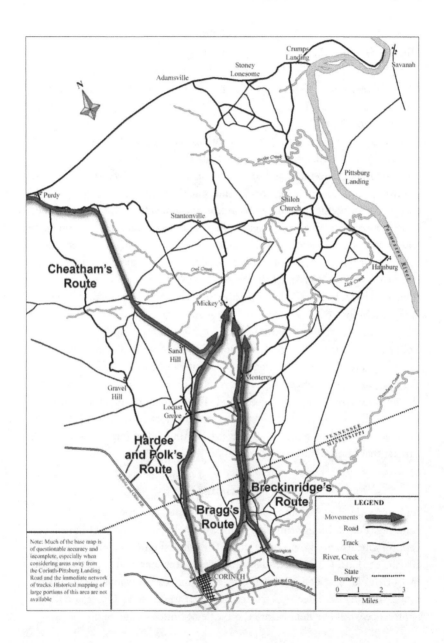

Crumps
Landing

Stoney
Lonesome

Adamsville

Savanah

Snake Creek

Pittsburg
Landing

Purdy

Shiloh
Church

Stantonville

**Cheatham's
Route**

Owl Creek

Hamburg

Lick Creek

Mickey's

Sand
Hill

Monterey

Gravel
Hill

Locust
Grove

**Hardee
and Polk's
Route**

TENNESSEE
MISSISSIPPI

**Breckinridge's
Route**

**Bragg's
Route**

Memphis and Ohio RR

Note: Much of the base map is
of questionable accuracy and
incomplete, especially when
considering areas away from
the Corinth-Pittsburg Landing
Road and the immediate network
of tracks. Historical mapping of
large portions of this area are not
available

Farmington

CORINTH

Memphis and Charleston RR

LEGEND

Movements

Road

Track

River, Creek

State
Boundry

0   1   2   3
Miles

Tennessee River

Chambers Creek

P. G. T. Beauregard Draws Up the Army's Deployment and Plan of Attack

Situation

As the Confederates marched out of Corinth on April 3, Albert Sidney Johnston dashed off a dispatch to President Davis in Richmond outlining his plans to attack Grant. In that wire, Johnston provided not only a quick outline of his intention to attack, but also a glimpse of his tactical plan. He wrote, "Confederate forces, 40,000, ordered forward to offer battle near Pittsburg. . . . Beauregard, second in command; Polk, left; Hardee, center; Bragg, right wing; Breckinridge, reserve. Hope engagement before Buell can form junction."[47]

That message clearly suggested that Johnston had a specific deployment in mind. Leonidas Polk's First Corps numbered 9,404 officers and men. Hardee's Third Corps contained 6,758, while Bragg's powerful Second Corps counted 16,279 officers and men present for duty—more than both the other corps combined. Breckinridge's reserve added 7,211 more soldiers. In keeping with the plan to turn Grant's left and drive the enemy army away from the landing into the flooded bottomlands of Owl Creek, Johnston's assignment of Bragg to the all-important right wing clearly demonstrated Johnston's desire to concentrate the bulk of his striking power on the right.[48]

And yet when the army marched out it did so under a quite different order, which served as the real blueprint for the Confederate attack plan. This order was written Thomas Jordan, a member of Beauregard's staff, who recounted its composition in a postwar letter: "[It was written from] notes you [Beauregard] gave me as the basis for the proper general order to be issued, directing and regulating the march, coupled with the order in which the enemy was to be attacked." Jordan's directive, which was also dated April 3, was issued under Johnston's signature.[49]

Far from adding weight of numbers to the right wing under Bragg, however, these instructions detailed a much different formation. Jordan specified that Hardee's Corps would form a single line with "its left resting on Owl Creek, its right toward Lick Creek." Since Hardee lacked the troops to cover the entire distance between those two watercourses, "a brigade or division . . . from the Second [Bragg's] corps" filled out the front line. The rest of Bragg's Corps "form[ed] the second line of battle about 1,000 yards in rear of the first line." Polk's First Corps came next, "halted in column or massed on . . . the Bark road, according to the nature of the ground, as a reserve." Breckinridge's Reserve Corps was similarly placed behind Polk.[50]

Jordan's orders deployed the main army in two parallel lines, one behind the other, with Polk's and Breckinridge's forces in reserve. Hardee, instead of commanding the center, was responsible for the entire front of the formation, including those of Bragg's men who had been moved up to extend his right toward Lick Creek. Instead of commanding the right wing, Bragg was now responsible for the entire second line. Polk and Breckinridge would go where needed.

Options

Johnston's choice of deployment would have an outsize impact on the Battle of Shiloh, and presumably he weighed his options carefully. Any battlefield is a chaotic place. Changing the direction of an attack or discovering that troops are out of place and trying to redirect them to a different sector of the field can consume precious time, time in which an enemy can recover or the day could slip away. The nature of linear warfare and the limited ability to control large bodies of men in battle, however, reduced Johnston's deployment choices to just a couple of options. Broadly put, they amounted to column and line. The first choice would be to adopt some form of column attack, with extra combat power assigned to one flank or the other, to strengthen the main blow. The second option called for a more balanced deployment in line across the entire front of the advance, which provided for continuous pressure across the enemy's line of battle. Support lines stationed behind the first line could then move to take advantage of any opportunity that arose. Over time, manuals and theorists offered variations and permutations on these two main themes; since the time of Frederick the Great these two basic orders of battle had constituted the main core of offensive tactics in the era of linear warfare.

Option 1:

The linear deployment detailed in Jordan's orders was at odds with Johnston's note to Richmond. With their men comprising the entire first and second lines, respectively, Hardee and Bragg were each responsible for a battle formation more than a mile in length. Moreover, Johnston's weighting of the Confederate right was now changed; instead, an equal number of Confederates were spread out across the entire front. The army reserve now consisted of both Polk's and Breckinridge's commands, which theoretically provided Johnston with more brigades that could be dispatched to deal with crises or opportunities, but at the sacrifice of some tactical control.

That loss of tactical control occurred primarily in two ways. The first was in that mile-long frontage for each of Hardee's and Bragg's Corps. Both corps commanders would have to range up and down the length of their commands, trying to monitor their formations as the battle developed; it was far too wide a span of command to control effectively. Additionally, for each brigade in line, the brigade directly behind it in support belonged to a different division from a different corps. These circumstances made for divided command at the tactical level, compounded by the fact that the senior divisional and corps commanders were likely to be elsewhere at a moment of crisis, trying to supervise other parts of their extended formations. It was a recipe for tactical chaos, and all too often, chaos ensued.

Option 2:

By contrast, a column attack would place each of Johnston's three corps side by side, holding a relatively narrow frontage, with other elements of each corps forming one or more support lines. This is the deployment Johnston described in his dispatch to Davis, in which he wrote: "Polk, left; Hardee, center; Bragg, right wing." While Johnston never elaborated on this idea (he died three days later), typically, each corps would deploy with one or two brigades in the front line and the remainder in support. Each unit would take up a relatively narrow frontage and could count on support from within its own command. Such a deployment would greatly simplify the corps commanders' job, limiting their command span and allowing them to focus on just their assigned sector of the front, not the entire line.

If there was any drawback to this deployment, it was in weighting Bragg's Corps on the right. Bragg's six brigades would have likely adopted a formation three lines deep—a front and two supports. With almost half his army on the right, Johnston would have fewer reinforcements to throw at any crisis or opportunity that arose along Hardee's or Polk's portions of the assault. He would still have his final reserve, under Breckinridge, but deploying in this manner unquestionably predetermined much of Johnston's course of action once the battle began.

Decision

When viewed against Jordan's final deployment, Johnston's telegram leaves us with many unresolved questions. Albert Sidney Johnston bled to death in a ravine on April 6 before he had time to answer any of these queries. What we do know is that at some point, he changed his mind about the deployment—either on the morning of April 6 or more likely during the march up from Corinth. We also know that Johnston did not see Jordan's written order until after he left Corinth, since it took Jordan some time to prepare it and make copies.

Instead, the army marched out under temporary movement orders. Jordan later wrote that Johnston, Beauregard, and Bragg all met in Beauregard's quarters on the morning of April 3. Beauregard laid out his plans during the meeting, even going to far as to draw "a sketch of the country, in pencil, upon [a] table." This was necessary, Jordan explained, since "I had taken to my office the sketch supplied by the engineers to enable me to write the order with the necessary precision." Presumably, Beauregard's drawing showed his intended broad front deployment.[51]

Since the actual attack orders were not fully circulated until April 4, Johnston did not see them until well under way. This circumstance has led a number of Johnston partisans to claim that the general simply didn't know of this change in plans until he was on the march, by which time he decided it was too late to change back. Some go so far as to charge that "Beauregard deliberately altered Johnston's plan" (why that would be is unclear, unless Beauregard were trying to secretly undermine Johnston, for which there is no evidence). Braxton Bragg later opined that "the general plan was admirable, the elaboration simply execrable." Historian and A. S. Johnston biographer Charles P. Roland argues that the confusion resulted from misunderstandings rather than animosity, but he points out, "Regardless of how the plan was formulated, Johnston was acquainted with it before the battle began; as commander of the army he must bear the ultimate responsibility for accepting it."[52]

Results/Impact

Whether Johnston agreed to the change in plans on the morning of April 3 at Beauregard's headquarters or while on the march the next day is not a critical distinction, for he did accept it. Whether he agreed to Beauregard's scheme because it was too late to correct a blunder or because he simply deferred to Beauregard in this matter as he had in so many others is also not significant. Johnston concurred, and the army formed on April 5 using Jordan's deployment order. Moreover, given the subsequent delays in attacking, there was indeed sufficient time to revise that disposition had Johnston chosen to do so; that he did not suggests he had no objections at the time.

The deployment had a profound impact on the outcome of the Battle of Shiloh. As might have been predicted, corps' arrangement in parallel lines created confusion on the battlefield. Troops from the different units became badly intermingled. Divisional and often brigade integrity broke down as well. Officers ranged over the battlefield seeking their commands or untangling them from other formations. As will be seen, the corps commanders ultimately gave up on exercising command of their own formations and simply agreed to assume control over geographic sectors of the field. Of necessity they settled on a scheme very much like what Johnston initially suggested, but without the clear lines of authority provided by the chain of command.

After the battle, criticism of Beauregard's deployment became widespread. As noted above, Braxton Bragg later opined that "the general plan was admirable, the elaboration simply execrable." Excusing his now-deceased commander, "Bragg insisted that Johnston had intended to concentrate on the enemy's left, but Beauregard muddled the details and Johnston hesitated to rearrange the details on the eve of battle." In his history of the Civil War, the French Compte de Paris summarized much of that criticism when he wrote that the Confederates "committed a grave mistake in deploying the different corps in successive lines along the whole front of the army, instead of entrusting a part of that front to each corps, itself formed on several lines." The impact, he felt, was obvious: "During the height of the engagement the three lines found themselves completely entangled with one another. Divisions, brigades, and even regiments being broken up and mingled, the generals could no longer get their commands together, and that system, the real sinew of armies, which is called the hierarchical organization, being destroyed, all command of the whole became impossible."[53]

There are a couple of other points worth considering when discussing the impact of the fateful deployment order. The man who drafted it, Col. Thomas Jordan, later wrote, "As I framed this order, I had before me Napoleon's order for the battle of Waterloo, and, in attention to ante-battle details, took those of such soldiers as Napoleon and [French Marshal Jean] Soult for [a] model."[54]

Jordan's comment has drawn sharp comment from historians, most notably Wiley Sword, whose seminal modern work on the battle, *Shiloh: Bloody April*, appeared in 1974. Sword argues that Jordan's reliance on Napoleon's order (really drawn up by Armee du Nord chief of staff Marshal Soult) "called for an attack by succeeding waves of infantry, with each corps aligned one behind the other across the entire front." It was assumed by all, said Maj. Edward Munford, also a member of Johnston's staff, that "'no force the enemy [could] amass could cut through three double lines of Confederates.' It was a fatal flaw," concludes Sword, "as events would later demonstrate."[55]

As so many have noted, Jordan's chosen deployment did indeed create problems during the fighting. But those problems had little to do with Napoleon or Soult. For one thing, in examining the actual disposition of Napoleon's corps at Waterloo, it is obvious that the French army was arrayed very differently than was the Army of Mississippi on the morning of April 6.

On June 18, 1815, Napoleon positioned his leading two corps side by side, not on single lines one behind the other. Moreover, while each French division deployed its two brigades abreast, each brigade formed with two battalions in the front line and two (most brigades had four battalions) behind. At the start of the Battle of Waterloo (about 11:30 a.m.) the French First Corps under the Count d'Erlon was formed across a narrow frontage three divisions wide (with a fourth coming into line on the right). Each brigade was in line with half in the front and half in support. Other corps were formed in column to the rear and held in reserve. All in all, while there are a few similarities between the two forces, the bulk of the French troops were formed much differently than what Jordan ordered for the Army of Mississippi.[56]

Instead, Jordan's choice of formation, while flawed, was conventional. He was simply relying on what was in 1861 the standard US (and Confederate) army doctrine. General Winfield Scott dominated the antebellum army, having served in the War of 1812, and having won everlasting renown by conquering Mexico City in 1847. He had served as the commanding general of the United States Army since 1841, a post he held until he retired in 1862. Scott also wrote the army's standard drill manual, first published in the 1830s. It held sway until supplanted by William J. Hardee's manual in 1855, and then only partially. Hardee's handbook, translated from the French, focused on company and battalion instruction for use with the new rifled muskets then coming into service; it did not supersede the third volume of Scott's work, which dealt with evolutions of brigades, divisions, and corps.[57]

Scott's manual stated quite clearly how a line of battle was to be deployed, and Jordan's deployment matched that description very closely: "A line of eight battalions, making up a *corps d'armee* of two divisions or four brigades, will be supposed, but the rules herein prescribed are equally applicable to a brigade, a division, or any number of battalions. . . . As often as one or more brigades or divisions, united in the same line, manouevre together, each battalion will be designated by its number according to its position in the line." Thus were the men of the old army taught, and thus would they fight, at least until the hard school of war taught them differently.[58]

Scott's influence can be seen on many Civil War battlefields, not just at Shiloh. For example, consider Lieut. Gen. Thomas J. "Stonewall" Jackson's deployment of Confederates in preparation for his dramatic assault on the Federal Eleventh Corps at Chancellorsville, just over a year later. Jackson commanded three divisions of between four and six brigades each. In addition, individual divisions were roughly the same size as Johnston's various corps formations at Shiloh. Deploying for the attack, Jackson arrayed his divisions one behind the other, each division formed in a single line of brigades, and each brigade with all the regiments/battalions in a single line abreast. The result was another long line of battle, more than a mile wide and three divisions deep, all in heavily wooded terrain not unlike Shiloh. Unsurprisingly, a great deal of confusion arose as Jackson's three lines became intermingled, confusion that, coupled with nightfall, forced the Confederates to halt. Even Jackson's wounding by his own men mirrored Johnston's demise at Shiloh. But Jackson's attack is considered one of the tactical masterpieces of the war, while Johnston's was, in Wiley Sword's words, fatally flawed. And yet both assaults used the same standard formation.[59]

Of course, Bragg's criticism was based on hindsight. At the time, there was little evidence that anyone objected to Beauregard's deployment. Johnston certainly did not; contrary to Bragg's assertion, he likely knew of Beauregard's intended formation when the army left Corinth. Further, even if Johnston only discovered Beauregard's "muddle" on the "eve of battle," Johnston still had plenty of time to adjust the plan, given the unexpected delays resulting from the march up. In his postwar essay concerning Shiloh for *Century Magazine*, later published in *Battles and Leaders of the Civil War*, Beauregard insisted in his own defense, "[Before the pertinent orders] were finally written, all the details were explained to and discussed by me with General Johnston." While the army commander thus had ample opportunity to modify the orders, he did not. Historians only have Johnston's terse telegram to President Davis from which to infer that Johnston intended a different deployment. But since Beauregard's plan was the one implemented, Johnston either changed his mind or again deferred to Beauregard.[60]

Johnston Overrides His Generals and Decides to Attack on the Night of April 5

Situation

Confederate troops began to march out of Corinth on the afternoon of April 3. Hardee's Third Corps led, since his three brigades would form the first line of the eventual assault force. They marched out via the Ridge Road, headed for a crossroads known locally as Mickey's after the farmer who lived there. (This site today is known as the community of Michie, though it is still pronounced as "Mickey.") Half of Polk's First Corps followed Hardee; the other half, under Cheatham, would march south from Purdy to rendezvous with his corps at Mickey's Farm. Bragg's Second Corps (the largest, with six brigades organized into two divisions) marched out via the Corinth Road and through the hamlet of Monterey, then joined the convergence at Mickey's.

Lieutenant General William J. Hardee.

Breckinridge's reserves marched from Burnsville to Corinth and then fell in behind Bragg's column.[61]

Mickey's Crossroads was thirteen miles from Corinth, and about six and a half miles from Sherman's and Prentiss's picket lines. Once at Mickey's, the Confederate attack plan next called for the assault columns to form up as follows: Hardee in the lead, his three brigades abreast; Bragg in the second wave, his six brigades also abreast; Polk's four brigades, all in brigade column; Breckinridge's three brigades, all similarly in column behind Polk. Johnston expected the march to be completed by the night of April 4, with a dawn attack launched on April 5.[62]

That plan proved wildly optimistic. Right from the start, the movement was marked by delays, straggling, and confusion. Hardee moved his corps off the Ridge Road on the night of the third to camp, but he failed to notify Polk, who marched past him—an error that took time to rectify the next morning. Rain on April 4 mired the roads, causing traffic jams, incurring delays that greatly affected the troops bringing up the rear. Breckinridge's trailing command was especially impacted, and it finally diverted to the Ridge Road. By the evening of April 4, while Hardee's leading elements were deploying into their attack positions, the rear of the army was still a day's march away. The Confederates changed their plans to attack at 8:00 a.m. instead of first light, but it was soon obvious that a morning attack on April 5 was impossible. Johnston's frustration grew as the hours passed. At midday on the fifth, somewhere near Mickey's, he was heard to exclaim, "This is perfectly puerile! This is not *war!*"[63]

To make matters worse, Confederates repeatedly clashed with Federal pickets and patrols. A significant alarm ran through the US camps on the evening of the fourth, when a patrol from the Seventy-Second Ohio clashed with the Fourth Alabama Cavalry. The Alabamians retreated through the ranks of Brig. Gen. Patrick R. Cleburne's brigade (of Hardee's Corps), pursued by the Ohioans, who soon stumbled into Cleburne's men. The discovery of Rebel infantry just a couple of miles from the Buckeyes' camps was soon reported up through the Union chain of command to Sherman. The firing "produced major reverberations. Numerous Federal units were called out to form a line in the rain, including [in] . . . Hurlbut's, [W. H. L.] Wallace's, and McClernand's divisions." Sherman, however, downplayed the incident, becoming "enraged at what he designated indiscreet conduct" on the part of the Seventy-Second Ohio's officers.[64]

With the Confederate attack again postponed until the morning of April 6, some of Johnston's officers were now convinced that surprise was impossible, and that the attack should be canceled. As the command group gathered on the evening of the fifth, Beauregard spoke out: "Surprise, which was the basis of his plan, was now scarcely to be hoped for. . . . [A]mple notice of our proximity" must have reached the Federals, he said, and "the Federal army would, no doubt, be found intrenched to the eyes, and ready for our attack." Bragg gloomily echoed Beauregard: "The delay of 36 hours will cause failure." Polk still wanted to attack, supported by an enfeebled Breckinridge, who joined the conference at about 4:00 p.m. but immediately lay down on a blanket. Ill, he only rose "occasionally" to "add a few words of counsel" in support of Polk. Hardee was apparently not present.[65]

Presented with such opposition from half his commanders, Johnston faced stark choices: stay and fight, or march back to Corinth. The Confederates would gain nothing by simply defending in place—i.e., holding the current ground but waiting for the Federals to come and attack them. Moreover, with the enemy presumably now fully aware of the Rebel presence, sidestepping Pittsburg Landing to strike at Crump's was impossible.

Options

Should Johnston continue with the plan or give it up and return to Corinth?

Option 1

Johnston had risked much on an all-out attack against Grant, and now he was at last ready to strike. And, despite Beauregard's gloomy assessment, Johnston knew that the Federals were not "intrenched to the eyes," a fact his own engineers uncovered while questioning Union prisoners. In fact, those prisoners were shocked to see the entire Rebel army massed so close to their front, with US forces oblivious to the enemy presence. Not even the skirmishes and reports of firing alerted the Federal army. If Johnston's men were raw, Grant's men were as well, and they were as prone to blunders and errors as his own command.

Moreover, returning to Corinth without attacking would damage the morale of Johnston's men, and probably see him relieved of command. The army—indeed, the whole Confederacy—expected Johnston to redeem the failures of Donelson and Henry by driving the Federal invaders back north. Could he simply turn tail and slink back to Corinth?

Option 2

But if the Federals were ready to receive him, Johnston could be marching into a trap, and retreat might well be the better choice. The intelligence concerning the lack of breastworks came on April 4. It was now the evening of the fifth. What if the Federals had used the past day to dig in, with those works cleverly concealed from outside observation? Beauregard spoke only accepted wisdom when he fretted that frontal assaults by raw troops against an entrenched foe were "unwise." The only thing worse than marching back to Corinth without a fight would be to launch a frontal assault that produced nothing but the army's self-butchery. Pressing the attack under these circumstances was a risky proposition at best.

Decision

If Johnston's resolve wavered, it went unrecorded. According to his biographer Charles Roland, "Johnston listened courteously to Beauregard and the others, and then said quietly that he yet hoped to find the enemy unprepared." According to Bragg, "Johnston declared, 'we shall attack at daylight tomorrow.'" To others, he expressed nothing but resolute confidence. Famously, "to one staff officer he said, 'I believe I will hammer 'em beyond doubt.' To another, 'Tomorrow at Twelve o'clock we will water our horses in the Tennessee River.'" And to yet a third, he insisted, "I would fight them if they were a million. They can present no greater front between those two creeks than we can, and the more men they crowd in there, the worse we can make it for them."[66]

Results/Impact

Whatever his reasoning, Johnston's final decision, taken that night of April 5, committed the Confederates to action and precipitated the Battle of Shiloh.

He made his choice believing that the Federals remained somnolent, un-aware—despite all that had passed—that the Confederates were camped just beyond their picket line.

The fault for this quiescence, and for Johnston's continued military good fortune, must lie primarily with William T. Sherman. He not only disre-garded any number of signs and warnings concerning the Rebel presence, but he also heaped scorn on those bringing him those reports.[67] The story of Shiloh is replete with examples of Sherman's derisive responses to various officers, perhaps the most infamous of which was sent to Col. Jesse Appler of the Fifty-Third Ohio. Appler's regimental camp in Rhea Field, south of the Shiloh Branch, was the closest to the Confederate lines. A mere thousand yards separated Cleburne's Brigade, on Hardee's left, from Appler's regi-mental street. A civilian in uniform whose age, lack of military experience, and nervous demeanor really rendered him unfit to command a regiment, Appler was nonetheless certain he was about to be attacked. On the eve-ning of the fifth, as Johnston was giving Beauregard his hearing, Appler was alerted to Cleburne's presence. He formed the Fifty-Third into line and sent an officer to Sherman's command tent to alert his divisional commander. Shortly, that staff officer returned with Sherman's derisive reply: "Colonel Appler, General Sherman says: 'take your damned regiment back to Ohio. There is no enemy nearer than Corinth.'" This retort elicited a burst of laugh-ter from the men of the Fifty-Third, who then "broke ranks without waiting for an order to do so."[68]

That same day, Sherman informed Grant, based on the recent activity, "The enemy is saucy, but got the worst of it yesterday, and will not press our pickets far. . . . I do not apprehend anything like an attack on our position." This breezy dispatch prompted Grant's own complacent telegraph to Halleck in St. Louis: "I have scarcely the faintest idea of an attack (general one) being made upon us, but will be prepared should such a thing take place." These words, and many other such dismissive comments would come back to haunt both Sherman and Grant after the fighting was over. What was clear, how-ever, is that Johnston's resolve paid off. He would get his attack and achieve his surprise.[69]

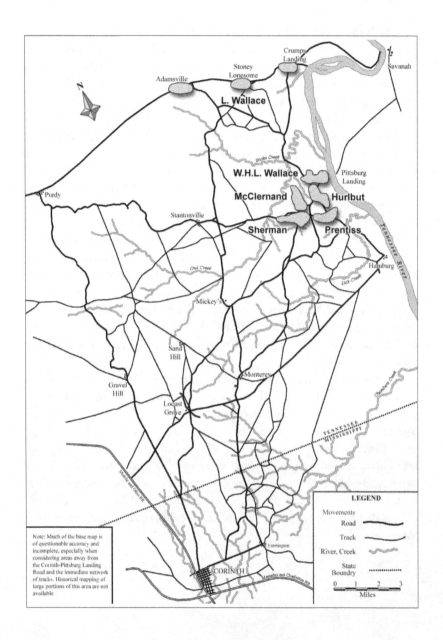

Note: Much of the base map is of questionable accuracy and incomplete, especially when considering areas away from the Corinth-Pittsburg Landing Road and the immediate network of tracks. Historical mapping of large portions of this area are not available

LEGEND

Movements
Road
Track
River, Creek
State Boundry

0   1   2   3
Miles

CHAPTER 2

MORNING, APRIL 6

Colonel Everett Peabody Sends Out a Reconnaissance

Situation

Col. Everett Peabody commanded the First Brigade in Benjamin Prentiss's Sixth Division, Army of the Tennessee. He got little sleep on the night of April 5–6. He was troubled by the steady flow of reports reaching him from uprooted civilians and jittery Federals, all of which insisted that a large Rebel army was gathered just beyond his picket line. On Saturday, April 5, he had asked permission of Prentiss to send out a patrol to investigate those reports. Prentiss did not answer, probably since as a divisional commander he was only too aware of the army's strict injunction not to bring on a general engagement, or even provoke a fight of any kind. This admonition, originating with Halleck in St. Louis, had been made clear to all Federal officers via Grant and Sherman.[1]

Peabody was the commander of the Twenty-Fifth Missouri and, as senior colonel, the acting brigadier. "It is funny to be called General," he wrote in a March 31 letter to his brother Frank, "but the boys are all delighted, and I think will do good service at the proper time." Peabody had seen action before. He had been wounded in the ankle at the siege of Lexington, Missouri, in 1861 and now walked with a permanent limp. There is also some evidence that in conversations with Prentiss, Peabody had already urged greater alertness,

Colonel Everett Peabody.

warnings which Prentiss ignored. In fact, according to at least one account, "Prentiss 'hooted at the idea of Johnston attacking.'"[2]

Options

Peabody could heed the wishes of his divisional commander and do nothing further. Alternatively, he could send out a patrol on his own initiative.

Option 1

Lacking definitive permission to reconnoiter, Colonel Peabody could simply have done his best to prepare his four regiments for a possible attack, then trusted that the army's more senior officers would safeguard the Federal camps. After all, he was not even a general; Peabody had been elevated to brigade command because he was the senior colonel. Further, as can be seen from Sherman's repeated reaction to other US officers who expressed concern, if Peabody did send out a patrol and it triggered some sort of engagement, he could be blamed for disobeying orders. Clearly, this was the safer option for the colonel's career.

Option 2

But it might not be the safer option for the army. Alternatively, Peabody could take the initiative and order out a patrol on his own authority. If the reports he was receiving were correct, the entire army could be in grave peril and oblivious to the looming threat. Though Peabody was a civilian in uniform rather than a professional soldier, he had served nearly a year, seen combat at the Battle of Lexington, Missouri, and certainly understood the dangers of a surprise attack. Ignoring the warning signs of that attack might be the safest choice for him personally—officers could hardly be punished for following orders—but inaction was charting a potentially dangerous course for the army.

Decision

Peabody was a man of confidence and firm opinions. Tall and robust, he was two months shy of his thirty-first birthday that April, with a decade's worth of life experience under his belt. Having graduated from Harvard in 1849, he had since worked as an engineer and an executive for railroad companies in Tennessee, Kentucky, and most recently in Missouri. He had lived and worked on the frontier and was no stranger to assuming personal responsibility for his actions. When Maj. James E. Powell of Peabody's own regiment, the Twenty-Fifth Missouri, asked permission to investigate the reports of Rebels, Peabody quickly authorized the reconnaissance. At 3:00 a.m. Powell led a mixed force of five companies drawn from the Twenty-Fifth Missouri and Twelfth Michigan out on a predawn patrol. Their mission was to scout off to the southwest of Peabody's tent line and across the front of Sherman's divisional camps. Peabody watched them depart, shaking hands with some and informing several patrol officers, "'I can not say anything more to General Prentiss, but he will soon see how near I was right.'" The colonel also bore a premonition of his own death: "'I must do this on my own responsibility, but I will not live to receive censure or credit for doing so.'"[3]

Results/Impact

Powell's patrol passed beyond the brigade's existing picket line, comprising companies drawn from another of Peabody's regiments, the Sixteenth Wisconsin, and pressed on, passing through Seay Field and into the southern end of Fraley Field. "We were sent out skirmishing about three o clock Sunday morning," wrote Michigan private Franklin H. Bailey on Monday, April 8, "and reached the rebals camp just before day light, they were out to meet us, and began to fire into us, we returned the fire and then comenced the battle, we with less than 1,000 men and they with at least 5,000."[4]

Bailey and his comrades first encountered Maj. Aaron B. Hardcastle's Third Mississippi Infantry Battalion, deployed as skirmishers and advance pickets across the front of Brig. Gen. Sterling A. M. Wood's Third Brigade of Hardee's Corps. Powell's appearance forced two small parties of advanced pickets to fall back to Hardcastle's main skirmish line, but the Confederates soon offered stronger resistance. The major reported, "The enemy opened a heavy fire on us at a distance of about 200 yards. . . . We returned the fire immediately and kept it up. Captain Clare, aide to General Wood, came and encouraged us. We fought the enemy an hour or more without giving an inch."[5]

This fighting began around 5:00 a.m., before full dawn. Johnston heard the first volleys and asked the time. One staff member's watch showed 5:14 a.m., while others' timepieces recorded 4:55. Beauregard, who was again advocating a retreat to Corinth, was cut off by Johnston's interjection: "The battle has opened gentlemen. It is too late to change our dispositions." Then the army commander mounted and headed for the front, leaving Beauregard to direct the flow of the reserves as needed. As he departed, Johnston reiterated a previous assertion: "Tonight we will water our horses in the Tennessee River."[6]

Powell's fight also affected the Federal camps, for the firing was plainly audible there as well. Sherman and Prentiss both heard it. Initially, those sounds were dismissed as yet another small clash, soon over; but when the volleys grew louder and more sustained, that casual dismissal was reversed. Powell fought long enough to witness much of Hardee's battle line emerging from the woods, several thousand strong, providing more than enough evidence to suggest a real attack. The major was reinforced by elements of the Sixteenth Wisconsin, still on picket, and subsequently part of the Twenty-First Missouri, with the unit's colonel, David Moore, at the troops' head. Moore took charge of the fight and asked for the rest of his regiment to be sent forward.

Upon hearing the firing, Prentiss became enraged. "He rode up to [Peabody], and reprimanded him as follows: 'You have brought on an attack for which I am unprepared, and for which I will hold you responsible.' . . . 'General, you will soon see that I was not mistaken,'" Peabody snapped back.[7] Prentiss's accusation was, of course, nonsense. The Confederate attack was happening, regardless of any Federal patrol. Instead Peabody had prematurely uncovered the Rebel movement, buying the unwary Federals time to begin forming up. The long roll began to sound in camp after camp, calling the men to duty. Peabody was killed in action that morning, and so for many years his critical decision to send out that reconnaissance was overlooked. However, modern scholars have given him his full due.

Johnston Orders the Army to Pivot in the Eighteenth Wisconsin Camp

Situation

Alerted (if just barely) by Peabody's predawn patrol, the Federal divisions of Prentiss and Sherman managed a credible defense during the opening Rebel assaults. Sherman's three brigades on the Federal right did well, aided by the local terrain. Buckland's and Hildebrand's brigades formed a solid defensive line along a high ridge overlooking Shiloh Branch, straddling the Corinth Road just south of Shiloh Church. Here, between about 7:30 and 10:00 a.m., intermingled Confederate brigades from Hardee's, Bragg's, and Polk's Corps all made unsuccessful assaults on that position. On Sherman's far right flank, McDowell's brigade confronted a single Confederate brigade under Louisiana colonel Preston Pond; neither command became heavily engaged.

Prentiss's two brigades had a less advantageous position and suffered more as a result. The ground here was flatter and uncut by ravines or streams, allowing the Confederates to approach in a more coherent manner. Peabody's men nevertheless held their own for some time despite the loss of Colonel Peabody, who fell here with a mortal head wound. Four Confederate brigades moved against Prentiss's two, however, and pressure was mounting, especially on Prentiss's left.

Here Col. Madison Miller's newly formed Federal brigade faced Confederate brigadier general Jones M. Withers's division of Bragg's Corps, consisting of three brigades: Brig. Gen. Adley H. Gladden's, Brig. Gen. James R. Chalmers's, and, moving up in support, Brig. Gen. John K. Jackson's. Recently arrived, barely organized, and in some cases lacking even a full issue of ammunition, Miller's men were among the newest in the Federal service. One private in the Eighteenth Wisconsin lamented, "We received orders to load. I had ten cartridges in my box, and I divided with the boys who had none, until I only had three left. . . . I don't think there were 2,000 cartridges in the regiment. On the way up the river we had twenty rounds given to each of us with instructions to try our guns, and . . . [those] twenty rounds were mostly shot away." The Eighteenth's soldiers only reached their new camps the day before and had received no new issue of ammunition or rations since landing. Now they entered Spain Field and deployed into a battle line for the first time in earnest.[8]

Even so, the first Rebel assault was repulsed. Sgt. Horatio Wiley of the Twenty-Second Alabama, a member of Gladden's Brigade, described a maelstrom of fire: "The 21st Ala. & the 1st La. suffered more than any other reg't engaged. Gen. Gladden's left arm was taken off about the first fire & Col. Adams of the 1st La. took com'd. Soon afterwards Maj. Armstead fell by a grapeshot thro' his bowell. In a few minutes more Col. [Zachary] Deas rec'd a slight wound in his left hand. Then Col. Adams had his horse shot from under him while leading a charge. . . . On both sides the slaughter was heavy."[9]

Miller's position crumbled when Chalmers's Mississippians stepped up to help Gladden's battered command. Chalmers came up on the Confederate right, striking the Eighteenth Wisconsin holding Miller's left flank. Sans bullets and attacked in the flank, the Eighteenth broke, taking with it the rest of Miller's command. Gladden's and Chalmers's men soon overran the Federal camps situated directly north of Spain Field. "As soon as our columns began to move the enemy fled," noted Sergeant Wiley. He continued, "Our forces took possession of their camp. Here was a perfect curiosity shop. Everything in the eating & wearing line, in fact every tent told of high & extravagant living."[10]

Albert Sidney Johnston witnessed this last attack, joining the men as they overran the Federal camps. Many Confederates now broke ranks to loot those richly laden tents, as if the battle were over and the day won. Johnston, of course, knew the battle was just getting started; he needed those troops back in line and pressing onward. Amid the debris of the Eighteenth Wisconsin's campsite, "an officer had brought from a tent a number of valuable articles, calling General Johnston's attention to them. He answered, with some sternness: 'None of that, sir; we are not here for plunder!' And then, as if regretting the sharpness of the rebuke, . . . he added, taking [a] little tin cup, 'let this be my share of the spoils today.'"[11]

With Miller's brigade routed, Johnston now contemplated what to do next. His plan had always been to turn the Federals' left flank, driving Grant's army away from the river and from Pittsburg Landing. Johnston intended to force the Federals back into the swampy pocket formed by Snake and Owl Creeks, where they could be destroyed or captured. This could not be accomplished if the Confederates simply advanced in a straight line from their starting positions; just driving forward would instead push the Federals to the northeast, directly toward the landing, not away from it. Hence, once Johnston found the Federal left flank, he needed to direct the Rebel right to pivot to the left and attack toward the northwest. Here, amid the Eighteenth Wisconsin's campsite, Johnston could sense heavy fighting to the west, where Sherman still held. He could detect no enemy troops or sounds of combat to the east. At 9:30, while halted among the fruits of that first success, Johnston had a decision to make.[12]

Options

Had Johnston found the Federal left flank or not? If he had indeed lapped the enemy's left, he could begin his pivot to the northwest. His own right flank was still a long way from the banks of the Tennessee, however, and he might only have stumbled into a gap in Sherman's and Prentiss's front. Johnston's second option was to wait, push farther eastward, and make certain he really had turned the flank before beginning his pivot.

Option 1

If Colonel Miller's brigade was indeed the left flank of the Federal line, then Johnston had achieved his goal and could begin the turn to the northwest. While moving along the lines earlier, the general had urged various officers to shift troops to the Confederate right, or eastward. Now he could begin to use those troops to outflank and drive the remaining Federal defenders to where he envisioned their destruction. If Johnston was correct, victory was within his grasp.

Option 2

If, however, Johnston was wrong, then he would be turning too soon, catching too few Federals in his trap while exposing his own right flank to more as-of-yet unengaged Yankees. Miller's camps were still a considerable distance from the Tennessee River, which curved away to the east at what was called the Upper Landing. A little over a mile of hilly, wooded terrain still lay between Spain Field and Lick Creek, the next major watercourse that flowed into the Tennessee. It was perhaps three-quarters of a mile from the field to the Hamburg Road, which passed for the next major thoroughfare in the area. Scouts found no new nearby camps east of the Eighteenth Wisconsin's, nor immediately to the north, but what about farther on? The safer course would be to push Confederate brigades as far as the Hamburg Road before pivoting to the northwest. Earlier, to make sure he was not himself surprised by Federal troops appearing from this direction, Johnston sent Col. George Maney and his First Tennessee Infantry (of which only five companies were present) to guard that road where it crossed Lick Creek. Maney and his men reinforced Nathan Bedford Forrest's cavalry regiment and an artillery battery already assigned that mission.[13]

Decision

By perhaps 10:00 a.m., Johnston concluded that he had indeed turned the Federal flank, and he began the pivot to the left. As William Preston

Johnston noted, "General Johnston was carrying forward the movement by which his entire right wing was swung around on the center, [Brig. Gen. Thomas C.] Hindman's brigade, as a pivot, so that every command of the Federals was taken successively, in front and flank, and a crumbling process ensued by which the whole [Federal] line went to pieces." Col. R. G. Shaver, who was commanding Hindman's brigade at the time, had just overrun Peabody's brigade camps when he was given a new task. As he reported, "I was ordered to make an oblique change of front to the left, with a view of making an attack on an encampment to the left and rear of the camp just captured." Shaver went on to assail the left of Hildebrand's brigade, thus beginning to unravel Sherman's first defensive line.[14]

Historian Timothy B. Smith, in his excellent study of the Battle of Shiloh, regards Johnston's decision to turn as "one of the major command decisions at Shiloh—one that would have a profound effect on the rest of the battle." In fact, it is not too much to argue that this was perhaps *the* key decision of the first day's fighting.[15]

Results/Impact

Johnston's decision to pivot certainly unraveled Sherman's line, just as Preston described. Federal infantry and artillery that had been successfully resisting the successive blows of a half half-dozen Confederate brigades for something like two hours, holding secure, now were flanked and driven back. Sherman's men retired between a quarter and a half of a mile, rallying on the lines of John McClernand's division, which had moved up to the Crossroads area to support Sherman's fight. Here, they stood ready to receive the next wave of Confederate assaults.

And yet Johnston had erred. He was not on the extreme left of Grant's army and did not turn the enemy flank. Instead, he was in the gap left between Miller's command and Col. David Stuart's brigade (detached from Sherman) which, it will be recalled, was stationed along the Hamburg Road. That gap was slated to be filled by the newly forming Third Brigade of Prentiss's Sixth Division. While several of the regiments intended to make up that force had landed that very morning, the brigade had not yet come into being, nor had they taken up any line.

Further, Johnston was unable to scout deeper into the Federal position, so he did not realize that Stephen Hurlbut's Fourth Division (twelve regiments in three brigades, many of them veterans of Donelson) was camped north of Stuart along the Hamburg Road leading back to Pittsburg Landing. Hurlbut was perfectly positioned to either extend the Federal line all the way to the river or, if left untended, to strike Johnston's pivoting flank in turn.

Johnston's decision and the subsequent pivot focused the fighting for much of the late morning and early afternoon over on the Federal right, against Sherman and McClernand. By contrast, the fighting on the far left began very belatedly—after 11:00 a.m. The relative inattention of the Confederate forces in this sector allowed a new Federal line to coalesce around Hurlbut's and, subsequently, W. H. L. Wallace's divisions, primarily along what has come to be known as the Sunken Road.

Had Johnston pushed his line all the way to the Hamburg Road before turning into his leftward pivot, he might have overrun Stuart's brigade sooner. He might then have outflanked the Hurlbut/Wallace line that subsequently formed along the axis of the Peach Orchard and Sunken Road.

Capt. Samuel H. Lockett Reports a Federal "Division" Farther to the Federal Left

Situation

The two outermost brigades of Johnston's pivot belonged to Chalmers and Jackson, both of Withers's Division. Withers's remaining brigade, formerly led by Brigadier General Gladden, now had its third commander of the day, Colonel Deas of the Twenty-Second Alabama. For the moment, Deas was too badly shot up to continue the attack. Chalmers and Jackson, however, pushed forward to the Hamburg–Purdy Road, angling to the northwest. They overran the camps of Prentiss's supporting cavalry (two battalions of the Eleventh Illinois) and emerged from the timber along the road near the southwest corner of Sarah Bell's Cotton Field. Once there, Chalmers's Mississippians took note of other Federals. To their north, either north of the cotton field or just entering it, they could see more US regiments moving about. These belonged Hurlbut's division, brigades led by Brig. Gen. Jacob G. Lauman and Col. Nelson G. Williams.

In response to Sherman's calls for support, Hurlbut sent his Second Brigade under Col. James C. Veatch westward toward the crossroads. The unit would be engaged on the Federal right the rest of the day, fighting no more with the rest of the division. Hurlbut then led his remaining two brigades south in response to a similar plea from Prentiss. This was the move Chalmers observed, reporting that "the enemy was reinforced and drew up in our front, supported by a battery of artillery and some cavalry." Passing word back to Johnston, who was still nearby in the Eighteenth Wisconsin camp or thereabouts, Chalmers then continued his duties: "We were about to engage them again, when we were ordered by General Johnston to fall back, which was done."[16]

Johnston recalled Chalmers and Jackson because he now had more detailed knowledge about the actual enemy positions, and that news was not
good. Capt. Samuel H. Lockett, an engineer on Bragg's staff, found Johnston
at about this time. Lockett had ridden out earlier that morning to reconnoiter
the Federal left. He traveled east on the Bark Road and then turned north
along the Hamburg Road, where he discovered Stuart's brigade. The captain
observed the troops for a time as they went about their normal camp rou-
tines, and then as they reacted to the sounds of the growing battle off to the
west. While Stuart's command included only three regiments, his brigade
numbered just under two thousand men, enough for Lockett to believe it represented all or part of another Federal division, unexpectedly placed to turn
Johnston's flank. "I then began to fear," Lockett recalled, "that the division in
front of me would swing around and take our forces in flank, as it was manifest that the Federal line extended farther in that direction than ours." With
that, Lockett headed back, finding Johnston along the way. After explaining
his bona fides, Lockett detailed his observations. His report had a profound
impact on the rest of the battle.[17]

Options

Given that his drive to the northwest was already under way, Johnston's
choices were limited. As his first and quickest option, he could simply have
the two brigades closest at hand (Chalmers and Jackson) halt and form a defensive shield for his own right flank while he continued destroying the Federal right. If needed, Gladden's battered command was available nearby as
a further support. Alternatively, Johnston could pull Chalmers and Jackson
out of the pivot, not to use defensively, but to shift farther east along the Bark
Road to strike the real Federal left flank. Doing so, however, would take
time and fragment the Rebel assault. Thirdly, Johnston could have Chalmers
and Jackson hold the Rebel center and guard the drive northwest while he
brought up all of Breckinridge's still-unengaged Reserve Corps to find and
strike the Federal left.

Option 1

Johnston had two brigades at hand—Chalmers and Jackson. He immediately halted their forward movement when they reported the new threat, and
he now placed them in the woods south of the Hamburg–Purdy Road. He
could leave them there to stave off any US attack against his own flank. Additionally, Johnston had Gladden's Brigade, now reorganizing under Deas,
as a further reserve. All told, Withers's Division took nearly 7,800 men into

action that morning, and even after subtracting the heavy casualties suffered while overrunning Prentiss, there were at least 6,500 to 7,000 Rebels here. While detaching Withers's Division from the drive against Sherman and McClernand certainly weakened Johnston's pivot, there were other reserves—Breckinridge's Reserve Corps—that could come forward.

Of course, there was also the question of what, exactly, the Federals would do. Their surprise appeared to have been complete. It was already 10:00 a.m., and heavy fighting had been raging for hours. These Yankees were just now showing signs of activity. How long would it take them to organize and mount a larger attack? Johnston was likely unaware that Grant did not even reach the battlefield until well after the fighting had begun, but clearly the Federal response so far had been very sluggish. With Chalmers and Jackson as a bulwark, it might be hours—perhaps all day—before these newly observed Federals could intervene over on the Federal right.

Option 2

But Johnston was here to crush the whole Federal army, not just part of it. Otherwise, he could simply have struck Lew Wallace at Crump's Landing. Those same two Confederate brigades could be moved farther east, guided by Lockett or some of his escorting cavalry squad, and used to strike at these new Federals before they mounted an attack of their own. Here, Johnston would have to depend on that same US sluggishness to give him time to shift thousands of Rebel infantry a mile or so to the east, form up, and attack via the Hamburg Road.

Moving Chalmers and Jackson was much the riskier gambit. Not only did Johnston need the Yankees to remain inert while he did so, but he was also creating a hole in the center of his line that would have to be filled with other troops, either from Breckinridge's command or by further weakening the pivoting force. If he simply left that two-brigade gap in his front, the now-exposed flank of that pivot would be dangerously vulnerable, and Johnston could not depend on the Federals' passivity lasting through the rest of day.

Option 3

There was a third option, one that split the difference. Johnston could leave Chalmers and Jackson in place, reoriented to guard the pivoting flank and defend the Confederate right. They could be further supported by Deas's (Gladden's) mauled command, which would have the additional advantage of keeping Withers's Division together as a tactical entity. Johnston could also use Breckinridge's Reserve Corps to move down the Bark Road to the east, and then the soldiers could come in somewhere on the Federal left when needed. If the Federals were attacking by the time Breckinridge was in position, then Breckinridge could move north to flank them in turn. If they had yet to organize an assault, then Breckinridge might still achieve a measure of surprise, attacking them in their camps from an unexpected direction.

Decision

Johnston did not hesitate long. He would not stand on the defensive, and he had no knowledge of how long it would take to move Breckinridge up the Bark Road to extend his own right as far as the Hamburg Road. Using the troops at hand to solve the immediate problem, Johnston turned to Chalmers's and Jackson's Commands. "[A] guide (Mr. Lafayette Veal) was sent to conduct us still farther to the right," Chalmers reported, "where we learned that the enemy was attempting to turn our flank." In his report, Withers noted only the following: "General A. S. Johnston . . . immediately ordered the division to move to the right. This movement was promptly and rapidly performed, over ground that was rough, broken, and heavily timbered." If other problems arose due to the shift, they would be dealt with as needed.[18]

Results/Impact

Of course, Johnston's decision to move Withers to the right (minus Gladden's men, who remained in Lost Field, re-forming) created a two-brigade gap in his center, leaving the now-truncated right flank of the pivoting force exposed. That problem was the next to be addressed.

Johnston's modus operandi at Shiloh was to lead from the front while his second-in-command, General Beauregard, orchestrated the flow of reserves from the rear. Johnston had already sent Beauregard several suggestions along those lines, carefully not couching them as orders. The commander felt that Beauregard, from his fixed position at the rear, might well have better or more timely information from other sectors of the field. In one such suggestion, Johnston directed Breckinridge's Reserve Corps to move toward the Confederate left opposite Sherman; Beauregard had fortuitously overridden this advice since it turned out the troops were unneeded there. Instead, Beauregard had posted two of Breckinridge's brigades, under Brig. Gen. John S. Bowen and Col. Winfield S. Statham, behind the right wing, holding them in reserve. He sent the remaining brigade under Col. Robert P. Trabue (which included four regiments of Confederate Kentuckians, already starting to be called "Orphans") to the left under the same orders.[19]

Now Johnston ordered the soldiers into the space left vacant on the right, sending Captain Lockett to help guide them into position. So far, Bowen's and Statham's men had done much marching but no fighting at Shiloh, and now more marching lay ahead of them. As Col. Isaac Dunlop of the Ninth Arkansas reported, "My regiment . . . was at daylight ordered to the anticipated battlefield. After a march of 2 miles our knapsacks, &c., were left. Soon after again reaching the road the roar of artillery broke upon the ear. We were ordered to the scene of action at double-quick for nearly 2 miles, when the scene of battle laid before and below us. We were here formed in line of battle."[20]

Johnston's gamble did pay off in one sense: Lacking any direction from Grant or any other senior officer, neither Hurlbut's two brigades nor David Stuart's brigade moved forward to exploit the gap left by Chalmers and Jackson. At 11:00 a.m., an hour after receiving Johnston's orders, Chalmers led the attack against Stuart's line, which was still in position near the brigade camp around Larkin Bell's Field. Jackson went into action on Chalmers's left. Stuart mounted stiff resistance, fighting for an hour before being forced back over very rough ground, where he joined a new line comprising Hurlbut's two brigades and Brig. Gen. John McArthur's brigade from W. H. L. Wallace's division. Statham and Bowen would eventually enter the fray that afternoon in the Bell Cotton Field, assaulting the western end of the Sunken Road position. All eight (four Confederate and four Federal) brigades faced tough fighting through the rest of that long and bloody day.

However, the most drastic consequence of Johnston's decision was additional fragmenting of the Confederate command structure. That led to a loss of coordination and control. Generals had difficulties organizing assaults or even in locating their troops. Confusion reigned as men who had straggled or fallen out could not find their commands, further reducing the firepower of the Confederate regiments on top of already staggering losses. Any military organization's combat effectiveness is a direct result of that formation's ability to exert command and control amid the extreme chaos of combat. Johnston's decision here, though it did not create the chaos (which had begun almost from the minute the first Confederate troops collided with the first Federal units), greatly exacerbated that chaos.

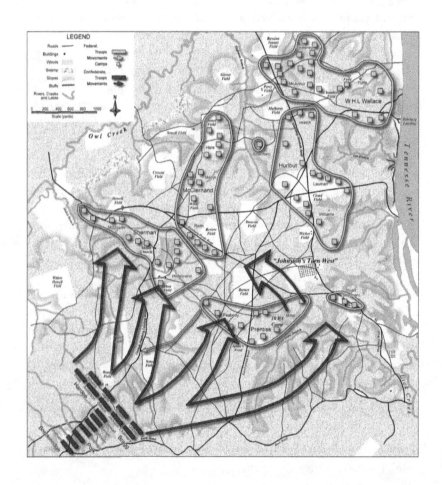

Braxton Bragg, William J. Hardee, and Leonidas Polk Divide Up Command

Situation

As described, Johnston's decision to shift Chalmers and Jackson eastward contributed greatly to the confusion overtaking the Confederate assault. By midday, the Rebel battle line stretched for more than two miles, and it was rare for more than two brigades of the same corps, let alone the same division, to fight alongside one another. Braxton Bragg's Second Corps, for example, had a brigade on each end of the line. Col. Preston Pond's (mostly) Louisiana brigade of Brig. Gen. Daniel Ruggles's First Division was on the extreme Confederate left, while Chalmers's Mississippians in Withers's Second Division occupied the extreme right. Brig. Gen. Patton Anderson's brigade of Ruggles's division was next in line to Pond's right, but Ruggles's remaining brigade under Col. Randall L. Gibson was more than a mile farther to the right, facing the Sunken Road near the Davis Wheat Field. Polk's and Hardee's Corps were equally fragmented, while elements of Breckinridge's force, as noted above, were simultaneously sent to both flanks. There were also examples of regiments becoming separated from their brigades, being left to roam the field looking for their commanders, or simply giving up that search to fall in with other commands.

Lieutenant General Leonidas Polk.

At the tactical level, Civil War armies communicated up and down the chain of command either via messenger or in person. Corps, divisional, and brigade commanders were legally allotted a set number of staff positions by Congress; the greater the leader's authority, the more staff members he was allowed. Commanders selected their staffs individually, based on various criteria. Younger officers who showed special promise were often chosen, especially those who were West Pointers or graduates of other military schools. For the Confederacy, institutions like The Citadel in South Carolina or the Virginia Military Institute were solid sources. But given the scope of the new war compared to the old military's previous needs, such officers were highly sought after. As likely as not, they were promoted to regimental and brigade command posts of their own. Younger sons, friends, sons of friends, and likely junior officers chosen from the rank and file were all alternative sources for these positions. William Preston, for example, lacked military experience but was a close friend of Johnston's, serving on his staff as a VADC, or volunteer aide-de-camp. Gov. Isham Harris of Tennessee also joined Johnston as a VADC.[21]

Leonidas Polk's staff exemplified much of this diversity. Over the course of the war, it included Lieut. William B. Richmond, a former US Navy officer and the treasurer of the Episcopal Diocese of Mississippi before the outbreak of hostilities; Lieut. Henry C. Yeatman, stepson to 1860 presidential candidate John Bell and son-in-law to Polk's brother Lucius; and, by 1863, Polk's own son-in-law William D. Gale. After meeting them in the summer of 1863, English army officer James Arthur Lyon Fremantle described "Richmond and Yeatman [as] . . . excellent types of the higher class of southerner." He further said of the two men, "Highly educated, wealthy, and prosperous before the war, they have abandoned all for their country. . . . They glory in speaking English as we do, and their manners and feelings resemble those of the upper classes in the old country. No staff officers could perform their duties with more zeal or efficiency than these gentlemen, though they were not educated as soldiers."[22]

Staffs were important not only because they carried messages, but also because an officially recognized staff officer, once his name was published in orders as serving a general, spoke with that officer's authority. In times of crisis, a staff officer could issue orders to other military leaders using the legitimacy of his own commander's power. This weighty authority made sense given the state of nineteenth-century battlefield communications and the confusing nature of combat.

But that same authority also meant that chain of command was important. An unknown officer riding up to a general during an action to deliver new instructions could produce confusion, even disaster. Commanders within the existing military hierarchy were more likely to know and recognize the staff officers assigned to their own superiors and acknowledge their authority. But by midmorning on April 6, that chain of command had largely broken down.

In military terms, every offensive has a culminating point at which disorganization, supply shortages, simple exhaustion, or all the above force an attacker to halt. The Army of Mississippi had not yet depleted its ammunition, and the men were not too prostrated to go on, but the command situation was quickly unraveling.

Options

Options for solving this organizational problem were limited. The army could either pause long enough to shift troops and restore lines of communication and command, or the senior officers could make the best of the situation presented them.

Option 1

After defeating Prentiss and Sherman, the Confederates could pause their offensive to redeploy. Brigades that had become detached from their divisions needed to regroup, and stragglers could be rounded up and returned to ranks. Meanwhile, generals and their staffs could take the time to get reoriented on the battlefield and locate their forces. Even soldiers who had been helping wounded men to the rear (a quite common occurrence, especially among green troops witnessing their friends and relatives mutilated or killed before their eyes) could be returned to the fighting ranks. Both the return of stragglers and the regrouping of combat formations would add greatly to the fighting power of the army going forward.

Of course, regrouping would take time, allowing that same process to play out on the Federal side of the battle lines. Grant's army was, if anything, even more disorganized than Johnston's command. Time to reorganize and regroup would arguably be even more precious for Grant's ability to defend than it would be for Johnston's capacity to maintain the attack. For a soldier trained in the shadow of Napoleon Bonaparte, who considered the offensive the primary method of war and who practiced the art of pursuit like no other general in history, pausing now could only be a blunder. Doing so would throw away the fruits of a victory on the verge of being a complete triumph.

Option 2

The more prosaic solution was obvious. Confederate corps and divisional commanders should simply take charge of those forces nearest to them, dividing the front into rough sectors, and press on with whatever troops were at hand. While this would do nothing to sort out the gigantic organizational mess that had developed, it would allow the attack to continue without significant pause. Of course, there would also be no time to round up stragglers and return them to the shattered ranks, thus leaving many regiments to continue as mere skeletons for the rest of the day. The Confederates could only hope their continued pressure denied the Federals the same opportunity.

Decision

There was no discussion of pausing, certainly not by Johnston or any of the corps commanders. Nor did Johnston attempt to define such a command reorganization. Instead, it fell to the three main corps leaders to decide how best to handle the creeping disarray. At about 10:30 a.m. General Polk reported, "I sought out [General] Bragg, to whose support I had been ordered, and asked him where he would have my command. He replied: 'If you will take care of the center, I will go to the right.' It was understood that General Hardee was attending to the left. I accepted the arrangement, and took part in the operations of that part of the general line for the rest of the day." Bragg's own version of that meeting agreed in substance, though he described it slightly differently: "Meeting at about 10:30 o'clock upon the left center with Major-General Polk, my senior, I promptly yielded to him the important command at that point, and moved toward the right."

Hardee never specifically mentioned any division of authority. However, Col. William Preston noted that "General Hardee reported in person to General Johnston . . . at the Wisconsin camp," and was apparently present when Captain Lockett subsequently reported the presence of Stuart's Federal brigade farther to the Confederate right. Since Johnston was personally "directing the battle" in this sector, Hardee reported that "a heavy cannonade soon attracted [him] to the left," where he took charge for the rest of the day. Either Johnston or Hardee must have sent word of that movement to Beauregard, who then similarly must have informed Bragg, Polk, and (presumably) Breckinridge.[23]

Results/Impact

Though the Confederate commanders' collective effort to reimpose order on the battlefield was only marginally successful, it was sufficient to retain offensive momentum and continue the assault. However, while those Rebel attacks continued throughout the day, each one grew increasingly disjointed and haphazard. Federal points of resistance drew Confederate attention, to be sure, but Bragg, Hardee, and Polk were all largely reduced to committing brigades into the fight as they came across them, instead of trying to orchestrate more substantial efforts.

In his postwar biography of his father, Capt. William M. Polk (who also served on his father's staff after Shiloh) attempted to explain the difficulties the corps commanders faced:

> When one of these officers had to concentrate a force for an assault on a difficult point, he had to gather men from almost every corps in the army. Conflicting orders were thus of necessity often given, and so it came about that, instead of the army being continuously projected in heavy masses upon the Federal divisions, its behavior was much like that of a balking team of horses: as one command went forward, the other was standing still. This defect was in part corrected by an arrangement made between Generals Bragg and Polk ... But it was twelve o'clock before the corps commanders had gotten into positions from which they could hope to accomplish anything definite, and only then by ... ignor[ing] the lines of the commands assigned to them for the battle.[24]

Arguably, the Confederates might have been better served by pausing at this point to try and reorganize. Doing so, however, would have risked losing the initiative and allowing General Grant to conduct a similar reorganization. The pressure was on, and the Confederates believed the enemy was crumbling. Now was not the time for a pause to consolidate.

Lew Wallace Marches to the Battle via the Shunpike

Situation

Ulysses S. Grant arose early on the morning of April 6—he had a busy day planned. First, he intended to meet with Don Carlos Buell. The first of Buell's divisions had reached Savannah the day before and settled into camps around the city. Grant intended to ride east and meet the arriving commander to confer, not knowing that Buell had ridden into town the night before. The two commanders would miss each other that morning, the first of many things that were about to go wrong for Grant. After his planned meeting, Grant at long last intended to transfer army headquarters to Pittsburg Landing, joining his command in the field. This movement would also be overtaken by events.[25]

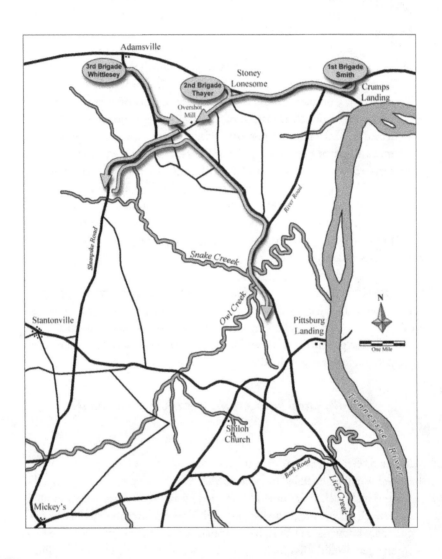

Major General Lew Wallace.

While at breakfast, suddenly the gathered commander and staff could hear cannon fire echoing from upstream. After a momentary pause to listen, "Grant set his cup down, stood up, and said: 'Gentlemen, the ball is in motion. Let's be off.'" Leaving notes for Buell and for Brig. Gen. William Nelson, commanding the first of Buell's divisions to arrive, Grant and his entourage boarded the riverboat *Tigress* and headed south.[26]

Grant's first stop was Crump's Landing, where at about 8:00 a.m. he found Lew Wallace on a steamer and awaiting orders. Until he reached Wallace, who confirmed that there was no firing on his front, Grant was still convinced that Johnston would never attack him at Pittsburg Landing. As he admitted in his memoirs, "Up to that time I had felt by no means certain that Crump's Landing might not be the point of attack." Disabused of this notion by Wallace, Grant promised to send the divisional commander further instructions once he himself had reached Pittsburg Landing and assessed the situation. In the meantime, Wallace should be ready to "execute any orders he might receive." To Wallace, Grant "seemed in a state of uncertainty."[27]

Grant reached Pittsburg Landing at about 8:30 a.m. The heavy fighting had just commenced. After conferring with W. H. L. Wallace, whose division was camped nearest the landing, Grant proceeded to Sherman's front, where he finally realized the full scope of the Confederate assault. At some point he issued a verbal order to one of his staff, quartermaster Capt. A. S. Baxter, to return to the landing, head downstream, and order Lew Wallace to come up.

At the landing, Baxter or possibly Capt. John A. Rawlins—a close confidant and friend of Grant's from his days in Galena, Illinois, and now another member of the general's staff—scrawled a written version of this order. Since virtually every aspect of Lew Wallace's movement to Pittsburg Landing was later the subject of immense and unending controversy, many of the key points of the directive are disputed or remain uncertain. Baxter then boarded a boat and hurried downstream to Crump's. At about 11:30 a.m. Baxter handed the order to Wallace, who read it and then handed it off to Capt. Frederick Knefler. Unfortunately for posterity, Knefler misplaced the order, and it was never seen again. If that note's exact wording were known today, one of Shiloh's greatest mysteries would be resolved.[28]

Wallace's command included three brigades. In the days prior to the battle, he left one brigade at Crump's Landing, one at Adamsville, and one halfway between, at a place atmospherically titled Stoney Lonesome. In dry weather the River Road ran south from Crump's Landing to Pittsburg Landing, but up until just a day or two before, that road had been largely underwater and unusable. In late March, Wallace improved a second route, called the Shunpike, that ran southwest from Stoney Lonesome before turning south to connect with the Hamburg–Purdy Road about a mile west of Sherman's camps. The Shunpike could provide quick access for forces moving between Wallace's detached camps and the main body of the army. Previously, Lew Wallace and Brig. Gen. W. H. L. Wallace had explicitly discussed the need for such a route. However, the main worry there was of reinforcing Lew Wallace's detached command if he was attacked, not of responding to a general assault on the main army.

Later, Grant would insist that his order intended Wallace to come to Pittsburg Landing via the River Road. In April 1863, Rawlins reconstructed the order, contending that it instructed Wallace to "move . . . [his] Division from Crump's Landing . . . to Pittsburg Landing, on the road nearest to and parallel with the river." Over the years, others of Grant's staff supported that version of the order. Wallace and his staff had a much different understanding. A week after the battle, Wallace stated that "[Grant] direct[ed] me to come and take position on the right of the army and form my line of battle at a right angle with the river." Wallace's staff all agreed with their general.[29]

Certainly, the two commanders were at odds in their understanding of what Grant intended Wallace to do. Baxter was unable to amplify and clarify those instructions verbally. Nor did Baxter stay to guide Wallace, but instead hurried back to Crump's so he could rejoin Grant via steamboat. Baxter later claimed he spent "less than three minutes" talking to Lew Wallace.[30]

Options

If Grant's order really did specify a route, then Wallace had little choice. It seems very likely, however, that someone blundered. One possibility is that Grant never explicitly mentioned the River Road because he assumed Wallace would automatically know to come to Pittsburg Landing, not Sherman's flank on the Hamburg–Purdy Road. Alternatively, Baxter's (or Rawlins's) efforts to transcribe Grant's verbal instructions went awry. Wallace now had two ways to reach the rest of the army: the River Road or the Shunpike.

Option 1

The River Road was Wallace's best option had he indeed been ordered to the landing, but this was the case only as of the past few days. For most of March, the River Road was at least partly unusable due to the spring floods. Had the Confederates attacked a week earlier, using the River Road would have been moot. In any case, from his position at Stoney Lonesome, Wallace would not use the River Road for most of his march since he would have to move back to Crump's Landing first. Instead, troops would travel a road extending from Stoney Lonesome to intersect with the River Road north of the bridge over Snake Creek. This route would lead to W. H. L. Wallace's camps stretched between Pittsburg Landing and Russian Tenant Field.

Option 2

The Shunpike followed higher ground, crossed Snake Creek and two tributaries above where they joined, and hence was less susceptible to flooding. Since it also allowed for more rapid access between the flanks of the army (Wallace's advanced brigade at Adamsville and Sherman's right on the Hamburg–Purdy Road), the Shunpike was more likely to be the fastest route to bring Wallace into the fight.

Decision

Much of the debate about what road to take is really a by-product of hindsight. At the time, Wallace thought his choice obvious; he must travel to the right of the army. In 1886, Captain Baxter, the man who delivered that first order, described his encounter with Wallace. Baxter recounted, "Adjutant-General Rawlins . . . requested me to . . . order General Lew Wallace to march his command at once by the River Road to Pittsburg Landing. . . . On meeting General Wallace I gave the order verbally, also handed to him the written order. General Wallace said, 'he was waiting for orders, had heard the firing all the morning, and was ready to move with his command immediately—knew the road and had put it in good order.'" In his memoirs, Wallace added one more detail: "How is the battle going?" he queried. "We are repulsing the enemy," replied Baxter.[31]

Baxter's account reveals that Wallace referred to the Shunpike, the only road "he had put in good order." The explicit references to River Road found in so many of the later accounts most likely were the product of clouded memories. Those same references also suggest that Grant and his staff were not familiar with the roads connecting the two forces, or with the arrangements made between the divisional commanders to connect their commands in a hurry if needed.

Captain Baxter reached Lew Wallace at around 11:30 a.m. Wallace began his march at about noon, heading out on the Shunpike. But this departure was not the critical decision; more was to come.

At the time of Grant's first order to Wallace, Sherman's line was holding. In fact, Grant noted that it had repulsed the Confederates. As the battle raged and the Federals were increasingly being driven, over the course of the day Grant sent four more officers to hurry Wallace along. The first of these was Lieut. Frank Bennett of the Second Illinois Cavalry, who departed the field around 11:00 a.m. and rode up the River Road to Crump's Landing, then west toward Stoney Lonesome. He found Wallace around noon, just ready to march, and urged the general to hurry. At noon, Grant sent Capt. William Rowley, who also rode up the River Road, across to Stoney Lonesome, then south on the Shunpike until he found the rear of Wallace's column. Rowley's message would trigger the most critical decision Wallace made that day.[32]

Rowley found Wallace at about 2:30 p.m., and for the first time Wallace was either informed or at last realized that he was on the wrong road. Rowley's news also included the facts that Sherman's line had collapsed, and that Wallace was headed not for the army's right, but instead for the enemy's rear. In his memoir, Wallace admitted he was shocked. Even more so, he admitted to being "*rattled*" by Rowley's news, declaring, "Beaten—that army? Incredible. The idea struck me dumb—too dumb for question."[33]

Wallace could choose to go on and perhaps strike the Confederates in their rear. A surprise attack from such an unexpected direction might well completely derail the Rebels and save the Federal army. But Wallace had only fifty-eight hundred men facing an enemy Grant estimated at seventy thousand strong. Under these circumstances, was it wise to go forward? Then, of course, there was the matter of Grant's most recent order, conveyed by Rowley: "[Grant] wants you at Pittsburg Landing—and he wants you there like hell," exclaimed the captain.[34]

Once he regained his composure, Wallace decided he had to countermarch. "The words were rough," Wallace wrote, "but the captain's excitement was great, and I passed them the more willingly," he admitted, "since they shifted the responsibility of action from me to General Grant." There was no crossroads near or ahead that would carry the soldiers across to the River Road, so Wallace's column would have to backtrack until, with local help, he could find a suitable crossover route. Here Wallace also chose to implement a countermarch by brigades, so that the entire column must file back on itself while jammed up on a narrow road. He did so to make sure that the leading brigade could remain in the lead. Wallace later admitted, "Referably to time, it [was] indefensible. A *right about* . . . would have expedited the march. My object, however, was to get certain regiments whose fighting qualities commanded my confidence to the front; for that I chose the countermarch."[35]

Results/Impact

All told, the countermarch ate up time, and the search for a crossroads consumed additional minutes, and the march along that unimproved country lane devoured still more time. Wallace admitted that the journey was slow going. When yet two more of Grant's officers, John Rawlins and Lieut. Col. James B. McPherson, found Wallace at about 3:30 or 4:00 p.m., they also fumed at the delays. But by now the damage was done, and the men's arrival did little to speed things up. Via the services of a local named Dick Pickens, Wallace found a connecting road that led into the route from Stoney Lonesome and then, a short distance later, into the River Road north of Wallace's Bridge, which carried the River Road across Snake Creek. The march also suggested why the Shunpike had been so necessary in the first place. Wallace's men now toiled on roads filled with mud that "the trampling of men and horses converted into mortar semi-liquid." A member of the Eleventh Indiana—one of those veteran regiments Wallace was eager to place in the lead—described the march as "mud and mire and backwater from Snake Creek and the river to the high grounds beyond Wallace's Bridge." Wallace also refused Rawlins's angry suggestion that he push forward the head of his column without regard to the rest of the division, insisting, "General Grant wanted my whole division, not a part of it." This necessitated periodic stops to allow the rear to close up. "There would be no piecemeal to the business," Wallace vowed.[36]

As a result, the first of Wallace's regiments finally reached the battlefield at 6:30 p.m., just as dusk was fading into full night. The troops found the bridge guarded by the Fourteenth Missouri Infantry (US), also known as Birge's Western Sharpshooters. Once across, they began to encounter some of the thousands of distraught stragglers that had fled the day's fighting, all of whom carried wild tales of defeat and disaster. Wallace sent word of his arrival to Grant, who ordered him to deploy along the road leading from Wallace's Bridge and wait for morning. In his memoir Wallace claimed he did not meet Grant that night, though many years later, when both men visited the battlefield in 1903, a fellow veteran of his division claimed otherwise. According to the veteran, Wallace told him of a personal meeting with Grant "that night at the landing. Grant seemed angry but did not rebuke Wallace, simply telling him that his division formed the right of the army and that he would attack at daylight."[37]

Wallace's failure to intervene in the battle on April 6 almost certainly tipped the fighting in the Confederates' favor, though they fell short of final victory. Grant maintained that he would have won the first day's fight if Wallace had been present, though this might be a stretch. Of course, even if Wallace had done exactly as Grant envisioned upon receiving the first order to move at 11:30, his men would not have reached the field before 3:30. As will be seen, Sherman's and McClernand's combined right wing had been driven out of Jones Field by that time, and the focus of the fight was turning to the Hornets' Nest. Given time to deploy, Wallace's division could not have joined the fight until 4:00 p.m. or later, at which point the battle had already gone decidedly against the Federals.

The most intriguing aspect of the question of delay really concerns that morning, before Wallace began his march. Why did it take Captain Baxter so long to reach Wallace in the first place? Grant issued the order at about 9:00 a.m. It was two and a half hours before Baxter delivered that order, traveling first to Crump's Landing by steamer and then inland. Lieutenant Bennett, who simply rode up the River Road expecting to meet the head of the column at any minute, still managed to locate Wallace within an hour of departing, and before Wallace set out on his own march at noon. Why was Bennett so much faster than Baxter? If Baxter had simply ridden up the River Road, as Bennett did, would he have reached Wallace at 10:00 a.m.? Would setting out an hour and a half earlier have made the difference?

It is also worth speculating what might have happened if Grant had moved his headquarters to Pittsburg Landing before the battle. He would have been alerted by the firing much earlier, and presumably have been able to assess the situation much more rapidly. With a much-improved decision loop, Grant might well have been able to summon Wallace to the field more quickly, and he probably would have had a better grasp of the road network as well. If Wallace had been able to join Sherman and McClernand on the right as early as midday, the fighting on that flank might have gone much differently. At that time, those two officers were organizing a counterattack out of Jones Field to retake the Crossroads area along the Hamburg–Purdy

Road, an assault that nearly succeeded. What might they have achieved if a fresh division had reinforced them?

Finally, we must acknowledge the largest what-if of them all: What if Wallace had disobeyed Grant, continued forward on the Shunpike, and then entered the battlefield from the southwest along the Hamburg–Purdy Road? Even with the late start, Wallace's column could have reached the Confederate rear around 3:30 p.m. The shock of an entire Federal division appearing in the Confederate army's rear would certainly have garnered Beauregard's attention, since his headquarters was by that time close to where these Federals would have shown up. Beauregard, who was also by then in command of the army (Johnston's wounding and death occurred at about 2:30 p.m.), would have had to react forcefully to any such arrival. Confederate troops that were historically shifted from the Rebel left over to the Rebel right, and who helped seal the fate of the Federal defenders in the Hornets' Nest / Sunken Road area, would instead have been diverted to face Lew Wallace. In turn, this likely would have meant that W. H. L. Wallace's and Prentiss's men would have been able to successfully disengage at 5:00 p.m., their path of retreat still open back to the landing.

Of course, such a move would also place the entire Confederate army between Wallace and the rest of Grant's command. If Wallace were exposed and vulnerable in his camps around Stoney Lonesome, how much more so would he be once he reached the Rebel army? With the other Federal divisions driven back in wild disorder to the landing, they could not possibly come to Wallace's aid if the Confederates managed to turn a sizable force against him. In short, while Wallace's appearance in the Rebel rear might have been a tremendous Federal opportunity to alter the course of the battle, it would also have been a tremendous risk.

Speculation is a dangerous path for any historian to tread, and it is impossible to predict such outcomes with certainty. But it is well within reason to see that Wallace's mere appearance in the Rebel rear could have had a dramatic impact on the outcome of the fighting on April 6—an impact that could have cut both ways.

CHAPTER 3

AFTERNOON, APRIL 6

William T. Sherman and John A. McClernand Decide to Counterattack

Situation

The collapse of Prentiss's division in Spain Field and along Peabody's brigade camps in turn unraveled Sherman's three brigades along the Shiloh Church line. Sherman's regiments subsequently fell back to the Crossroads, named for the intersection of the Corinth, Pittsburg Landing, and Hamburg–Purdy Roads. These units were met by Maj. Gen. John McClernand's division, drawn up in line. Some of Sherman's men fell in alongside McClernand's troops, and the men readied to meet the next attack.

McClernand's three brigades were encamped in a long line from Jones Field down to Review Field. The modern Sherman Road runs the length of McClernand's camps. Col. A. M. Hare's command set up in Jones Field, with Col. C. C. Marsh's brigade in the woods just to the south. Both brigades faced generally west toward Owl Creek. Col. Julius Raith's brigade camped to Marsh's left and was nearest to Sherman. Moreover, Raith's camps were laid out facing southwest, fronting the Hamburg–Purdy Road. Raith's men were the first of McClernand's forces to become engaged.

At Sherman's request, Raith moved his troops forward, going into action east of Shiloh Church, where they were also flanked and driven back.

Major General John McClernand.

Raith fell, mortally wounded, near the intersection of the Corinth and Hamburg–Purdy Roads. Part of Hare's brigade formed a new line along the north edge of Review Field, while Marsh took up a supporting position north of the Corinth–Pittsburg Road. Both commands provided a rallying point on which McDowell's, Buckland's, and Raith's units partially re-formed. Hildebrand's more fragmented Ohioans did not re-form as a brigade, though elements of his regiments fell in with other commands.

"While this disposition was being completed," McClernand reported, "the enemy were rapidly advancing at all points, supported by several batteries. The action, both by infantry and artillery, became general all along the line, and the conflict was desperate." Desperate indeed, for thanks to Johnston's pivot, the attention of all or most of twelve Confederate brigades now focused on McClernand's position. By contrast, McClernand's only available support arrived when Col. James C. Veatch's brigade of Hurlbut's division, dispatched earlier, appeared. However, as noted in chapter 2, Veatch would be the only of Hurlbut's men to fight here; Hurlbut moved his other two brigades to reinforce the Federal right, where other troops were currently engaged in Bell's Cotton Field.[1]

While holding the embattled Shiloh Church line, at around 10:00 a.m. Sherman was visited by Ulysses S. Grant, who provided him with two important pieces of information. First, Lew Wallace's division would be up soon to support Sherman and the Federal right, traveling via the River Road to the bridge over Snake Creek, in the army's rear. "It was paramount," notes park historian Stacy Allen, "that [Sherman] hold both the road and the bridge, otherwise Wallace's men could not cross the flooded creek." Grant also relayed heartening news concerning Buell; the first elements of his army were even now en route to the east bank of the Tennessee opposite Pittsburg Landing, where his men could be ferried across the river to join the fight. Thus, vital reinforcements were available—if Sherman and McClernand could buy sufficient time for them to arrive. With that, Grant rode on to the left, where "the situation did not look as good." The army commander trusted to Sherman's acumen and would not pay a return visit to the Federal right until much later in the day, near 4:00 p.m. Shortly after Grant took his leave, Sherman's men made their disordered retreat to McClernand's crossroads position.[2]

By 11:00 a.m. the Sherman-McClernand line at the crossroads, hammered by repeated Rebel assaults and again threatened from the flanks, became untenable. By this time, another segment of Federal line had formed on McClernand's left when two brigades of W. H. L. Wallace's division came into position along the Sunken Road. There Wallace bolstered the remnants of Prentiss's force (perhaps five hundred men) and connected with Hurlbut. In turn, Hurlbut connected with the brigades of Brig. Gen. John McArthur (from W. H. L. Wallace) and Col. David Stuart, still positioned on the Federal far left. Now forced into another retreat, Sherman and McClernand managed to retain tenuous contact with Wallace and Hurlbut as they swung their line back like a gate, with the Federal right—McDowell's brigade— swinging the farthest.[3]

By 11:30 a.m., Sherman and McClernand's combined right fell back through Crescent Field to Jones Field, halting amid Hare's orderly rows of canvas tents. Here the two divisions received some welcome reinforcements, though not from Lew Wallace or Buell. The Thirteenth Missouri, earlier detached from Hurlbut's division to guard a section of artillery, now reported to McClernand. Also, the Fifteenth and Sixteenth Iowa Infantry, about 1,500 men in all, had just come up from the landing, ordered by Grant to report to McClernand. These last two units were among the rawest of the raw—one of them had reached the landing the evening before, and the other had literally arrived on the battlefield that morning. Yet their numbers were welcome. Even better, when McDowell reported in, Sherman discovered that his three regiments had barely been engaged thus far and were still organizationally intact. Freshly reinforced and with the Confederate attacks flagging, Sherman and McClernand now had a chance to confer.[4]

Options

So far, while the fighting had been desperate, neither Federal division was completely hors de combat. There were, however, tough choices to be made. Union troops' efforts at stationary defenses had crumbled, first along the Shiloh Church line, and then at the Crossroads. Most Federal camps were in Rebel hands. What should the two generals do? They could retreat, they could choose to defend Jones Field, or, more daringly, Sherman and McClernand could even mount a counterattack to recapture their original camps.

Option 1

The Federals could retreat farther, perhaps back to Pittsburg Landing, where fresh troops were expected. There they could rally, recover some of the thousands of stragglers that had broken from the ranks, and organize a more substantial defense. A controlled retreat would be better than falling back under the weight of renewed enemy pressure, but only just.

The drawbacks to a further retreat were obvious. A new line would have to form on the high ground of the landing and along the ridge that carried the River Road toward Snake Creek; behind them, Union soldiers would only find more river bottoms. Once at the landing, the Federals would have no other line to fall back to. If it turned out that they could not hold the landing, then the army would be destroyed, with Confederates surrounding H. L. Wallace, Hurlbut, Stuart, and what was left of Prentiss's force. This would be especially likely if Grant's promised reinforcements were not yet on the scene. And having already been driven from multiple defensive positions so far, could Sherman's and McClernand's remaining effectives hold the landing unaided, if it came to that? An immediate retreat might buy a bit more time, but it might also be the recipe for unmitigated disaster.

Option 2

Holding in Jones Field was the cautious course of action. At 11:30, McClernand's leftmost regiment, the Eighth Illinois of Col. Abraham Hare's First Brigade, was still in the woods a few hundred yards south and slightly east of Jones Field. The brigade's men had fallen back only about two hundred yards from their 11:00 a.m. position at the north edge of Duncan Field, and they represented a tenuous connection with the Seventh Illinois of Col. Thomas Sweeny's Third Brigade of W. H. L. Wallace. This connection needed to be maintained, even strengthened, to prevent yet more Confederates from wedging their way between the two halves of the Federal army and forcing open a path to the landing.[5]

But a static defense also offered no guarantee of security. At least two lines (McClernand counted three in his report, but one was an interim position) had already been compromised through frontal and flank attacks. Each time, the combination of temporary Confederate disorganization and frantic Federal efforts to rally cobbled together a new defense, but could that happen a third time? If the line in Jones Field gave way, could the troops be rallied short of the landing, if at all?

Option 3

The third option was the most aggressive: a counterattack. Circumstances also strongly argued that now was the time for such a strike. At least two of McClernand's brigades were still in relatively good order, as was Col. John McDowell's command. The lack of immediate pressure from the Rebels suggested that the enemy was equally disrupted. It is a truism of military theory that no attacker is as vulnerable as at the culmination of a successful assault; when the attacking formations have lost cohesion, their ammunition is depleted, and key commanders have been wounded or killed. Moreover, the Yankees might be able to recover their camps or, at the very least, buy some of that additional time Grant needed to bring up those reinforcements.

Of course, both Sherman's and McClernand's men had already suffered much. Asking them to strike now was asking a great deal. If that offensive was repulsed or fell apart, could the troops once again be re-formed to mount a further defense? In risking too much, the two generals might be gambling with the survival of Grant's whole army. Attacking was clearly a risky option.

Decision

There is no stirring account of Sherman and McClernand meeting to discuss these options. For this reason, interpretations of the Battle of Shiloh have for many years de-emphasized what came next, instead focusing on the drama of the Sunken Road and Hornets' Nest. Nor did the two men report on this decision in any detail. Summarizing several hours of combat in a short passage, Sherman merely wrote, "Finding [McClernand] pressed, I moved McDowell's brigade directly against the left flank of the enemy, forced him back some distance, and then directed the men to avail themselves of every cover. . . . We held this position for four long hours, sometimes gaining and at other times losing ground, General McClernand and myself acting in perfect concert and struggling to maintain this line." McClernand offered a more thrilling description of the counterattack, though he omitted the details of arranging it: "I rode along my line and gave the order, 'Forward;' responsively to which it rapidly advanced, driving the enemy a first and second time for half a mile with great slaughter."[6]

According to historian Stacy Allen, Sherman and McClernand simply carved up the patchwork Federal line using the same principle that had guided the Confederate corps commanders: geographic expediency. With no time to sort out all the fragments of regiments, Sherman took the right half of the line and McClernand the left, "and [they] counterattacked from Jones Field at noon." Given the details found in the various reports, it seems that McClernand's segment of the line carried the assault's momentum; even Sherman's report noted that he advanced McDowell's brigade to aid McClernand and take pressure off the latter's flank. McClernand biographer Richard Kiper notes that the general "initiated a counterattack with a portion of his Second and Third brigades . . . [with] Sherman and the remnants of his command join[ing] the advance."[7]

Essentially, then, it was either a joint or a simultaneous decision, perhaps made instinctually rather than after a detailed discussion or sober weighing of options. In any case, it proved to be the right choice at the right time.

Results/Impact

The attack surprised the Confederates. McClernand's assault first struck Bushrod Johnson's brigade, now commanded by Col. Preston Smith, driving it south to Woolf Field along the axis of modern-day Sherman Road. Along the way, the Federals recaptured Marsh's brigade camps and McClernand's own divisional headquarters tents. They also overran Capt. Robert Cobb's Battery of Kentucky Confederates; as the unit's park tablet states, "At 12 m. its horses were all killed and guns taken." These pieces were not permanently lost, since the Federals had no way to move them, but the battery was ineffective for the rest of the battle.[8]

On the Federal right, McDowell pressed south through the timber west of the modern road, outflanking Johnson's (Smith's) brigade until the Federals encountered a flanking threat of their own. Here, Confederate colonel Robert P. Trabue's brigade of Breckenridge's Reserve Corps engaged McDowell's men from the direction of Crescent Field. Beauregard dispatched Trabue to the Rebel right that morning when the rest of Breckinridge's force was directed eastward, and despite hiving off regiments to various missions, Trabue's men were still fresh and relatively intact when the Union counterattack began. Turning to meet Trabue's threat, McDowell took up a north–south line facing west and overlooking a ravine. Trabue's men swung into position against this formation, facing east. The resulting overall Federal line took on the shape of a rough fishhook as McDowell protected McClernand's right. The fighting here raged for at least an hour, if not more.[9]

Elements of up to fourteen Federal regiments were involved in this attack (the exact number will never be known, given the disorganized state of the army by this point), and they faced all or part of seven Confederate brigades. As a result, this action was one of the largest sub-engagements of the battle. Most sources agree that the attack began at about noon, with Sherman and McClernand finally falling back again into Jones Field sometime after 2:30 p.m. The assault not only bought Grant time and space for the long-anticipated reinforcements, but it also diverted half the Confederate army away from the exposed right flank of the Sunken Road–Hornets' Nest line, allowing W. H. L. Wallace and Hurlbut to hold their ground. McClernand's and Sherman's gamble paid off handsomely.

Johnston Decides to Lead from the Front on the Critical Right Wing

Situation

Though this decision was really made in Corinth well before the battle commenced, its full consequences were not manifest until the afternoon of April 6, when the battle's fury reached its zenith. The roots of the problem lay in the Army of Mississippi's unusual command structure, and in Johnston's habit of deferring to Beauregard in most tactical matters.

The Confederacy had two full generals present: P. G. T. Beauregard and Albert Sidney Johnston. Beauregard had been transferred west precisely to avoid a similar situation in Virginia. At the Battle of First Manassas, Gen. Joseph E. Johnston had brought his Army of the Shenandoah to join with Beauregard's Army of the Potomac. Joseph Johnston ranked Beauregard, even though the latter general had the larger army. During the fight, Joseph Johnston essentially let Beauregard run the show since he was more familiar with the ground. Subsequently, with the Federal army defeated and the Rebel forces consolidated into a single unit, Joseph Johnston assumed command of the combined Confederate army. Frustrated at being supplanted and by the lack of offensive action in Virginia, Beauregard, still hailed as the "Hero of Manassas," eventually asked to be transferred west. He got his wish, but only to come up against the same situation at Corinth—too many generals.[10]

As a compromise, Albert Sidney Johnston offered to remain as overall departmental commander while Beauregard assumed direct command of the newly assembled army. This gesture, possibly symbolic, was perhaps just a chivalric courtesy. In any case, Beauregard declined. This left the second- and fifth-ranked officers in the entire Confederacy to jointly lead the army. Rather than have Beauregard step down to a corps command and thus supersede either Bragg, Polk, or Hardee, Johnston instead retained him as second-in-command. To further complicate matters, Johnston chose Braxton Bragg, head of the newly organized Second Corps, to take on the additional role of chief of staff. Since a chief of staff drafted the army's orders and could issue directives in the commander's name, this situation created a potentially awkward command arrangement. As corps commander, Bragg was Beauregard's subordinate, but as chief of staff, he could issue orders to the army with Johnston's imprimatur.

As we have seen, however, neither Johnston nor Bragg penned the army's marching orders or spelled out the intended final deployment. Instead, Beauregard's man Jordan drafted those orders, working from the general's notes and effectively (if informally) supplanting Bragg as chief of staff. Perhaps this was because Bragg still retained command of the army's largest corps, having never relinquished that responsibility. It was generally understood that Bragg would command his corps in the coming battle, and so would abandon his chief-of-staff duties once the shooting started. In any case, Beauregard's attack orders proved especially controversial. They called for Hardee's Corps to lead, arrayed in a single line with one of Bragg's brigades brought up to lengthen Hardee's front, and for Bragg's other five brigades to be deployed in a single line a thousand yards behind Hardee. Polk followed, and then Breckinridge, each corps in column of brigade.[11]

Johnston did not survive to explain this discrepancy, but as already noted, Bragg later criticized Beauregard heavily. "Bragg insisted that Johnston had intended to concentrate on the enemy's left, but Beauregard muddled the details and Johnston hesitated to rearrange the details on the eve of battle." Johnston's dispositions would have massed his largest command, Bragg's Second Corps, against the Federal left. Under Beauregard's arrangement of forces, the army was evenly distributed across a broad front. Worse, each corps commander's line of battle was too long for effective command, and as each came into action it would—exactly as it happened—become badly intermingled. As "Bragg explained, 'no commander, in a wooded country, could possibly exercise supervision over his own troops, even, and he had no control over those in his front or rear.'"[12]

Then there was the matter of how the army fought. At First Manassas, neither Confederate army had any intermediate structure; all brigades reported directly to their army's commander. It immediately became obvious that this was not the way to direct a battle, and Confederate forces adopted divisional and corps levels of organization shortly thereafter. Certainly, that is how Johnston structured the Army of the Mississippi as it assembled in Corinth in late March: the sixteen brigades were organized into four corps, though only two of those corps also included divisions. Hardee's and Breckinridge's Corps, each of only three brigades, omitted division-level command.[13]

But, even well before battle chaos disrupted the chain of command, the senior Rebel commanders were guilty of committing brigades individually. They were trapped in a mind-set more suitable to junior officers acting as brigade and at times even regimental commanders. As a result, even if Johnston's hinted alternative deployment were used at Shiloh, would it have made a difference in command and control? Or would the command situation have degraded much as it did historically, forcing the army's corps commanders into the rough sector arrangement they eventually settled on?

Finally, there is the question of the troops themselves. Even brand-new Civil War soldiers were unquestionably brave, committed fighters. The casualty lists produced in battle after battle for four long years of bloody war amply demonstrate that commitment. But raw troops experiencing battle for the first time will—understandably—behave unpredictably. Acts of courage can give way in the next instant to panic and despair, and both extremes were amply demonstrated on the field of Shiloh. At moments like those, the presence of a senior commander can have a profound impact on the outcome of a fight. Johnston, who had previously led soldiers in three different armies, certainly understood this unpredictability. Further, given the loss of the Rebel force at Fort Donelson, virtually all the men assembled at Corinth were green. Most of them were drilled to reasonable efficiency, but they were unbloodied by real combat.

Options

All the factors listed above influenced Albert Sidney Johnston's decision on where best to exercise command of his army in its baptism of fire. He had to balance leading from the front with directing the flow of combat from farther back.

Option 1

Johnston's proper place was a position from which he could best command the whole army and direct the commitment of his reserves. Army headquarters needed to be close enough to the fighting for soldiers to reach it quickly and locate it easily. Messages to and from the front should be able to reach the commander in minutes, with reserve troops kept close enough to be dispatched equally rapidly. A commander who placed himself too far forward risked getting caught up in the action swirling around his immediate vicinity but neglecting the larger picture.

By the same token, a commander who moved around too much would prove hard to locate, forcing inevitable delays as couriers sought to deliver messages, request reinforcements, or seek new orders. A commander who could not be easily found might as well be in Corinth, or dead, if he were unable to receive information and issue new orders.

These factors dictated that Johnston should remain with the army headquarters, where he could best monitor the flow of combat. On April 6, the Army of the Mississippi's headquarters advanced slowly, establishing locations at the Two Cabins just north of Fraley Field, subsequently near Shiloh Church, and at the Crossroads that afternoon. If frontline leadership was required, Beauregard remained available to inspire the troops and provide Johnston with his own observations, without Johnston losing control of the army.

Option 2

Alternatively, Johnston could choose to lead from the front, leaving Beauregard behind to orchestrate the larger battle. Johnston could roam the battlefield, making important decisions on the spot and motivating his men as they entered combat for the first time. Doing so would surrender yet more control of the overall battle to Beauregard, who would route reserves and collate information while at army headquarters. In essence, Johnston would be sacrificing greater overall authority to provide personal inspiration where he thought it was needed most.

Decision

Here, too, Johnston did not overly ponder the choice. He fully intended to lead his army from the front, leaving Beauregard behind to coordinate things at headquarters. On the evening of April 5, Col. Jacob Thompson, a volunteer aide on Beauregard's staff, recalled that because of the evening's discussions, "General Johnston determined to lead the attack in person, and leave General Beauregard to direct the movements of troops in the rear." Arguably, since Beauregard had already drawn up the original battle plan, the Creole general would likely have a firmer grasp of the larger picture than would Johnston. Additionally, two other factors argued against Beauregard adopting the forward role. First, the Louisianian was ill on April 6 and unlikely to be as active or wide ranging as Johnston. Further, Beauregard had no faith that the army would achieve the necessary surprise—in fact, before first light on April 6, he was still counseling a retreat. Could Johnston trust him to press the attack with the same grim do-or-die determination that characterized Johnston's own mind-set that morning? As far as Johnston was concerned, the fate of the Confederacy rested on this battle. It was only natural that he would give his utmost to achieve the needed victory.[14]

Results/Impact

Johnston understood that he was turning over much of the direction of the battle to Beauregard. He said as much at about 9:00 a.m. on the first day of fighting, while watching Patrick Cleburne's men engage Sherman's line south of Shiloh Church. While there, he instructed Colonel Thompson to have Beauregard send up Breckinridge's men. "'Say to General Beauregard,' Johnston yelled, . . . 'that the enemy is moving up in force on our left, and that General Breckinridge had better move to our left to meet him.' As Thompson turned his horse, Johnston added: 'Do not say to General Beauregard that this is an order, but he must act on what additional information he may receive. The reports to him are more to be relied on than [those to] to me.'"[15]

Johnston spent his time that day inspiring individual units instead of developing strategy. In fact, his single most influential strategic decision, made from the camp of the Eighteenth Wisconsin, proved a mistake. He thought he had turned the Federal flank, only to discover shortly thereafter from Major Lockett that there were many more Yankees farther to the right.

That afternoon, while trying to dislodge Hurlbut's Federals from the Peach Orchard, Johnston exerted his final influence on the outcome of the battle. Since Beauregard had not taken the earlier call for Breckinridge to go to the left as an order, at midday Breckinridge was available to lead two of his three brigades to the Rebel right, appearing at about 1:30 p.m. Federal colonel Isaac C. Pugh's brigade had clung stubbornly to the Peach Orchard for the past two hours. Johnston wanted the force dislodged. Riding among some of Breckinridge's men, he called for the Ninth and Tenth Arkansas regiments to use their bayonets, clinking the tin cup taken from the Wisconsinite camp that morning against those same bayonets as he went. "'These must do the work,' he shouted. . . . One of [Col. Winfield S.] Statham's Tennesseans remembered Johnston telling them that this position was the 'key' to the landing and they should 'unlock it' with their bayonets." Johnston then led them partway forward in the next charge.[16]

That effort proved successful—and fatal. Somewhere during that assault, Johnston was struck by at least two bullets. One tore the heel of his boot. The other struck the back of his knee, partially severing the popliteal artery, which commenced bleeding into the boot. The bullet strike on the heel drew Johnston's attention, masking the knee wound. As the wound was draining into the boot rather than down the outside of his leg, his blood loss went unnoticed as well. Even when Johnston began to sway in the saddle, orderlies and aides had trouble finding the dangerous injury. It need not have been fatal had it been found in time, but at least a half hour passed before it was uncovered. The delay was too much, and at about 2:30 p.m., while lying in a ravine just behind the battle lines, Johnston expired from blood loss.[17]

Within a half hour, Beauregard was informed of Johnston's death. Though the lore of the postwar former Confederacy would often cite Johnston's loss as a key reason why the South lost the Battle of Shiloh, initially, at least, the general's demise changed very little. In the words of historian Edward Cunningham, "Contrary to what many of Beauregard's critics said during the war and after, the new army commander possessed a fairly good picture of how the battle was developing." However, Johnston's demise removed any last semblance of senior command on the front line, since Beauregard remained well to the rear and, as will be seen, removed a key decision-maker from the scene for the day's final critical decision.

The main point of resistance among the Federals had by now shifted to the Union center, where W. H. L. Wallace, along with Prentiss's remnants, still held the Sunken Road and Hornets' Nest positions. Beauregard now began concentrating Rebel troops against that line, pulling them from the Confederate left, where McClernand and Sherman had already fallen back to Jones Field.[18]

The great unknown concerning Johnston's death is in what happened later in the day as the fighting ended. As will be seen, the Rebels broke off the attack near dusk, leaving Pittsburg Landing in Federal hands. Had Johnston lived, would the day have ended differently?

W. H. L. Wallace and Benjamin M. Prentiss Hold the Hornets' Nest

Situation

Brig. Gen. William H. L. Wallace was not a professional soldier, though he had seen service in the Mexican-American War. The lawyer from Ottawa, Illinois, had joined the Eleventh Illinois Infantry in 1861. He proved his capability under fire at Fort Donelson, earning plaudits for steadiness and courage. When C. F. Smith's injuries proved more severe than first thought, Wallace was assigned to command the Second Division in Smith's absence.

Major General Benjamin Prentiss.

With their camps located just west of the landing, Wallace's command was farthest from the front when fighting erupted that Sunday morning at Shiloh. Only Lew Wallace's men, at Crump's, were farther away.[19]

Col. James M. Tuttle of the Second Iowa Infantry, commanding Wallace's First Brigade, later recounted, "On awakening about sunrise . . . my attention was attracted by severe firing at the front. . . . I ordered my horse immediately and rode to General Wallace's tent to report myself ready to take command of the brigade. He did not seem to think that a general engagement was on, but that it was only some picket firing, such as we had experienced a day or two before." Shortly thereafter, with the brigade formed in line, Tuttle rode out to the main road, "which," he noted, "I found full of fugitives, among whom where [sic] quite a number of wounded men belonging to the regiments first engaged." Wallace now hurried his brigades forward.[20]

Though General Prentiss would later garner many accolades for the stubborn defense of the Sunken Road, the lion's share of that credit really belongs to Wallace's division. While the approximately five hundred Sixth Division survivors who rallied with Wallace certainly contributed, they alone could not have held that position against a serious assault. The severity and number of Confederate strikes on the Hornets' Nest have been exaggerated over time. Nonetheless, at least seven and perhaps as many as thirteen separate attacks were launched against the line prior to 3:00 p.m., with the largest coming at about 11:30, led by Brig. Gen. Alexander P. Stewart and roughly 3,700 men assembled from elements of four different brigades. Thanks to Wallace and his Second Division veterans, each was repulsed. Prentiss and Wallace also worked well together, perhaps in part because they had been captain and lieutenant in the same company of Illinois infantry in the Mexican-American War, where Wallace had once referred to Prentiss as "the best officer in the two regiments" then serving together.[21]

About 11:00 a.m. Grant visited the position, having come from Sherman's portion of the field. He met with both Prentiss and Wallace. Prentiss later said of the encounter, "I received my final orders [from Grant], which were to maintain that position at all hazards." Undoubtedly, Grant conveyed that same emphatic message to W. H. L. Wallace.[22]

By 3:30 p.m., circumstances were considerably different. On Wallace's right, the Seventh Illinois of Col. Thomas Sweeny's brigade had lost contact with the Eighth Illinois of McClernand's division. On Prentiss's flank, his troops witnessed the retreat of Hurlbut's Federals back through the Peach Orchard and into Cloud Field, several hundred yards north of Prentiss's left. There was also a growing Confederate artillery presence in Wallace's and Prentiss's combined front. At 3:00 p.m., about the time he learned of Johnston's death, Beauregard tasked Brig. Gen. Daniel Ruggles with coordinating Confederate efforts against what appeared to be the last knot of Federal resistance at the Hornets' Nest. Ruggles's solution was to round up as many Confederate artillery pieces as he could find—postwar lore says anywhere between fifty-seven and sixty-two guns were eventually employed—to blast the Federals out of the way.[23]

Options

With both flanks exposed and facing a growing Rebel threat to their front, Wallace and Prentiss conferred again. They now faced a choice akin to the one McClernand and Sherman had been presented with earlier, in Jones Field: Should they retreat toward the landing; remain and defend their position at all hazards, as Grant had instructed earlier; or counterattack?

Option 1

The two commands could retreat, falling back to realign with Hurlbut and perhaps reestablish a connection with the Federal right, thereby safeguarding their exposed flanks and once again presenting a unified line to the enemy. Indeed, a controlled retreat would likely be the best course, if the men could pull it off, but it did pose other significant risks.

Managing a retreat in the face of an aggressive enemy is a difficult, perilous feat. If Prentiss and Wallace began to withdraw and were attacked, or if they proved unable to halt their line as desired, or even if they simply could not locate McClernand and Hurlbut to tie in with, they might endanger Grant's entire army. With their current position strong and well supported by their own artillery, Prentiss and Wallace had already held firm in the face of repeated Rebel attacks.

Option 2

Grant's orders were an additional argument in favor of staying. As Prentiss reported, the last word the army commander imparted was to "hold . . . at all hazards." Prentiss and Wallace both understood what Sherman and McClellan had known when they faced a similar decision in Jones Field: Grant needed time to bring up Lew Wallace and Buell. With fresh troops, the battle could be won. Without them, the army might be doomed.

Of course, holding entailed risks. With both flanks exposed, Prentiss and Wallace risked being surrounded even if they rebuffed further frontal attacks. If that happened, their loss would rip a far larger hole in Grant's center than that produced by a retreat. Hence, in opting to stand pat, they could potentially create a larger disaster.

Option 3

The last option, counterattacking, was also the least likely. It had proven successful for McClernand and Sherman. However, had Wallace and Prentiss even known of that success (there is no evidence that they did, as communications between the wings were haphazard at best), circumstances were much different across their own front. Plenty of Confederate infantry were arrayed against them, as well as a growing enemy artillery presence. Both Federal commanders witnessed how quickly the Rebels' own attacks fell apart in the face of withering defensive fire. Launching a counterattack of their own seemed likely to end in disaster.

Decision

W. H. L. Wallace did not survive the battle to relate his version of what happened next. Prentiss later reported, "When the gallant Hurlbut was forced to retire General Wallace and myself consulted, and agreed to hold our positions at all hazards, believing that we could thus save the army from destruction; we having now been informed for the first time that all others had fallen back to the vicinity of the river." Thus, Prentiss framed the moment as one of deliberate sacrifice on his and Wallace's part, a desperate but necessary choice required to "save the army."[24]

Results/Impact

Between 3:30 and 4:00 p.m., McClernand's division fell back out of Jones Field to occupy an interim position in Cavalry Field and extending into the woods to the south—which broke the connection with Colonel Sweeny's brigade around Duncan Field. What was left of Sherman's division (McDowell's brigade, the remnants of Hildebrand, and the Fifteenth and Sixteenth Iowa) was arrayed in Perry and Mulberry Fields. This line was also unconnected with McClernand or with any Federals on Sherman's right. The Federals were opposed by elements of at least five Confederate brigades, including Col. Preston Pond's large Louisiana command of the Second Corps, which had been on the extreme Rebel left flank all day, but so far had been only lightly engaged. Three of Pond's regiments drifted south through the timber to strike McClernand's right, now uncovered by Sherman.[25]

McClernand's men, not yet fought out, met this new assault fiercely. As one Federal soldier noted: "Advancing in heavy columns, led by the Louisiana Zouaves, [they tried] to break our center, we awaited his approach within sure range, and opened a terrific fire upon him." The Sixteenth and Eighteenth Louisiana, accompanied by the Confederate Guards Response Battalion of Louisiana state militia, "were repulsed with heavy loss," falling back to the north end of Jones Field.[26]

But that proved McClernand's last act. The stand in Cavalry Field was temporary. Sherman stated, "About 4 p.m. it was evident that Hurlbut's line had been driven back to the river, and knowing that General [Lew] Wallace was coming up from Crump's Landing with reinforcements, General McClernand and I, on consultation, selected a new line of defense, with its right covering the bridge by which General Wallace had to approach." W. H. L. Wallace's right and rear were now entirely exposed, with several Confederate brigades now moving to take advantage of that fact.[27]

Hurlbut was also now falling back. As early as 3:00 p.m., when he received word that Colonel Stuart could no longer hold, Hurlbut warned Prentiss that he was going to have to retreat, telling him, "Reach out toward the right and drop back steadily parallel with my First Brigade." Instead, Wallace and Prentiss elected to remain in place. Hurlbut recorded subsequent events: "Perceiving that a heavy force was closing on the left, between my line and the river, while heavy fire continued on the right and front, I ordered the line to fall back. The retreat was made quietly and steadily and in good order. I had hoped to make a stand on the line of my camp, but masses of the enemy were pressing rapidly on each flank." Now threatened with encirclement, Hurlbut fell back across the Dill Branch Ravine to rally on what is now known as Grant's final line.[28]

Encirclement is exactly what happened to Wallace's and Prentiss's men in the Sunken Road. Hurlbut's retreat allowed Jackson's and Chalmers's Confederate brigades to pivot toward the northwest. Prentiss responded by refusing his right flank. "The Second and Sixth divisions were now in the strange position of fighting back to back," observed historian Edward Cunningham. The Hornets' Nest line was now fatally compromised.[29]

In the absence of higher authority, Confederate general Braxton Bragg orchestrated this final move against the Hornets' Nest. Bragg, who had been directing Rebel efforts to reduce the Federal position for much of the day, soon realized the enemy's vulnerability. "General Bragg dispatched me to the right," recollected Capt. Samuel Lockett, "and Colonel Frank Gardner . . . to the left, to inform the brigade and division commanders on either side that a combined movement would be made on the front and flanks of that position. The movements were made, and Prentiss was captured."[30]

Wallace now bowed to the inevitable. Col. James Tuttle of the Second Iowa recalled, "It became evident that our forces on each side . . . had given way, so as to give the enemy an opportunity of turning both our flanks. At this critical juncture General Wallace gave orders for my whole brigade to fall back." The soldiers did so under a severe cross fire that brought down Wallace. William Wallace's brother-in-law, Cyrus Dickey, recounted the moment to Wallace's wife, Anne: "[I] had just directed Will's attention to some move of the enemy and he raised in his stirrups apparently to see better; but a shot had reached him, and the next moment he fell upon his face on the ground. He was in full view of the whole division at the time, and from that time confusion reigned."[31]

Trabue's Brigade, the leftmost element of this Rebel pincer movement, and Chalmers's Brigade, the rightmost, effectively sealed the trap near the southwest corner of Cloud Field. Today their tablets mark the closing of that trap, positioned only a couple of hundred yards apart. Regiment by regiment, the ensnared Federals now began to surrender. Prentiss seemed bewildered by this turn of events. To one Rebel he "admitted, 'I can't understand how you have surrounded us.'" By about 6:00 p.m., the surrender was complete, netting the Rebels nearly 2,200 prisoners, as well as many muskets, flags, cannon, and other trophies.[32]

Despite Prentiss's later claim that their stand was a deliberate sacrifice, both Wallace and Prentiss did, in fact, order a retreat once they realized the extent of the danger; but those orders came far too late. As a result, most of the Federals who fell into Rebel hands did not do so while in line along the Sunken Road. Instead, they were captured in the low ground well behind that position, in what is now called "Hell's Hollow."[33]

Still, Wallace's and Prentiss's sacrifice bought Grant precious time. By 3:00 p.m., the army commander had already begun to organize a final line on the high bluff overlooking Pittsburg Landing. Further, Hurlbut's, Sherman's, and McClernand's divisions, however battered, were re-forming to defend the landing. And, at long last, by 6:00 p.m. the first of the promised reinforcements was arriving. Elements of William Nelson's division from the Army of the Ohio were unloading at the landing, having been ferried across the river by steamboat. Buell had arrived.

Would the Confederates have been able to break this line had Wallace and Prentiss elected to fall back earlier? The answer, of course, can only be left to speculation. Grant's final line would have been stronger by some 2,200 men, but the Confederates might have had a couple of extra hours of daylight to organize a final assault if the Hornets' Nest had been cleared at 3:30 or 4:00 p.m. instead of 5:30 or 6:00 p.m.

CHAPTER 4

AFTERNOON AND EVENING, APRIL 6

Grant Builds a Final Line

Situation

Historian Timothy Smith has described the battlefield of Shiloh as shaped like an hourglass, with the main plateau of the site—the same high ground that induced the Federals to select it as a campsite in the first place—segmented by the deep ravines of various tributaries feeding into Snake Creek, Lick Creek, and the Tennessee River. McClernand, Sherman, Prentiss, and one of Hurlbut's brigades all camped in the southernmost portion of that hourglass, formed by Shiloh Branch and Locust Grove Branch. Behind them, Dill and Tilghman Branches pinched off the terrain and formed the uppermost, or northern, portion of the hourglass. W. H. L. Wallace's and most of Hurlbut's camps occupied that space, which also included Pittsburg Landing. A narrow stretch of high ground, described by Grant as "the ridge which divided the waters of Snake and Lick Creeks," ran southwest from Pittsburg Landing toward Corinth. This divide separated the drainages of Dill and Tilghman Branches and then Shiloh and Locust Grove Branches, so that there was a narrow gap of high ground between each of the two sets of watercourses. The "neck" of the hourglass, then, was the narrow stretch of high ground between Dill and Tilghman Branches. Dill Branch flowed east into the Tennessee above (south of) Pittsburg Landing, while Tilghman

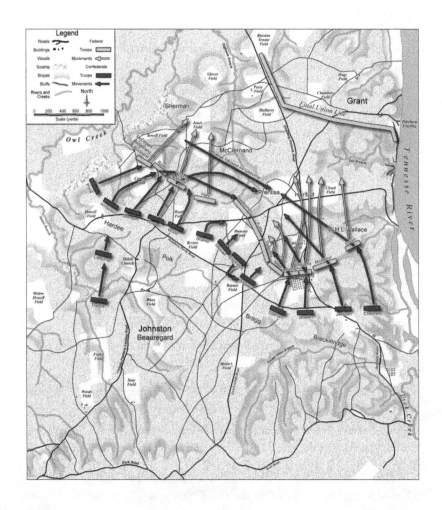

Branch flowed north into Owl Creek, which then flowed into Snake Creek, ultimately draining eastward into the river below (north of) the landing.[1]

So far, all the fighting had been confined to that southernmost bulge of the hourglass. Sherman's line at Shiloh Church, McClernand's line at the Crossroads, and the fight for the Hornets' Nest /Sunken Road were all south of the Dill-Tilghman plateau. And though the fighting had been intense, and the Federals had been driven from those positions, Albert Sidney Johnston's original plan had failed. The Federal army was not cut off from Pittsburg Landing. Instead, formation by formation, troops were falling back to take up new positions around the landing. Grant was building a new, final line of defense.

This critical decision differs from the other decisions discussed in this monograph for one important reason: it does not fall into the traditional series of choices confronting the decision-maker at a critical point in the battle. At first glance, in fact, it might be considered no decision at all—after all, what other choice did Grant have? Once battle was joined, there was not really a safe retreat path from Pittsburg Landing for an army under fire. There was only the risk of trading one kind of disaster for another. The fact that Grant gave thought to building a final line of resistance on which to anchor his battered command and receive the long-expected reinforcements from Lew Wallace and Buell highlights the importance of foresight in a commander. Good commanders anticipate and plan for outcomes both positive and negative. However, this seemingly obvious skill often gets lost in the swirl and confusion of combat, where stress undermines effective decision-making.

Options

Grant's choices were not so easily defined as either stay and fight, or retreat. In fact, retreat—at least a controlled withdrawal before night fell, with an intact army surviving the operation—was virtually impossible. From the landing, there were only two possible avenues of retreat. The first method was via steamboat, and it involved ferrying troops and equipment across the Tennessee to the east bank, where the Rebels could not follow. The second path lay overland; soldiers could move north along the Hamburg–Savannah Road over Snake Creek and then up the River Road to Crump's Landing. But the steamboats could only load and unload so many men in a given period of time, while the bridge over the creek could only be crossed by a limited number of troops and wagons at a time. These limits created dangerous choke points, exposing thousands of men to enemy attack while they waited to either board or cross. It was a classic recipe for military disaster, especially with an army of raw troops, many of whom had already panicked and left the ranks to crowd the landing, desperate for escape. Grant therefore had no choice but to stand, at least until full dark.

Thus, Grant's Choice, if he was to stave off disaster until nightfall, was to fight—somewhere. All day long he sought to bolster his forward line, repeatedly instructing commanders to hold their positions while he forwarded reinforcements. Even the debate over Lew Wallace's orders and where Grant expected him to arrive is part of this focus on a forward defense. Wallace, after all, initially expected to join Sherman's right flank somewhere near the crossroads or Shiloh Church, and did not conceive of the idea that he might be needed at the landing instead. Should Grant continue to bolster the forward line, or should he plan for a fallback position?

Option 1

Grant could continue this policy of moving to shore up the forward line, defined as the Hornets' Nest / Sunken Road / Jones Field line, that the Federals occupied for most of the afternoon of April 6. When Hurlbut's division and Stuart's brigade retreated northward into Cloud Field between 3:00 and 3:30 p.m., for example, they had a chance to reorganize. Grant could order them to try and push back south and reconnect with Prentiss's left. Similarly, at about the same time, McClernand's and Sherman's disorganized forces fell back out of Jones Field across the Tilghman Branch to eventually take up a new line along the Hamburg–Savannah Road. As they did so, Confederate pressure eased, with most of those Rebels turning to the south and east to collapse W. H. L. Wallace's right flank in the Hornets' Nest. Grant could send both divisions (such as they were by that point in the battle) back to try and retake Jones Field.

Option 2

This second option has more to do with presence of mind and foresight, rather than a simple binary choice. Combat is a confusing, extremely stressful experience for everyone involved. Command pressure only heightens that stress, since no commander ever has all the data needed to make the most informed choice at any given moment. Combat authority is about weighing uncertainties and acting. Military history is replete with examples of men who simply froze under the weight of those uncertainties.

In other cases, a commander might focus on the immediate fighting and fail to anticipate other needs or circumstances. Perhaps the greatest example of this loss of focus can be found in the career of one of the greatest soldiers of the era, the French emperor Napoleon I, during the twin Battles of Jena and Auerstedt. Napoleon fought the Battle of Jena against what he thought was the bulk of the Prussian Army, while a few miles away one of his corps commanders, Marshal Louis Davout, was engaged at Auerstedt. Napoleon believed that he was facing the main Prussian Army, only to learn after the fact that his 40,000 men had fought 53,000 Prussians while Davout, with a mere 26,000 men, engaged 66,000 of his foes. Davout held his own, allowing Napoleon to triumph at Jena, but among trained military men there was no hiding the fact that Napoleon had—uncharacteristically—badly misread his enemy's intentions. Even the greatest general can lose sight of the larger picture amid the swirl of combat.[2]

Around Pittsburg Landing the terrain offered up a second option: to create a final line of defense. The bluff at the landing opened onto another high plateau, this one protected from the south by the Dill Branch. The branch's deep ravine offered perhaps the most daunting geographic obstacle yet faced by any attacker at Shiloh. Running westward to connect with that Shiloh divide, the landing plateau offered another piece of flat defensible ground overlooking the Tilghman Branch. By re-forming his lines along these two ridges, Grant could effectively protect both the landing and the Hamburg–Savannah Road. Even better, there was already an impressive amount of Federal artillery clustered around the landing, including some guns of very heavy caliber. Among them were the five 24-pound siege guns of Battery B, Second Illinois Light Artillery, commanded by Capt. Relly Madison.[3]

Decision

Grant was determined to hold the landing at all costs. Col. Joseph D. Webster was his ace in the hole. Webster, an 1832 graduate of Dartmouth College, was a civil engineer by trade, but he joined the United States Army in 1838, serving as a topographical engineer until he resigned in 1854. He had been living and working in Chicago when the war erupted, and he immediately returned to uniform, acting as the State of Illinois's chief engineer in 1861. He met Grant at Cairo and accepted the offer of chief of staff. Webster almost certainly accompanied Grant when the general met with Don Carlos Buell sometime close to 2:00 p.m. Informed that Buell had arrived on the *Tigress*, Grant rode to the landing. Both men, along with their entourages, then rode back up the bluff, passing thousands of dazed, exhausted, and frightened Federal stragglers as they did so. Buell, dismayed, asked, "'What preparations have you made for retreating—?' 'Why,' interrupted Grant eagerly, 'I haven't despaired of whipping them yet.'" The two men then discussed bringing over the first of Buell's troops to reinforce the landing.[4]

Major General Joseph Dana Webster.

In addition to the swarms of frightened, discouraged soldiery, numerous Federal artillery batteries occupied the bluff above the landing. Since the army was amid a complete reorganization of that arm when the battle opened, some of the more recently arrived batteries simply camped on the bluff, awaiting orders; others had just disembarked as recently as the previous evening. Madison's massive siege cannon were, in fact, still aboard a steamer. At some point, Grant decided, "Webster was placed in special charge of all the artillery." Though in Grant's report he never specified when exactly he charged Webster with this mission, it seems very likely that the assignment occurred at about the same time as the meeting with Buell. Further, "Grant put . . . Webster . . . to work forming the line" destined to be Grant's final defensive position.[5]

Results/Impact

Grant could not have made a better choice. Webster began by organizing the various artillery batteries and assigning them positions. Webster posted one battery, Capt. Louis Margraf's Eighth Ohio, on a spur projected southward from the bluff above the landing from which their six pieces could fire up the length of the Dill Branch Ravine. Webster later reinforced Margraf with Capt. Emil Munch's First Minnesota Battery, adding an additional five cannon to any potential enfilade. After getting Madison's heavy guns unloaded, Webster placed them several hundred yards farther from the landing, near the intersection of the Corinth–Pittsburg Road and the Pittsburg Landing

Road. From this location, Madison's howitzers could fire into the ravine and command "the neck of the hourglass"—that level ground that offered the best approach for any attacker. Over the next couple of hours, Webster placed approximately a dozen batteries of artillery along the length of the plateau overlooking Dill Branch, as well as dispatching Capt. Edward Bouton's Battery I, First Illinois Light Artillery to the far end of the line to help protect Lew Wallace's path to the battlefield. In all, Webster assembled approximately fifty cannon of all sizes and calibers, mustering an impressive show of force.[6]

Webster's line also accumulated infantry. While little could be done with the mass of stragglers, many members of the Army of the Tennessee were still willing to fight. The Fifty-Fourth Ohio and Fifty-Fifth Illinois of David Stuart's brigade, after retiring from Cloud Field, took position on the extreme left, near the modern National Cemetery, supporting Munch and Margraf. Other regiments filled in along the gunline, intermixed but still effective. These were mostly Hurlbut's men, plus whoever had escaped the Hornets' Nest. Ultimately, that line stretched all the way to the Hamburg–Savannah Road, connecting with Sherman's and McClernand's similarly battered but still effective formations, which now angled to face more west than south. This line eventually formed a giant *L*, with the base of the *L* arrayed facing south along the Dill Branch, and the vertical part, facing west, running north along the Hamburg–Savannah Road. This formation controlled all the level ground between the Dill and Tilghman Branches, as well as protecting the bridge over Snake Creek.[7]

However, the most important arrivals were the first troops of Buell's army. William Nelson's division reached the eastern bank of the Tennessee opposite the landing at about 5:00 p.m. There, the soldiers viewed quite a scene: steamboats in midstream, with masses of men thronging the west bank. At first, some of Buell's men took these for Grant's reserves, ready for combat; closer inspection revealed that these individuals were really an unformed mob of stragglers. Col. Jacob Ammen's brigade was the first to cross, with the Thirty-Sixth Indiana in the lead, followed by the Sixth Ohio. A member of the Sixth later recorded his impressions of that moment: "The *debris* of a broken army were comingled in the utmost disorder. . . . It was a sickening sight—one that has never been adequately described." As the leading companies of the Sixth debarked, General Nelson, who accompanied them, raged at stragglers who sought escape and tried to swarm the steamboat. "'Get out of the way, you d—d cowards!' he exclaimed, furiously. . . . 'Get out of the way. If you won't fight yourselves, let these men off that will. Sixth Ohio, follow me!'" Atop the bluff, Nelson and Ammen met with Buell, who sent them forward to support Webster's gunline. Agitated, an unidentified Army of the

Tennessee staffer met Ammen there, declaring, "'Don't stop to form, colonel, don't stop to form! . . . We shall all be massacred if you do!'"[8]

Buell's army would develop something of a rivalry with and a bit of a grudge against Grant's army, which doubtless colored the narrative above. It took some time to get even the leading elements of Buell's forces across, and it was close to 6:30 p.m. before Ammen's leading regiment and a half (only part of the Sixth Ohio crossed in time to witness any fighting) could be said to have joined the defenses. By then, Federal confidence in the ranks of the Army of the Tennessee had rebounded. Several "despondent" Federals described their surge in confidence upon seeing the gunline. "When we came to this our last line," wrote a member of the Seventh Iowa, "and seeing a line of 20 or 25 cannon to support us I had more hope." Webster himself continued to inspire the men. "Riding along behind the artillery, he shouted encouragingly, 'Stand firm, boys. They can never carry this line in the world.'"[9]

Confederates did make some effort to storm this line, but the reality was that they were as disorganized and exhausted as Grant's troops. The Rebel attack on Grant's last line was not a full-fledged, all-out assault that fully tested the strength of Webster's deployment (and General Beauregard's decision regarding this attack was destined to become very controversial). Yet it became clear to those few Rebels who tested it that the final line was very strong, perhaps impregnable. To Webster must go much of the credit for organizing the troops and deploying them, but Grant's foresight in making sure that some prominent officer handled this important task was equally significant.

Grant's final line impacted the outcome of the battle in two vital ways. First, it discouraged the Rebels from making any final effort that night to storm the landing before the bulk of Buell's army arrived. Second, the Federals gained moral confidence from knowing that they still held the landing and, despite everything, the battle was not lost.

Beauregard Breaks Off the Attack

Situation

For many Confederates, the capture of 2,200 Yankee soldiers in the Hornets' Nest signified victory and a triumphant end to a very trying day. This was not so for General Beauregard, who understood that if Grant held the landing, the battle was not over.

It was also clear, however, that the Army of the Tennessee held no monopoly on exhaustion and confusion. The "closing in of the Confederate lines," recounted Alfred Roman, Beauregard's wartime staff officer and postwar biographer, "had brought the extreme right and the left centre of the line of battle unexpectedly face to face. . . . Much confusion ensued, as well as delay for the replenishment of ammunition, before the commands were extricated and directed anew against the enemy." Things were no better farther south. "But in the rear of the victorious Confederate line," continued Roman, "was a scene of straggling and pillage which, for a time, defied all remonstrance and all efforts at coercion. The disorder and plunder that had followed the capture of Prentiss's Sherman's, and McClernand's camps were now all the greater, as the troops, fasting since dawn—and some of them since the previous evening—were exhausted from incessant fighting and marching." Worse yet, "the commands were broken and mixed; among many the idea prevailed that the battle had been won and was virtually ended."[10]

Bragg, Polk, and Hardee all still intended to press their attacks. Afterward, Bragg reported, "The prisoners were dispatched to the rear under a proper guard, all else being left upon the field that we might press our advantage." He claimed that "the enemy had fallen back in much confusion and was crowded in unorganized masses on the riverbank, vainly striving to cross." This was guesswork, of course: neither Bragg nor any other Confederate could observe Pittsburg Landing directly. Still, Bragg claimed that he was not prepared to quit for what little remained of the day. He stated, "As soon as our troops could again be formed and put in motion the order was given to move forward at all points and sweep the enemy from the field."[11]

As noted, Grant certainly did not consider the battle at an end. Nor were the Federals—except perhaps for the stragglers—"vainly striving to cross." In fact, the first of Buell's men were beginning to arrive. Nor would Colonel Webster's defensive line succumb to any but the strongest pressure the Confederates could bring to bear. Moreover, daylight was now running out. The sun was due to set at about 6:15 p.m. Twilight lasted for about another hour, though by 7:00 p.m. it would simply be too dark to conduct any effective attack.

All attacks have a culminating point, defined by the United States military as follows: "Every offensive operation will sooner or later reach a point where the strength of the attacker no longer significantly exceeds that of the defender, and beyond which continued operations therefore risk overextension, counterattack, and defeat." The factors now at play in the Confederate ranks indicated that the offensive had reached this stage. Exhaustion, supply shortages, command confusion, and disorganization all wear down the combat power of the attacker.[12]

There is no question that the Federals were still capable of putting up a fight. Bragg admitted that Grant's men "were covered by a battery of heavy guns, well served, and their two gunboats, which now poured a heavy fire upon [the Rebel] supposed positions." Bragg insisted that this fire, "though terrific in sound and producing some consternation at first, did [the Confederates] no damage." Other officers differed. Brigade commander James R. Chalmers, trying to lead his troops across Dill Branch to assault the Federals, asserted, "We were met by a fire from a whole line of batteries protected by infantry and assisted by shells from the gunboats." Subsequently, Chalmers noted this as "the heaviest fire that occurred during the whole engagement" on April 6 or 7. In a private letter written on April 9, General Hardee admitted that the firing "was perfectly appalling to [his] men."[13]

There is some evidence that Beauregard was at the forefront of the fight for at least part of the time between Prentiss's surrender and the organization of the next assault. But Beauregard did not occupy this position for long. He was instead still trying to control the larger battle from the rear. He soon returned to his headquarters near Shiloh Church, where he discussed the events of the day with newly captured General Prentiss. Prentiss boasted that the Federals would turn the tables on the Rebels tomorrow, since Buell's army was up. Beauregard discounted this news as mere braggadocio, because the Confederates had received a report that morning stating Buell was still in northern Alabama near Decatur, far from any juncture. That report was incorrect; only a portion of Buell's force was headed for Decatur, but Beauregard had no better information at hand. This piece of incorrect news played an outsize role in Beauregard's next decision.[14]

Options

The key question now facing the Rebel commander was whether to press the issue to the utmost or break off the attack for the night. If he chose the first option, Beauregard could mount one final attack with every last bit of combat power the Army of the Mississippi could muster in the scant daylight remaining. If he chose the second option, he could rest the troops and renew the fight the next morning.

Option 1

Beauregard could elect to end the fighting for the day, recover his army, and renew the fight in the morning. If he halted now, he would give his troops time to rest, resupply, eat, and reorganize his badly scattered line. Johnston and Beauregard brought about forty-four thousand men to the battlefield on April 6, suffering about eight thousand casualties in the first day's fighting. This loss, coupled with the thousands of stragglers knocked loose from their commands by the shock of combat (a number likely equal to Grant's stragglers, though that fact gets less attention) probably reduced Beauregard's effective numbers to no more than half of his starting strength at best. Some of those loose men would rejoin their formations overnight, improving Beauregard's numbers for April 7 if he chose to wait. The next morning, should Grant still be present, Beauregard could reorganize his forces and finish the job with plenty of daylight.

Pausing, however, gave the Federals the same advantages. And even without the arrival of Buell, who Beauregard believed was out of immediate reach, Lew Wallace's division at Crump's Landing would surely be joining the battle tomorrow, which would give Grant a boost in fresh troops. Beauregard could count on no similar Confederate reinforcements. His nearest major friendly force was under Gen. Earl Van Dorn, still en route from Arkansas. Worse, Beauregard would have to fight on April 7 without the benefit of surprise. Every Federal soldier would be expecting a fight.

Option 2

Conversely, Beauregard could press on. If he elected to make one last all-out assault on Grant's final line, he retained at least one critical advantage—the initiative. Beauregard, not Grant, would continue to call the shots in what had over the course of a single day become the bloodiest battle in American military history. The Federals, despite stubborn resistance and fierce fighting, had undeniably been driven from position after position all day. There was reason to believe that they could be driven again, and this time there was no fallback. If Grant lost the landing, thousands of his men would be captured, killed, or driven into the Tennessee River. His army might be irreparably shattered.

However, a continued attack posed real dangers. Foremost, Beauregard risked a night action, something at which even veteran Civil War armies proved notoriously inept. He might forgo all the benefits of a halt with daylight remaining and still fail to achieve anything more. The deeper into the night the Rebels fought, the less chance they would have to renew the combat effectively the next morning. Exhaustion and disorganization would increase dramatically in the dark. The Federals, defending a static position and supported by the tremendous firepower of Webster's gunline, would have a much easier and less confusing fight than the Rebels attempting to scramble their way across the Dill Branch Ravine.

And any attack would have to be mounted primarily across Dill Branch. This was the case because, given the final positions of the two armies after Prentiss's capture, there was simply no time to reorganize the army to bring more than a handful of troops to bear against Sherman's and McClernand's portion of the line, which was both relatively easier to approach and not so heavily studded with Federal artillery. But there was simply no time to launch a well-formed, deliberate assault; it was only possible to push regiments, brigades, and fragments of brigades haphazardly against the new Federal position and hope it collapsed.

Decision

Initially, it appeared as though Beauregard was prepared to let Hardee, Polk, and especially Bragg press on. Capt. B. B. Waddell, acting as one of Beauregard's aides-de-camp, later recalled that close to 5:00 p.m., Beauregard and Bragg met somewhere near the Hornets' Nest. Waddell wrote that "General Bragg expressed a difficulty he experienced in forcing his men across a depression by which gunboats were firing shells; it was regarded as important that the desired point be carried. He left you [Beauregard] with the order to *press forward*, using his discretion as to the possibility of carrying the point." Waddell's comments suggest that Bragg was already trying to force Dill Branch (though Waddell's time sense might well have been off by as much as an hour, writing as he was in 1878) and that it was not going well.

Yet as noted above, shortly after this encounter Beauregard returned to his headquarters (where he spoke to Prentiss) and decided whether to press on or fall back. Here, at 6:00 p.m. Maj. Numa Augustin, another aide, received Beauregard's unequivocal order to break off the fight. As Augustin explained on April 10, "At dusk, about 6, [I was] sent by General Beauregard to the front, to order 'to arrest the conflict and fall back to the camps of the enemy for the night.' [I] transmitted this order to Generals Bragg, Polk, and Hardee; returned, and was happy to congratulate the general upon the success of our army on that day." The fight would have to wait until tomorrow.[15]

Results/Impact

Beauregard's order definitively ended all fighting for the day, but it also ignited a storm of after-the-fact criticism. Whether or not the order shut down a last-gasp, all-out Rebel assault on the Federal position, however, is much less certain. Two significant movements rose to the level of an attack on that last Union location. The first such effort was more of a preliminary stab and came at 4:30, even before the curtain fell on the final act at the Hornets' Nest. General Hardee sent a trio of Louisiana regiments commanded by Col. Preston Pond against an amalgamated brigade of four regiments (from three different brigades) currently commanded by Federal colonel James C. Veatch. Veatch's men occupied a hill east of Cavalry Field, though only temporarily—they were themselves in the process of falling back to the final line. Pond protested the strike, which forced his men uphill against more numerous defenders, but he failed to dissuade Hardee. The attack went in and was duly repulsed "with heavy loss." Combat was over within half an hour, and except for some limited cavalry engagement, this affair ended action on the Confederate left against Sherman and McClernand. Their final line along the Hamburg–Savannah Road remained untested, no other attack being able to be mounted before Beauregard's halt order arrived.[16]

The single largest effort targeting Webster's line came directly across Dill Branch. It was mounted by Chalmers's Brigade, as described above, supported by elements (none were full brigades by this late in the day) of Jackson's, Anderson's, and Gladden's (now Deas's) Brigades. Rebel soldiers struggled manfully across Dill Branch to try and assail the Federals on the far crest, but despite Bragg's later dismissal, the Federal fire was overwhelming. Few troops got within even distant rifle range, and the Confederate attack was already unraveling by the time Major Augustin reached Bragg.

Arguably, Beauregard's decision to break off the attack has become *the* major controversy of Shiloh. Many of the participants (as well as subsequent historians) later argued that Albert Sidney Johnston, had he lived, would have refused to halt, and that the battle would have ended on April 6 as a decisive Confederate victory. In his report, Bragg insisted on his men's good showing in battle despite their exhaustion and hunger: "Our troops . . . mostly responded to the [attack] order with alacrity, and the movement commenced with every prospect for success . . . [until] just at this time an order was received from the commanding general to withdraw. . . . As this was communicated, in many instances, direct to brigade commanders, the troops were soon in motion, and the action ceased." Bragg clearly believed that Beauregard snatched defeat from the jaws of victory with that order. Polk was even more blunt: "Nothing seemed wanting to complete the most brilliant victory of the war but to press forward and make a vigorous assault on the demoralized remnant." Hardee remained noncommittal, stating, "[Our] advance lines were within a few hundred yards of Pittsburg, where the enemy were huddled in confusion, when the order to withdraw was received."[17]

Alfred Roman, Beauregard's faithful defender, amassed considerable evidence that circumstances were perceived differently at the time. The fighting on April 7 revealed a heavily reinforced Federal army on the counterattack, recapturing all that had been lost the previous day. Only once back in Corinth, and with the benefit of hindsight, did these generals fully grasp the significance of Beauregard's decision. In the heat of the moment no one disputed the order. Bragg's medical director, Dr. J. C. Nott, informed Roman that he was present with Bragg "at the close of the day." The doctor recalled, "When beside him on horseback, I heard him give an order to withdraw the troops. . . . My impression at the time was, that General Bragg gave the order on his own responsibility." Further, Nott said that the men were far from eager to attack: "[They instead] were much demoralized, and indisposed to advance in the face of the shells. . . . my impression was (and this was also the conclusion of General Bragg) that our troops had done all they would do and had better be withdrawn."

Nott believed that Bragg gave the withdrawal order on his own initiative, but if Bragg did indeed receive Beauregard's order after that, he made no objection at the time. "If he had received and disapproved of such an order," Nott argued, "it is probable that something would have been said about it." Col. Jacob Thompson of Beauregard's staff concurred. In an 1880 letter to the general he wrote of that evening, "I heard no one express the slightest discontent with your order. . . . All the complaints of your drawing off the troops on the evening of the 6th were afterthoughts."[18]

Beauregard's decision ensured that the Federal Army of the Tennessee would live to fight another day. But could the Confederates have finished off Grant's command in one final push? For all the reasons favoring the defense—especially in a night action—reiterated above, it seems highly unlikely that the Rebels could have overrun Pittsburg Landing. Perhaps veteran troops with more experienced commanders could have done so, but then they would almost certainly have been facing equally seasoned defenders and opponents. That would have been a quite different Battle of Shiloh.

Grant Decides to Stay and Fight

Situation

As the sounds of combat died away, replaced by the sounds of suffering, both armies sought what shelter they could for the night. Confederates roamed the field. They now had thousands of captured Federal tents available to them, though many were already filled with the wounded of both armies. The few more permanent dwellings and other structures—including Shiloh Church—were filled to overflowing with casualties and stragglers. The movement to seek shelter was haphazard, scattering Confederate units across much of the field without rhyme, reason, or a nod to reconstituting brigades, divisions, and corps. Though Beauregard intended to reorganize the army, the first priorities were food and sleep. After all, the men of the Army of the Mississippi believed there would be ample time the next morning to finish off the Federals, if they remained on the field.

The Federals had fewer sleeping options. Certainly, they had fewer tents. The Army of Tennessee's positions that morning comprised five divisional camps. Four of them were now firmly in Rebel hands. Only the bulk of W. H. L. Wallace's campsites remained within the final Federal perimeter. Further, Union forces occupied a smaller space than the Rebels. Constricted by the Tennessee River to the east and swampy low ground to the north, Grant's army was now crammed into less acreage than it had been on April 5. Moreover, the Federals remained to man the battle line, bracing for an attack at any moment. To further complicate matters, it rained overnight, a cold, pelting downpour.

The Fifteenth Illinois, one of Hurlbut's regiments, typified the Federal experience. Having lost their field officers and 250 of the 600 men that began the day's fighting, the soldiers of the Fifteenth finally moved to a position behind Captain Madison's siege battery, where they spent the night. Capt. George C. Rogers, who now commanded the Fifteenth, recorded his experiences in an April 10 letter home: "The enemy were in our camp, sleeping in our tents, and we had to lay down on the wet ground, but not to sleep, with our blankets over us." Rogers had been struck twice by shell fragments or spent bullets, and his wounds were not sufficient to render him unfit for duty. "Then," he wrote, "my breast and arm commenced to pain me very much, but I thought I should be able to go into battle in the morning without any trouble. In the night it rained very hard, and I was wet all over, and took cold and could not speak out loud in the morning or use my right arm. I did not complain—there were so many worse off than I was."[19]

Thousands of men shared Rogers's experiences. The Federals also had thousands of wounded, and still thousands more stragglers, who thronged the area but could not—or would not—rejoin their regiments. Grant's army was a mess. There was, however, reason for optimism. Buell's first men were already present, and more arrived throughout the night. By 9:00 p.m., all of Nelson's infantry were across the river and formed along the northern rim of Dill Branch Ravine. Brig. Gen. Thomas L. Crittenden's Fifth Division, Army of the Ohio immediately followed; the troops began landing at 9:00 p.m., forcing their way through the mob of stragglers to take a position farther up the bluff. "We stood at our arms on the road," reported Crittenden, "half a mile from the landing." As Crittenden's men debarked, each boat chugged back downstream to pick up the next wave, Brig. Gen. Alexander McDowell McCook's Second Division, expected to reach the battlefield sometime early the next morning. Behind them, the lead elements of Brig. Gen. Thomas J. Wood's Sixth Division were also close at hand. Nelson and Crittenden combined brought roughly 8,400 men to the field; McCook would add 7,500 more troops once he appeared.[20]

And, at long last, Lew Wallace reached the field. His leading regiments arrived at the Snake Creek Bridge around 7:00 p.m. They finished moving into position on Grant's right flank by 1:00 a.m., April 7. Wallace might be tardy, in Grant's eyes, but he was now present, adding 5,800 men—many of them veterans of Donelson—to Grant's strength. By dawn, the Union commander would have 14,000 fresh troops with which to renew the fight, plus many more on the way. These were heartening numbers.[21]

There are numerous recorded instances of Grant's stubborn optimism in the face of adversity, all of which suggest that his spirit remained intact. At one point, while John Rawlins and Grant were near the landing watching Webster assemble artillery, Rawlins "asked . . . 'do you think they are pressing us, general?' Grant replied, casually, 'they have been pressing us all day, John, but I think we will stop them here.'" Others offered similar recollections, but perhaps none so epitomized Grant's mood as Sherman's famous anecdote, recounted in an interview three years later. Encountering Grant sitting in the rain (Grant had been driven to leave his nominal headquarters by the sights and sounds of medical teams working on the wounded), Sherman commented, "'Well, Grant, we've had the devil's own day, haven't we?' Grant said, 'Yes,' and his cigar glowed in the darkness as he gave a quick, hard puff at it. 'Yes. Lick 'em tomorrow, though.'"[22]

Options

With nightfall and the lapse of Confederate pressure, Grant's options increased to three. Retreat was now possible overnight, using the cover of darkness and his reinforcements to safeguard a total withdrawal toward Crump's Landing and Savannah. The second, probably safest choice was to simply stay put, hoping that the fresh troops would further render Grant's final position impregnable. This was also a relatively risk-free proposition, given the presence of Buell's men. The third, and most aggressive option was to counterattack, using those same reinforcements to turn the tables on the Confederates.

Option 1

Retreat was not in Grant's nature, but it had to be considered nonetheless. Darkness would provide cover, and the rain would only further muffle the noise of the move. Part of the army could retreat over Snake Creek toward Crump's Landing, where troops could prepare a more defensible position. More men and equipment could also be evacuated via Pittsburg Landing to Savannah or some other point on the river. Some part of the army could be saved.

But a retreat would have three major drawbacks. It would abandon large quantities of arms and equipment to the Rebels, including thousands of the most modern rifled muskets, of which the Confederacy was in short supply. Rebel troops were already eagerly trading their antiquated converted weapons for the newest Enfield and Springfield models, as well as numbers of cannon. Some stores might be destroyed, but there was no time, over a single night, to destroy everything that would have to be left behind. Withdrawal also abandoned many stragglers and many of Grant's wounded to the Rebels; inevitably, not everyone would get away safely.

Finally, a retreat would unequivocally concede the battle to the Confederates and be recorded as a crushing defeat for Federal arms, hardly offset by the fact that Grant might save a portion of his command. Such a disaster would likely cost both Grant and Sherman their jobs. Aside from the political and career ramifications, a Rebel victory could have a tremendous impact on Southern morale and resolve, and a conversely disastrous effect in the North. After two months of apparent defeat, Shiloh could mark the beginning of a Confederate resurgence in the West.

Option 2

Remaining in place held less peril than a retreat. The army would be ensconced in a compact position with secure flanks and no chance of a repeated Confederate surprise. The Federals could no longer be cut off from the landing since they were defending its very doorstep. Moreover, the Rebels had no way to interdict steamboat traffic between Pittsburg Landing and Savannah. Grant's supply line was secure. In time, he could reorganize his battered divisions, return all those stragglers to the ranks, and, if Beauregard did not attack him, choose the place and time of his own assault.

But with limited deployment space and with his army's back to either the river or the impassable swamp, Grant was still in a difficult position. Some of the line's strengths were also potential weaknesses. The more densely the Federals were packed, the more vulnerable they were to enemy artillery fire, and the less room they would have for battle deployment. The army would have virtually no rear area—no space to place reserves, bring up ammunition, or provide for the wounded. If the Confederates attacked again and were successful, there was no room to retreat. Disaster could strike easily in such circumstances. And again, just as a retreat would do, inaction would effectively concede the day to the Rebels. April 6 would still be viewed as a Federal defeat. Perhaps it would not be as decisive of a loss, but it would still be a hugely significant one.

Option 3

Grant's remaining option was the most aggressive: a counterattack. By dawn he would have fourteen thousand new men, with at least ten thousand more on the way. Given that he fought Sunday's battle with forty thousand men, against a like-numbered opponent, these reinforcements more than made up for his losses. The additional manpower nearly doubled his remaining strength, without a like gain for Beauregard. This was a huge advantage and a strong argument for going over to the offensive on Monday, April 7.

A successful counterattack would also go a long way toward reversing the opprobrium sure to ensue over the Army of the Tennessee's failings on April 6. If Grant could recapture his camps and drive the Rebels off the field—let alone crush them as they intended to crush him—the battle might yet become a Federal victory.

Of course, there were hazards. Most of those reinforcements belonged to Buell's army, not Grant's own; Grant would have to depend on Buell for effective cooperation and coordination on the battlefield. In addition, Grant's authority over Buell was tenuous. Both men were major generals, and both were departmental commanders, Grant of the Tennessee and Buell of the Ohio. Halleck, the overarching commander, was still far away in St. Louis. Buell was expected to collaborate with Grant, and since Buell was now outside his own departmental boundaries and within Grant's sphere of operations, he was expected to at least defer to Grant. But Halleck, who never intended or wanted these forces to engage in a battle before he arrived, did little to establish a clear chain of command between the two subordinates. Thus, much like McClernand and Sherman had to do on the first day, Grant and Buell would have to learn how to cooperate on the fly, in the heat of battle. Divided command is never a good recipe for battlefield success.

Then there was the question of surprise. n April 6, Grant's army was surprised and unprepared for an attack. No one could count on a similar surprise befalling either army on April 7. Reasonably speaking, even if he beat Beauregard to the punch in launching an assault the next day, Grant could still expect to face a determined, prepared opponent. He might add heavily to his own casualty lists without achieving a decisive counterstroke.

Decision

Grant chose to counterattack. His aggressive nature demanded the most aggressive solution, a determination only enhanced by both Buell's reinforcements and his own previous experiences. Grant subsequently claimed that he decided to strike "before firing had ceased on the 6th," an optimism founded on his experiences at Fort Donelson. There, despite an initial reverse, the contest had been decided by fresh troops and a vigorous counterattack. Grant recalled, "To Sherman I . . . said that the same tactics would win at Shiloh."[23]

Grant expressed his intentions to many different people who later recounted those exchanges. Newspaperman Whitelaw Reed overheard one such conversation, which also occurred near the landing late in the afternoon. "Does not the prospect begin to look gloomy?" queried one worried Federal. "'Not at all,' was the quick reply. 'They can't force our lines around our batteries tonight—it is too late. Delay counts everything with us. Tomorrow we shall attack them with fresh troops and drive them, of course.'" A bit later, after the firing had ended, Lieut. Col. James B. McPherson offered up a gloomy report and then asked, "'Under this condition of affairs, what do you propose to do, sir? Shall I make preparations for a retreat?' Grant snapped back, 'Retreat? No. I propose to attack at daylight and whip them.'"[24]

The issue was settled. The Federal army would attack.

Results/Impact

Grant intended to advance with his whole army, but the main weight of his blows would rest with Buell's men on the Federal left and Lew Wallace on the right. William Nelson reported that after his men deployed and the firing ceased, Buell ordered him to throw out "heavy pickets" and "to move forward and attack the enemy at the earliest dawn." Buell next brought up Crittenden's division on Nelson's right, and as McCook's men arrived, Buell would place them on Crittenden's right. Buell's numerous infantry were short of artillery, a factor that hampered the advance later in the day. The troops in Nelson's command, having marched overland from Savannah and then ferried across the river in great haste, were forced to leave their batteries behind.[25]

Wallace's three brigades deployed in a single line on the far right, facing more west than south, along the Hamburg–Savannah Road. Wallace was in a sour mood, his spirits dampened by the rain and perhaps by the accusations of foot-dragging that were beginning to be whispered among some of Grant's staff. "Chilled and dissatisfied," Wallace wrote, "I confess myself in a very unjoyous spirit. Indeed, I would have willingly shuffled off what was before me, could it have been done leaving a good taste in my mouth."[26]

Between Buell and Wallace, Grant deployed Sherman, McClernand, and Hurlbut, in that order from right to left. These were the Federal commander's remaining three divisions. Sherman was to connect with Wallace, while Hurlbut tied in with McCook's division once it arrived. One potential complication was the fact that Wallace, on the right, faced mostly west, while Buell, on the left, faced south and would have to cross Dill Branch. If all the units simply started forward, they would advance on divergent angles, open-ing gaps in their lines as they went. To compensate, Wallace's men executed what amounted to a large left wheel, which eventually brought them into line with Buell's southward-oriented command.

Despite Grant's intention to attack at daylight, the Federals in fact got off to a much slower start. As it turned out, very few Rebels were in their immediate front. Only Lew Wallace's men could see any enemy troops as the sun rose—elements of Preston Pond's brigade and Capt. William Ketchum's Alabama battery. Ketchum opened fire, and Wallace's artillery replied. Then, about 6:30, Wallace's infantry began to advance, wheeling toward Jones Field.

Meanwhile, Buell's men had to cross the Dill Branch Ravine, which proved no easy feat. Buell began his advance about 6:00 a.m., but it took the better part of two hours for his brigades to scramble down into the ravine, cross the creek, and claw their way up the far slope. The first elements of the force began to emerge at about 7:30, but it would be 8:00 a.m. before the Army of the Ohio was fully formed and ready to resume the attack. As it turned out, soldiers still had to advance anywhere between a half to a full mile before they met resistance.

If Beauregard intended to finish off Grant's army on April 7, he took no action to translate intention into reality. The Confederates were badly scat-tered by the night's haphazard bivouac, which only compounded the straggler problem. Even if they intended to return to the ranks, many of those men shaken loose in the previous day's fighting now had no idea where to find their units. The officers they encountered could rarely tell them where to find their commands. Even though the Federals took far longer than anticipated to close with the enemy and attack, the Confederates were in little better tac-tical shape to receive that attack than they would have been at dawn, despite the extra hours.

Grant's decision changed the nature of the battle. He irrevocably wrested the initiative from the Confederates, who would not regain it. At best, Beauregard's forces would manage limited counterattacks on April 7. By as-suming the offensive, Grant also recaptured the lost ground and retained possession of the field, with all the political import that entailed.

CHAPTER 5

APRIL 7 AND BEYOND

Lew Wallace Chooses to Maneuver

Situation

Brigadier Gen. Lew Wallace and his subordinate commanders, having reached the battlefield just as the daylight waned on April 6, had little opportunity to reconnoiter the terrain in front of them. Wallace knew that he was Grant's right flank, that his mission was to wheel south as he advanced to conform to the movements of the rest of the army, and that he was to attack the enemy when encountered. He did not know the Rebels' location or strength.

Unlike elsewhere on the field, the enemy was in close proximity. About half of Col. Preston Pond's mixed Louisiana and Tennessee brigade was positioned just north of Jones Field, supported by Captain Ketchum's Alabama battery. At dawn, as the visibility increased, Ketchum came under cross fire from two Federal batteries, which he promptly returned. After about thirty minutes he retired to a better position and resumed firing. Here, the Alabamian reported that he received support from both Pond's men and Col. John Wharton's regiment of Texas cavalry, though they did no shooting. This "duello" (as Ketchum termed it) lasted another half hour.[1]

In the meantime, Wallace formed his troops and waited for the order to attack. After a breakfast with the First Nebraska Infantry, Wallace recalled, "[In order] to be found easily, I betook myself to the road to Crump's." The

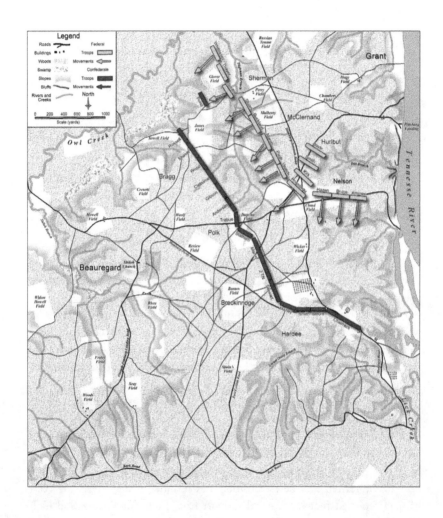

road ran directly behind his front, and Grant soon found him there. "'Good morning,' [Grant] said, pulling rein. He spoke in an ordinary tone, cheerful and wholly free from excitement. From his look and manner no one could have inferred that he had been beaten in a great battle only the day before. . . . 'You are ready?'" Grant queried. "'Yes sir.'" He and Wallace rode forward together, with Grant indicating a line of advance westward. Wallace recalled having only two questions: "'Pardon me, General,' I said, 'but is there any special formation you would like me to take in attacking?' He replied, 'No, I leave that to your discretion.'" Then Wallace asked, "'I will be supported, of course?' 'I will see to that,'" answered Grant. Later, Wallace would complain that Grant failed to inform him of the nature of the ground to his front, the exact troops who were to support him, and even the fact that Buell's army was present.[2]

At 6:30 a.m. Wallace's three brigades stepped off. Their first challenge was to cross Tilghman's Branch; it was not as severe an obstacle as Dill Branch, but the task still proved arduous. Wallace, trailing the Eleventh Indiana of Col. Morgan Smith's brigade, experienced some trepidation when climbing a hill overlooking the creek. He was expecting stout resistance but met none. Greatly overmatched, Colonel Pond had retreated, ordering Ketchum's artillery to fall back as well. Wallace pressed on until Col. Charles Whittlesey's brigade, on the extreme right, was pinched off by Snake Creek, forcing Wallace to shift Whittlesey's line behind his remaining two brigades. Whittlesey could support the first line and also protect Wallace's right flank if needed from this position. Wallace then halted in Jones Field, from which he could see more Confederates in the far tree line, to await the promised support.[3]

While halted, Wallace reconnoitered. Calling the bottomland of Owl Creek a "muddy sea," he observed, "[It] could be relied upon to take care of my right flank. . . . It was physically impossible for the enemy to establish themselves in the backwater and undergrowth." Of further note, "the woods occupied by the Confederates . . . did not reach to the creek by many hundreds of yards." "It seemed possible to get on their [the Rebels'] flank," Wallace wrote, "force them out of position, and possibly help myself to a lot of prisoners. All the project required was to swing the Second and Third brigades to the left, pivoted on the First. Making no doubt of Sherman's appearance with his division on my left in time for the manoeuvre, I set about it at once. Whittlesey advanced promptly."[4]

Wallace's plans soon foundered. His promised support failed to appear. Moreover, he could hear the rising sound of battle to the south, which seemed to be "creeping into the west, which was forward," or toward his own still-unsupported left flank, "whereat," Wallace recalled, "my impatience turned to anxiety." Still waiting, Wallace advanced the rest of his line to midfield to bolster Whittlesey and again brought up his artillery to silence the Rebel guns who had opened fire once more. Wallace watched nervously as infantry and cavalry moved on the far side of the field; these men were apparently reinforcements sent to help Pond, or perhaps even to attack Wallace's own left. By now, Wallace recalled, it was 10:00 a.m., and still there was no sign of support. Fortunately, the Confederate efforts to attack were slight and easily repulsed. At last, more Federals arrived. "The support for which I waited . . . To this day," Wallace admitted, "I do not know who composed it or by whom it was commanded—whether by Sherman or McClernand." Conforming his advance to that of the new arrivals, Wallace finally ordered his division forward. "Again the enemy disappointed me," Wallace stated, adding, "He yielded the woods to us without opposition, except of skirmishers."[5]

Grant's stated intention to "attack them and whip them at daylight" proved to be easier said than done. Buell's advance shared much in common with Wallace's. Reaching the field after sundown and deploying through the night, Nelson's Fourth Division and Crittenden's Fifth Division also had no chance to reconnoiter. Nevertheless, Buell ordered them forward just after 5:00 a.m.; Nelson navigated the Dill Branch Ravine, while Crittenden moved along the Corinth–Pittsburg Road. It was after 7:00 a.m., however, before they encountered the first Rebel pickets. Enemy cannon opened, and Buell ordered his own guns to reply. Then, just as along Wallace's front, an artillery duel ensued. Buell used this time to better align Crittenden and Nelson's brigades, as well as to bring up McCook's Second Division, which had reached the landing about first light. All this maneuvering ate up more of the morning.[6]

Exhausted, the Confederates had done almost nothing to sort themselves out overnight and prepare for the next day's contest. Had Beauregard somehow been able to form an effective line in and east of Cloud Field on the tableland overlooking Dill Branch, Nelson's division might have had a much more difficult time of it. Of course, the Confederates believed that they would have to do nothing more than finish off Grant's battered Army of the Tennessee on Monday morning, and they were therefore unprepared for Buell's attack. Col. Nathan Bedford Forrest awoke General Hardee in the night with the news of Buell's arrival, prompting Hardee to instruct Forrest to find the army commander and inform him in turn. Forrest, however, was unable to find Beauregard. The colonel returned to Hardee at 2:00 a.m., whereupon Hardee ordered the cavalryman "to return to his regiment, keep a vigilant, strong picket line, and report all hostile movements." As a result, the army was not in good shape to receive any attack the next morning.[7]

Fortunately for Beauregard and his fellow Confederates, the slow prog-
ress of the Federal advance allowed time to form a patchwork battle line by
midmorning. The first significant fighting erupted between Nelson's division
and some of Hardee's men in the vicinity of the Peach Orchard and the Sarah
Bell Cotton Field at about 8:30. By 10:00 a.m., the fighting had become general. A Confederate line ran from Larkin Bell's Field on the east, extending
along the south and west edges of Sarah Bell's Cotton Field, then through
the woods to and across Duncan Field, and finally terminating in Jones Field,
where Wallace confronted Pond. Through the forenoon the Federals launched
a series of frontal attacks against portions of this line. Periodic Confederate
countersallies answered these assaults, adding up to a stalemate.[8]

One more Federal element must be considered in addition to Wallace's
and Buell's contingents. The battered remnants of McClernand's, Hurlbut's,
and Sherman's divisions re-formed as best they could and expected to join in
the general Federal advance. These troops made up the very center of Grant's
line, becoming the glue between Buell's right and Lew Wallace's left. But as
Wallace discovered, despite a relative lack of terrain obstacles in their path,
these divisions moved the slowest of all. Almost certainly the shock of yesterday's combat and the tremendous losses already suffered induced a great deal
of caution on Monday morning. As Wallace noted, McClernand, Hurlbut,
and Sherman finally appeared on his left by late morning, engaging Confederates in the southeast corner of Jones Field and the woods between Jones and
Duncan Fields after 10:00 a.m. Historian Timothy B. Smith describes their
advance on April 7 as "lackluster," perhaps made the more so because Grant,
instead of providing overall leadership and direction to the three divisional
commanders, "chose to remain at Pittsburg Landing much of the day, for-
warding the arriving troops to the front." When the commanders did become
fully engaged, it was again via a series of disjointed piecemeal frontal attacks
answered by similar Rebel sorties. This situation mirrored the deadlock on
Buell's portion of the line.[9]

Though he certainly knew little enough of them at the time, these were
the facts of the tactical situation when Lew Wallace again advanced to encounter the next Rebel line at about noon. He was simply groping forward,
trying to fulfill Grant's orders, and listening to the now full-fledged roar of
combat off to his left.

When the Confederates attacked over this same ground on April 6, they
pushed the Federals back into a narrowing peninsula of land between Owl
Creek and the Tennessee River, both of which provided unassailable flank
protection to the constricting Federal line. In fact, the Federal flanks were
never turned; instead, the center was captured when the flanks fell back but

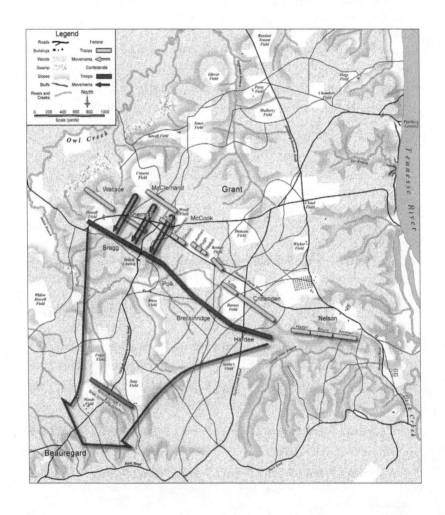

Prentiss and W. H. L. Wallace did not. Now, however, those circumstances were reversed. The Owl Creek drainage angled much farther west the farther south one progressed, leaving far more open space to the west of the Confederate line than Beauregard had troops available to occupy. Wallace's right advanced into Sowell Field, recently cleared of Rebels. "The enemy's left had rested upon the bluff," he reported, "and as it had been driven back, that flank was now exposed."[10]

Options

While Wallace's orders from Grant were to attack, troops were not to do so blindly or unsupported. Wallace could wait for the rest of the army to come up on his left here. Alternatively, he could follow Grant's last instruction and simply attack without pausing, or he could use more care and attempt another flanking move.

Option 1

Wallace's safest course was to again halt, engage the enemy line with his artillery, which had already prevailed against Ketchum's Alabamians, and await reinforcements. Wallace knew that support was on his left and could be expected to marry up with his left flank soon. Then a joint advance would protect his left from any enfilading fire or sudden counterattacks. In the meantime, his artillery could soften up the enemy position. There was also the constant battle noise off to Wallace's left to think of; should he get too far in advance of the rest of the army, he could become isolated and exposed to destruction.

There was a cost to this plan, of course. Grant had ordered Wallace to attack. So far, the advance had been slow—not unrealistically so given the terrain, but still consuming much of the morning. Nor could Wallace know how the fight was progressing elsewhere. His attack could be the very thing needed to divert Rebel reserves and take pressure off beleaguered Federals elsewhere. Further, Wallace had to reflect on the previous day's disappointments and frustrations. His delayed arrival—no matter who was at fault—angered Grant and led the army commander to question Wallace's fitness for divisional command. What would Grant think of a second day's disappointment and delay?

Option 2

Wallace's easiest choice was to simply attack—though at potentially great cost to his men. Charging onto Crescent Field certainly would fulfill Grant's intentions. It was the quickest way to come to grips with what had been so far an elusive opponent. Grant wasn't interested in simply chasing Beauregard's army away, leaving the Confederates to evacuate the battlefield at their leisure. He wanted to hit them hard and damage them, perhaps even to turn the tables on the Rebels and destroy their army if he could.

However, frontal assaults were costly, as thousands of soldiers had already learned the day before. At this stage of the war, enthusiasm tended to override tactics, even assuming that the half-trained—in many cases untrained—regiments and brigades were capable of more sophisticated tactical efforts. Wallace might certainly prevail in his assault since his men were both fresh and veteran, still unblooded at Shiloh. However, that success would be purchased at a high price. And if the Federals were repulsed, what other fresh troops did Grant have with which to stave off disaster?

<u>Option 3</u>

There was a third way, as evidenced by Wallace's own observations. The Rebel line stopped in the woods well short of Owl Creek, leaving him room to move around the Rebel left flank instead of simply charging straight ahead. Turning an enemy flank was the primary goal of linear warfare, forcing an opponent to either maneuver in kind to face the threat or retreat. Maneuvering offered Wallace a way to continue his attack without resorting to a bloody frontal assault.

But moving against the flank would require more time than would a frontal assault, and the morning was already gone. Furthermore, as noted, Wallace's own left flank might be turned, especially if he maneuvered farther west and lost contact with the army. The decision to maneuver carried inherent risks of its own.

Decision

Having observed that exposed flank, however, Wallace didn't hesitate. As he explained, "I resolved to attempt to re-turn it. For that purpose it became necessary for me to change front by a left half-wheel of the whole division." Doubling his skirmish line, Wallace further resolved to make this assault in open order (i.e., not in a dense, two-rank shoulder-to-shoulder battle line) to make the most of the undulating terrain and reduce losses. It was a profoundly powerful choice.[11]

Results/Impact

Wallace's division actually conducted multiple flanking movements. The first occurred in Glover Field around daylight, but Pond's men, far in advance of the main line, retreated too quickly to be engaged. A second took place in Jones Field around 10:00 a.m., again levering Pond out of position. The next transpired around noon, proceeding through Sowell Field and into Crescent Field. Due to space constraints, Wallace was forced to shift Whittlesey's brigade from his right to his left, and he subsequently returned two of Whittlesey's three regiments to the far right as the move progressed.

Colonel Deas of the Twenty-Second Alabama, now in command of Gladden's Brigade, was posted on the Rebel left. After moving to the front that morning, Deas found himself adjacent to an ad hoc division now commanded by Col. Robert M. Russell of Polk's First Corps. Ordered by Russell to advance, Deas complied until difficulties arose. "Perceiving the enemy's skirmishers on our left and rear," the colonel recalled, "[we] fell back to our first position." Alexander Oliphant of the Twenty-Fourth Indiana, a member of Wallace's division, observed that retreat somewhat differently. "The whole Rebel Army broke and ran for their lives," he exulted. "A soldier knows when he is flanked and wont stand for it." Perhaps not the whole Rebel army broke and ran, since Col. John M. Thayer of the First Nebraska Infantry, one of Wallace's brigade commanders, reported—with some exaggeration as to time—that the battle here "raged with unabated fury for nearly two hours." He described at least two efforts by Rebels to stand and fight, noting that "the enemy's battery was exceedingly well served, it having obtained excellent range."[12]

The Confederates now formed a second battle line along the Hamburg–Purdy Road, but here the westward bow of Owl Creek opened up even more usable ground beyond their left flank. Having had success with turning movements so far, Wallace was happy to stick with what had worked. It was now 1:00 p.m. Confederate colonel Robert Russell was on the left in the woods between Crescent and Ben Howell Fields. Wallace's line again overlapped Russell, allowing Wallace to send a portion of Thayer's brigade, as well as Colonel Whittlesey and the Twentieth and Seventy-Eighth Ohio of his brigade, out beyond the flank to enfilade Russell. "The enemy had now forced a line across our left flank," reported Russell, "and was planting a battery in an open field [Ben Howell Field] in that direction." Russell recounted his attempt to place a Rebel battery to oppose this move: "Before it could be placed in position and unlimbered, the opposing battery opened a terrific fire upon our line, killing and wounding many of our men. This, with the heavy flank fire on the left and the direct fire in front, caused a retreat to a ravine a short distance in front of Shiloh Church."[13]

This last retreat carried out under Beauregard's "immediate eye" forced a larger Confederate withdrawal to a more compact line south of the Hamburg–

Purdy Road, extending from Prentiss's camps to the Shiloh Church. Pressure from the stalled Federal center and left was renewed as Buell's divisions pressed forward in the wake of this movement. In forcing the Rebels back, Wallace's flank movements had done what all of Buell's frontal attacks failed to accomplish.[14]

Wallace's maneuvering completely changed the nature of the day's action, though many observers at the time and since have been slow to recognize that fact. Up to 1:00 p.m., however, all the other Federal efforts had failed to break or even seriously dislodge the Confederate line. Since at least 10:00 a.m., repeated Federal attacks hammered at the Rebels to no avail. Whatever local success that might be claimed was quickly offset by a Confederate riposte that restored the line and returned things to deadlock. Casualties, furthermore, were heavy. Of the 16,000 men in Buell's army that were heavily engaged, 2,103 were killed, wounded, or missing on April 7. Yet another of Buell's divisions was arriving (the Sixth, under Brig. Gen. Thomas J. Wood), but only one brigade came under fire, suffering four wounded. And even if Wood's division was thrown in to eventually attrit the Rebels into breaking, there was no reason to think the unit's losses would be less.[15]

Wallace has been strongly criticized for not playing a greater role in the fighting on April 7. This criticism begins with a look at his casualty figures. The Third Division suffered 296 killed, wounded, and missing at Shiloh: a mere fraction of the losses suffered by other commands. Wallace was chary with his men's lives, used cover where possible, adopted open-order formation when the opportunity beckoned, and generally fulfilled the spirit of Grant's order. And yet, far from lagging, Wallace's repeated flanking efforts produced the only solid Federal successes of the day's fight.

Beauregard Quits the Field

Situation

By 2:00 p.m. General Beauregard had seen his troops driven back almost to their starting positions of April 6, giving up nearly all they had captured in those overrun Federal camps the previous day. The Confederates fought well on April 7, launching repeated counterattacks. Even so, Beauregard—and everyone else on the field—knew now that Buell was present, and the Army of the Mississippi was heavily outnumbered.

Beauregard had been surprised by the morning's attack. He expected to do the attacking, not be assailed himself. The rest of the army felt likewise, and soldiers did little more besides eat and catch what rest they could that night. There was no order to the bivouac, nor even decent communication among the commanders. Colonel Forrest, for example, was able to warn Hardee of Buell's arrival, but when Hardee instructed him to pass that news on to the army commander, Forrest was unable to locate Beauregard's headquarters. Similarly, when Leonidas Polk received word that divisional commander Benjamin F. Cheatham was moving his two brigades back to their April 5 bivouac sites for food, rest, and ammunition, Polk decided to accompany them. He attempted to inform Beauregard of his whereabouts via a staff officer, but that messenger was also unable to locate Beauregard. As a result, for some time the next morning, Beauregard had no idea where Polk was, even speculating that he might have been captured. Only at about 8:00 a.m., when Polk led Cheatham's men back onto the field, were those fears allayed.[16]

Exhaustion, inexperience, and complacency explain why the Confederate army was so poorly situated regarding either attack or defense on the morning of April 7. Timothy B. Smith censures Beauregard strongly for this inaction, noting that even a modicum of effort to place troops on the southern rim of the Dill Branch Ravine overnight could have seriously—perhaps fatally—disrupted Buell's advance. Such an effort would have required an extensive sorting out of troops during the night, however, amid driving rain and under fire from the Federal gunboats. Complacent, Beauregard felt no need to put the men through that ordeal. He told one officer "that 'the enemy were making a stand at only one point, and he expected to capture them that morning.'"[17]

Subsequent fighting soon confirmed the news that Buell was present, especially after the noise of the combat spread across the entire Confederate front. In his report, Beauregard claimed, "[As early as 6:00 a.m.,] a hot fire of musketry and artillery . . . assured me of the junction of his [Buell's] forces." Certainly Federal general Prentiss, who spent the night with Confederate staff officer Thomas Jordan at Beauregard's headquarters, thought so. "When the firing first of musketry and then of field artillery roused us," recalled Jordan, "General Prentiss exclaimed: 'Ah! Didn't I tell you so! There is Buell!'" Caught by surprise, the Confederates scrambled to get a defense organized. Another staff officer, Capt. Samuel Lockett, stated, "I, as a great many other staff officers, was principally occupied in the early hours of the second day in gathering together our scattered men and getting them into some sort of manageable organization." Lockett proved singularly successful in this endeavor, assembling a scratch force "about a thousand strong" that he dubbed the "Beauregard Regiment." Lacking any field officers, Lockett himself was assigned to command this ad hoc task force.[18]

Despite the thrown-together nature of this defense, however, the Confederates managed to counterattack vigorously and often, effectively blunting the Federal advance. It was evident that the Confederates still had some bite left, and that Beauregard had not yet wholly abandoned the idea of his own attack. According to Smith, "Beauregard had always planned on renewing the battle on April 7." And notwithstanding this unexpected Yankee combativeness, "Beauregard was still in an offensive mind-set, and despite a slow, stuttered start to the morning's operations, he was ready to make his major attack. . . . Breckinridge['s Division] would be his hammer" attacking the enemy center. The rest of the Confederate army was supposed to watch for and support this move when it came. This intention explains why so often that morning, Rebel troops lashed out at advancing Federals instead of standing on the defensive.[19]

Even as late as 1:00 p.m., while Wallace was moving to turn Colonel Russell's left, Braxton Bragg ordered Brig. Gen. Sterling A. M. Wood's brigade, currently in reserve, to launch one such counterblow. Wood's command was a mixed force of Arkansans, Alabamians, Mississippians, and Tennesseans; and though it started the battle with more than 2,000 men in the ranks on Sunday morning, it was down to no more than 650 men now. The attack, launched out of the timber just north of Shiloh Church, caught the Federals by surprise. Wood moved through the Crossroads, splashed across Water Oaks Pond, and charged into Wolf Field, striking the seam between McCook's division of Buell's army and Sherman's battered formations of Grant's force. "The enemy gave way and fell back in disorder," Wood reported, "but soon rallied on our left so as to pour into us a cross-fire." These Federals on Wood's left were Wallace's men, moving to follow Russell's retreat and turning to deal with this new threat. The result was that Wood fell back in turn. He stated, "We retired to the edge of the woods and here maintained for nearly three hours a most unequal contest." Wallace's men followed, which, Wood noted, "forc[ed] my brigade to sustain a galling cross-fire." Eventually, their combat power spent, Wood's men fell back to the final Rebel line.[20]

There was also some fleeting hope that Beauregard might receive Confederate reinforcements to offset Buell's appearance. Maj. Gen. Earl Van Dorn's Army of the West had been ordered to join the concentration at Corinth. His earlier decision to reinvade Missouri, which resulted in a Rebel defeat at the Battle of Pea Ridge in early March, disorganized his army and precluded him from arriving in time to join the attack on April 6. But he was still en route, and rumors of his army's possible presence were being whispered in the Confederate ranks. Close to 2:00 p.m., with the situation growing more desperate by the minute, Beauregard "sent messengers rearward in the vain hope they might encounter Earl Van Dorn's army approaching the battlefield. . . . Word soon arrived from Corinth that he had yet to even arrive there."[21]

Options

Beauregard now faced a choice. His troops had stood all day, taking any damage the Federals could offer and meting out like punishment in return. But could they stand more? Van Dorn's force might have made all the difference, but that hope was now dashed. Beauregard's most aggressive option would be to launch yet another attack, gambling that Grant's and Buell's forces might break before his own men did. Alternatively, he could abandon the idea of attacking but still stand on the defense, hoping that the Yankees would exhaust themselves in fruitless attacks before his own force collapsed. If neither strategy worked, however, Beauregard was risking complete destruction if his army came apart first. His last, safest option would be to retreat now, abandoning the field but saving his troops. Each of these options had pros and cons.

Option 1

A final, all-or-nothing counterattack might just win the day. All the Federal assaults so far had fallen short of driving the main Rebel line, and when the Confederates launched their own attacks, they had met with at least limited success. Given the chaotic nature of the field and the Confederate dispositions, Beauregard had so far been unable to assemble the kind of massive general assault he envisioned, which might explain why his counterattacks so far had only met with local success.

But such an attack might also produce nothing but heavy additional casualties and exhaust the last combat power in the army's arsenal. If the Rebels attacked, failed, and subsequently broke, there might be no army left. Albert Sidney Johnston had been willing to bet the army's survival on a high-stakes, all-or-nothing attack the day before, and he had come up just a hairbreadth short. Could Beauregard do better now?

Moreover, Wallace's success on the Confederate left had already forced Beauregard's line back twice—three times, counting Pond's initial withdrawal. While each retirement shortened Beauregard's line, it also brought the Federal right flank closer to the Corinth Road, which angled off to the southwest as it left the battlefield. Should Grant's forces gain control of the Corinth Road, they would occupy the quickest route to Beauregard's base of operations. The Rebels would then be left with the Hamburg Road, which ran east along the curve of the Tennessee River, as their best retreat option. If Beauregard lost control of the Corinth Road, Grant would have an open road to Corinth. And if Grant managed to seize the town before Beauregard arrived to defend it, the Army of the Mississippi almost certainly faced complete destruction.

Option 2

Beauregard could elect to stand fast, betting instead that his men would continue to resist, and that Grant and Buell would break off their own attacks first. If Beauregard chose this option and outlasted the Federals, at the least he could claim a measure of victory and many of the spoils of war that the Confederates still controlled. Weapons and supplies still littered the field along the line of Sherman's and Prentiss's camps.

But again, if his army broke first, that break might be complete. Beauregard roughly estimated his remaining strength at no more than twenty thousand men, or half the army he had brought to the field on April 6. No one knew how many of Buell's men were already on the field or would be there by dark. If the Confederates yielded first, standing fast posed all the risks of an all-out attack with none of the potential gain. And, just as with option one above, if Beauregard lost control of and access to the Corinth Road, his own base was in great peril.

Option 3

Conversely, a retreat now would probably save the army. Beauregard could fall back to Corinth via the best, most direct route, reorganize his own badly straggled ranks, integrate Van Dorn's reinforcements into his command, and again take the war to the Federals when he was ready. While they would leave Union troops in possession of the field and likely give Grant some grounds for claiming success, Johnston and Beauregard had undeniably dealt the Federal commander a very damaging blow on April 6. That might prove victory enough.

But retreating was also an acknowledgment that the Confederates had failed to achieve their intended objective, and that the initiative would once again pass to the Yankees. Buell's reinforcements were only the first wave of what would probably be a massive Federal concentration for the showdown at Corinth; once he arrived to take personal command, Halleck would draw on additional troops from the Mississippi River valley and Missouri to reinforce Shiloh. A retreat might save the army, but for how long? And how many more blue-clad soldiers would the Rebels face when the next clash came? And how much more of the new Confederacy's territory would have to be surrendered when that happened? These were all difficult questions that had to be weighed when contemplating a retreat.

Decision

At about 2:00 p.m. or a little before, Col. Thomas Jordan and Gov. Isham Harris (who joined Beauregard's staff after Albert Sidney Johnston's death) conversed. Jordan recalled the exchange as follows: "[Isham] asked if I did not regard the day as going against us irremediably, and whether there was not danger in tarrying so long in the field as to be unable to withdraw in good order." Jordan agreed with the governor and then approached Beauregard. "'General, do you not think our troops are very much in the condition of a lump of sugar thoroughly soaked in water, but yet preserving its original shape, though ready to dissolve? Would it not be judicious to get away with what we have?'"[22]

Beauregard had already come to the same conclusion: "'I intend to withdraw in a few moments.' Was his reply." In his report, the Creole commander wrote, "[By noon,] my last reserves had necessarily been disposed of, and the enemy was evidently receiving fresh re-enforcements after each repulse; accordingly about 1 p.m. I determined to withdraw from so unequal a contest, securing such of the results of the victory of the day before as was then practicable." Beauregard chose the safest course open to him at the time.[23]

Results/Impact

Beauregard's decision to retreat did not precipitate a wholesale withdrawal, since that might have incited the very panic he was trying to prevent. Instead, he opted for a continued retirement in stages. Beauregard boasted of the retreat, "Never did troops leave a battlefield in better order." He noticed that "even the stragglers fell into the ranks and marched off with those who had stood more steadily by their colors," and that "the enemy made no attempt to follow." However, the Rebels did not extricate themselves from the field entirely scot-free. Sometime after 2:00 p.m., Stanford's Mississippi Battery lost four of the unit's six pieces to Crittenden's Federals while buying time for General Breckinridge's Reserve Corps to establish a final line south of Shiloh Church. At about 4:00 p.m., Beauregard committed a scratch force built around the Thirty-Eighth Tennessee Infantry and numbering about one thousand men to a final counterattack north through the woods east of the church. That assault failed to dent the Federal lines, but it probably precluded a rapid forward movement by the Yankees.[24]

Still, the Federals were largely content to let the Rebels escape. As the army filed south, Breckinridge withdrew to a second position near "the intersection of the Hamburg and Pittsburg Roads." Beauregard noted that this position was also near "the ground [the Confederates] had occupied the night preceding the first battle." On April 8, after another heavy overnight rain-storm, Breckinridge took up a third line at "Mickey's, which position [he] continued to hold, with . . . cavalry thrown forward." The lead elements of the army trudged into Corinth on the eighth, and by April 9 virtually the whole army was present, "with only small groups walking on over the next few days."[25]

Almost certainly, Beauregard made the best choice possible in deciding to retreat. If a fresh, numerically advantaged Rebel force failed to finish off Grant's surprised divisions on April 6, an exhausted, battered, half-strength Confederate army was not likely to prevail against Grant *and* Buell on April 7. Standing in place was likely no better an option, given that Wallace was working around the Rebel right flank. If given enough time, he would sever the all-important Corinth Road.

Grant Limits Pursuit

Situation

Ultimately, Federal efforts to pursue the retreating Confederates came to no more than a couple of feeble attempts, hardly worth the name. It is a maxim of military science, of course, that no battlefield victory is complete without a rigorous pursuit. Certainly no nineteenth-century military professional— or even well-read amateur soldier—failed to understand the importance of such an effort. Any student of Napoleon's greatest campaigns (which by mid-century were the blueprint for all professional study) understood that fact. Despite having fresh troops and a decided numerical advantage, however, neither Grant nor Buell managed to mount any effective pursuit on April 7. Nor did anyone do much better on April 8.

Grant's earliest communications suggest that at best, he intended to ex-ercise great caution in mounting any pursuit. He was still thinking about defense. To Halleck, he wrote on the seventh, "I shall follow [Beauregard] to-morrow far enough to see that no immediate renewal of an attack is con-templated." Grant sent the following to Buell, also on the evening of the seventh: "When I left the field this evening—[headed back to Savannah] my intention was to occupy the most advanced position possible for the night with the infantry engaged through the day, and follow up our success with cavalry and fresh troops expected to arrive . . . [overnight.] The great fatigue of our men . . . would preclude the idea of making any advance to-night with-out the arrival of the expected re-enforcements. My plan, therefore, will be to feel on in the morning [April 8] with all the troops on the outer lines until our cavalry force can be organized. . . . Under the instructions which I have previously received, and a dispatch also of to-day of General Halleck, it will not then do to advance beyond Pea Ridge, or some point which we can reach and return in a day."[26]

Thus, Sherman, McClernand, and Hurlbut merely reoccupied their former camps by the end of April 7. Nor did Buell's men do much more. Buell, after all, was subordinate to Grant and as mindful of Halleck's admonitions as anyone. Beauregard was correct in stating that the Federals did not pursue. Col. Jacob Ammen, commanding one of General Nelson's brigades, recorded that the fighting ended "about 3:30 p.m. Parties were sent in pursuit, but there was no fighting except slight skirmishing." James A. Garfield's brigade of General Wood's Sixth Division reached the field at 3:00 p.m. Garfield reported that after the Rebels retreated "I moved my command to the front of our line and bivouacked during the night, having sent forward 200 men, deployed as skirmishers, a few hundred yards in advance of our position." In fact, Buell expected more fighting the next morning, taking care to select positions and arrange his divisions in order "to commence the terrible work again" on the morning of April 8.[27]

Lew Wallace, still on the Federal right, expected to be ordered forward, but he was baffled at the seeming indifference of the army commander. He declared, "To-morrow there would be pursuit—that of course—and, as I was farthest out, why should not the duty be entrusted to me? Besides that, I was unwilling to retire a step without an order. In the end, I sent an officer with a report to General Grant. To my great disappointment the officer returned with a direction for me to retire the division to the line the army had occupied Sunday morning."[28]

Thus, General Halleck's strictures seemingly precluded any actual pursuit. However, Halleck was also hundreds of miles away, headquartered in St. Louis; he was in no position to determine the situation on the ground. Moreover, it was also a well-understood precept of nineteenth-century military affairs that field commanders often had to use their own initiative, dictated by circumstances, to override a far-off commander's orders. It was also a precept of military strategy that no victory was decisive without a successful pursuit. While the combined Federal armies might have fended off the Confederates and avoided complete catastrophe, they had not destroyed the Rebel army; only an aggressive and vigorous follow-up could achieve that.

Options

While Shiloh had been a bruising, hard-fought battle that had all but wrecked five of Grant's six available divisions, his losses had had been more than made good by reinforcements. Lew Wallace's Third Division suffered 296 total casualties on April 7, while Thomas Wood's Sixth Division of Buell's command suffered only 4 wounded. Further, Maj. Gen. George H. Thomas's First Division, Army of the Ohio had begun to arrive at 11:00 a.m. on the seventh, though it did not become engaged that day. It was fully available for operations on the eighth. Buell's other three divisions, though they had been more heavily engaged, were also still intact and ready for action. Thus, Grant had plenty of fresh manpower at hand should he wish to follow up Monday's success.

Option 1

Grant could elect to join forces with Buell and push all his fresh troops forward as quickly as possible. This would still leave some twenty thousand men to defend Pittsburg and Crump's Landings, clean up the battlefield, and begin the process of returning stragglers to the ranks. There were ample signs that the Confederates were in no better shape after two days' hard fighting than were Grant's men, and following up hard might well net thousands of Confederate prisoners. Even if the Confederate Army of the Mississippi escaped all the way back to Corinth, it might be dramatically weakened in the process.

Two significant obstacles stood in the way of this option. Halleck was reiterating caution with every communication, all but forbidding anything but the most limited pursuit. Further, Grant and Buell were not working well together. Buell's first impression of the Army of the Tennessee was that of masses of frightened men huddled on the Tennessee riverbank, clamoring for escape—hardly an inspiring image. Any strong pursuit would necessarily require Buell's Army of the Ohio to take the lead, since most of the fresh troops belonged to that army.

Option 2

Grant's other choice was to consolidate. He had redeemed the field on April 7. His army had suffered severely, and most of it was in no shape to advance. It was not even clear to some Federals that the Confederates were done attacking; they might have simply undertaken a tactical withdrawal to regroup. Certainly, Buell's nighttime orders to Colonel Ammen suggested as much. The safest option would be to follow the Rebels much more cautiously, obeying Halleck's injunction to advance no farther than Pea Ridge / Monterey, and avoiding another major action at all costs.

The drawback of such a limited effort was in letting the Rebels reconstitute their own battered formations, reintegrate their stragglers, and absorb reinforcements in the shape of General Van Dorn's army from Arkansas.

When the time came for the Federals to advance toward Corinth, the job of taking the town would be much more difficult due to the delay.

Decision

Grant chose caution. Despite having three fresh divisions at his disposal, he merely instructed Buell to send out Wood's command of two brigades, plus an artillery battery, "to discover the position of the enemy, and press him if he should be found in retreat. General Sherman," noted Buell, "with about the same force from General Grant's army, was on the same service." Neither Grant nor Buell would direct the pursuit in person. Instead, Grant turned once again to his most trusted subordinate: William T. Sherman. "With the cavalry placed at my command and two brigades of my fatigue troops," Sherman reported, "I went this morning out on the Corinth Road." The two brigades of infantry accompanying him were Col. David Stuart's and Col. Jesse Hildebrand's commands, both drawn from Sherman's own division. These units had been hard hit on April 6; each brigade now numbered less than 1,500 men and probably closer to 1,000. The cavalry was Col. Lyle Dickey's Fourth Illinois, attached to Sherman's division. All told, Sherman led perhaps 2,500 men forward for the morning's reconnaissance. Wood's force numbered about the same, given that one of his brigades had only two regiments. The combined force contained perhaps 5,500 men.[29]

Grant had at his disposal fifteen thousand completely fresh troops (Lew Wallace, Wood, and Thomas) and roughly fifteen thousand more who had fought only on April 7 and not suffered unduly (Buell's remaining three divisions). Even so, he chose to pursue the Confederates with but a fraction of that force. Worse yet, half of the men selected were in no condition for additional action after two days of bloody fighting. Further, being senior in rank to Wood, Sherman would be in overall charge.[30]

Results/Impact

The results were predictable. Sherman ventured forward very cautiously, marching south past the now-abandoned enemy camps marking the Confederate positions of April 5, the night before the battle. All were now makeshift hospitals. Sherman reported that "at all we found more or less wounded and dead." A mile out, Sherman met up with Wood and, coming to a fork in the road, directed the latter's column down the left-hand lane while his own force bore to the right. A half mile farther on, Sherman found a "clear field, through which the road passed, and immediately beyond a space of some 200 yards of fallen timber, and beyond an extensive camp."[31]

Making for the camp, Sherman's advanced skirmishers were in the open field when 350 Confederate cavalrymen under the command of Col. Nathan Bedford Forrest charged into them. The fight quickly degenerated into a swirling brawl at close quarters, but perhaps the most alarming thing to Sherman was the fact that the Seventy-Seventh Ohio, "without cause, broke, threw away their muskets, and fled" when faced with this onslaught. The general was appalled, noting that "the ground was admirably adapted to a defense of infantry against cavalry, it being miry and covered with fallen timber." Only the quick response of Col. Dickey's Illinois cavalry and the presence of the rest of Hildebrand's brigade turned Forrest back. Clearly, however, Sherman's troops were not ready for another hard fight.[32]

When Forrest's men withdrew, Sherman discovered that the camp in question was another field hospital. Beyond that, the last of Beauregard's forces under John C. Breckinridge had spent the night, acting as rear guard, but they were now withdrawn. Sherman, however, had had enough fighting. "The check sustained by us at the fallen timbers," he wrote, "delayed our advance, so that night came upon us before the wounded were provided for. . . . Our troops being fagged out by three days' hard fighting, exposure, and privation, I ordered them back to camp." The Battle of Shiloh was at an end.[33]

At the time, Sherman accomplished all that Grant intended—which is to say, not much. Caution ruled the day on April 8; Grant had no intention of violating Halleck's instructions. Not everyone felt that this was the correct choice, but those that did wish a stronger effort also believed they had no chance of inducing Grant to take up a more aggressive posture. In time, even Grant admitted that he should have mounted a stronger pursuit. He even indulged in a bit of historical revisionism, arguing in his *Century Magazine* article, "I wanted to pursue, but had not the heart to order the men who had fought desperately for two days, lying in the mud and the rain whenever not fighting, and I did not feel disposed positively to order Buell, or any part of his command, to pursue." Here, Grant admitted to feeling a bit insecure in his position vis-à-vis Buell: "Although the senior in rank at the time, I had been so only a few weeks. Buell was, and had been for some time past, a department commander, while I commanded only a district. I did not meet Buell in person until too late to get troops ready and pursue with effect; but had I seen him at the moment of the last charge, I should have at least requested him to follow."[34]

Buell, in his rebuttal to that article, flatly rejected both this line of reasoning and any hint of blame for the decision not to follow up. First of all, he insisted, "It is always to be expected that the chief officer in command will determine the course to be pursued at such a juncture, when he is immediately upon the ground." That chief officer was unquestionably Grant. Moreover, Buell was quick to point out that Grant's confidence was hardly at a high point even two days after the battle. On April 9, Grant informed Halleck that he did not want to retreat across the river to the east bank of the Tennessee, stating, "It would be demoralizing . . . [to] our troops here." It would also be "unsafe to remain [on this bank] . . . without large reinforcements" over and above Buell's command. Indeed, for some time Grant believed that the Confederates attacked him with a force of at least one hundred thousand, far stronger than his army and Buell's combined. That number was, of course, greatly exaggerated, but at the time, Grant was not thinking of pursuit. Indeed, concluded Buell, "General Grant's troops, the lowest individual among them not more than the commander himself, appear to have thought that the object of the battle was sufficiently accomplished when they were reinstated in their camps."[35]

CHAPTER 6

AFTERMATH AND CONCLUSIONS

The Battle of Shiloh produced a staggering casualty count, inflicting a toll that stunned both the North and the South. Grant's and Buell's combined losses tabulated 1,754 killed, 8,108 wounded, and 2,885 missing, for a total of 13,047 fallen officers and men from a total of 66,812 engaged. Confederate losses were hardly fewer: 1,728 killed, 8,012 wounded, and 959 missing for a total of 10,699 out of 41,699 engaged. As a percentage, the Federals lost 19.5 percent of their force, while Johnston and Beauregard's casualty rate amounted to a staggering 25.6 percent, one of whom, of course, was the army commander.[1]

While such casualties were not unheard of in war—the more than two decades of conflict known as the Napoleonic Wars produced similar bloodbaths—for Americans, the slaughter was unprecedented. The Mexican-American War, for example, produced 1,733 combat deaths over the course of nearly two years' struggle. In contrast, Shiloh matched that total in two days. Nor had any earlier battle in the Civil War reaped such a staggering toll, though within months even more savage engagements would sadly become commonplace. Unsurprisingly, the shock of such heavy losses unleashed widespread criticism, especially of Grant, who had failed to entrench his force and was not even on the field when the battle began. Lurid stories flooded the Northern newspapers, with sometimes-intense rivalries springing up as soldiers from one state pointed fingers at those from another. Sherman's division included many new Ohio regiments, and stragglers from his brigades were prominent among those who swamped the landing on April 6. Many Federals subsequently expressed disgust over Buckeye conduct. Ohioans were stung by the criticisms, and the state's newssheets spread tales of extreme surprise—of men being attacked at breakfast and bayonetted in their tents. They largely blamed Grant, and to a lesser extent Sherman, for these disasters.

Sherman's decision to end pursuit at Fallen Timbers concluded the fight and introduced a month-long pause in operations. When Henry Halleck reached Shiloh on April 11, "carefully dressed in a new uniform, wearing his sword, and carrying himself erect, with a distant and somewhat austere manner," he made his first observation about the troops and confided it to his wife in a letter home: "[Grant's] army is undisciplined and very much disorganized, the officers being utterly incapable of maintaining order." Intent on restoring that discipline, Halleck concentrated on drilling his men and summoning all available troops to Shiloh; he had no intention of undertaking any offensive until everything was organized to his compete satisfaction.[2]

Though Halleck did not overtly censure Grant, he made his disapproval with the latter's performance clear in other ways. Halleck spent the rest of April assembling an enormous field army at Shiloh, incorporating additional regiments into the shattered Army of the Tennessee divisions, and bringing up the rest of Buell's Army of the Ohio troops. The commander also drew even more forces from Missouri and from Maj. Gen. John Pope's column operating along the Mississippi, most recently successful in capturing the Rebel garrison of Island No. 10 near New Madrid, which surrendered on April 8. By May, Halleck had amassed a huge force of one hundred thousand troops.[3]

Beauregard was also reinforced, though not in numbers enough to match Halleck. Van Dorn's Trans-Mississippians arrived in mid-April, as did other minor forces from the Deep South, but Beauregard's strength never climbed much above seventy-five thousand men. Still, despite the favorable odds, when Halleck finally advanced, he did so with extreme caution. Once within striking distance of the town, he built repeated lines of entrenchments, halting every mile or so to dig in again—there would be no surprise attacks on his watch. The Rebels proved equally adept with shovels, building extensive lines of defensive earthworks and redoubts, bracing for a full-scale battle that never came. Beauregard certainly sought opportunities to strike, hoping to catch Halleck's legions on the march or while maneuvering around the city. But each time he was thwarted by Halleck's caution and the tide of blue uniforms moving south. Finally, on the night of May 29, fearing the overwhelming power of the siege artillery accompanying Halleck's army and the vulnerability of his own rear to Federal cavalry raids, Beauregard evacuated Corinth and set up a new base at Tupelo, fifty miles to the south.[4]

That retreat cost Beauregard his job. Shortly after arriving at Tupelo, the general took sick leave, his health further wrecked by the stress of the campaign. President Davis, already dismayed by the loss of Corinth, used that leave as a pretext to relieve Beauregard of command. Braxton Bragg took the helm of what would soon become the Army of Tennessee. He remained in command for a year and a half, until he was defeated in the Battle of Chattanooga. Then Bragg resigned his post in early December 1863. During his tenure, he transferred operations to Kentucky and Middle Tennessee, never returning to the Mississippi River valley. In time, a new Army of Mississippi was built up from the core of troops who accompanied Earl Van Dorn from Arkansas. They would face Grant again, at Vicksburg, this time directed by Lieut. Gen. John C. Pemberton, who surrendered that fortress city and the army defending it to Grant on July 4, 1863.

But that triumph was in the future. For a time immediately following Shiloh, Grant despaired of saving his career. Halleck removed him from direct command of the Army of the Tennessee, replacing him with George Thomas. Halleck then elevated Grant to second-in-command of all the assembled forces, a nominal position without any real control over troops or planning. According to Sherman, Grant grew frustrated and nearly resigned at this time. Sherman persuaded his fellow officer to stick things out a bit longer—advice that proved prescient. On June 10, Halleck returned Thomas to the Army of the Ohio under Buell, restoring Grant to command of the Army of the Tennessee. At the end of July, Halleck was called to Washington to take charge of the entire Federal war effort, which left Grant in operational command of affairs in Mississippi and West Tennessee. In July, Halleck assigned Grant to lead the District of West Tennessee, and in October elevated that command to a full department. As noted, Grant captured Vicksburg the next year, led a combined Federal force to defeat Bragg at Chattanooga, and eventually replaced Halleck as the overall Federal commander in 1864. By war's end he had become the man who saved the Union, a reputation that in turn propelled him to the presidency in 1868.[5]

Though all the decisions presented in this book are deemed critical to the battle's direction and outcome, several early choices had perhaps the most dramatic impact of all. Unquestionably, the Army of the Tennessee's failure to entrench, reorganize camps, or place veteran troops at the outer edge of the encampment all contributed not only to how the battle progressed on April 6, but also to whether it was fought at all. Grant and, to a lesser extent, Sherman were certainly at fault here. Their combined failures to take even rudimentary precautions flew in the face of Halleck's natural caution and ignored the army's prewar doctrine, not to mention Grant's own experience mere weeks before at Fort Donelson. Had the Confederates received credible reports of heavy fortifications surrounding the Federal camps after the night action on April 4, Johnson might, however grudgingly, have accepted Beauregard's and Bragg's pessimistic counsel of retreat. Alternatively, had Johnston's attack stepped off only to run headlong into veteran infantry behind prepared defensive works, the outcome of that day's fighting would have been vastly different. Grant's lapses in this area made Johnston's success on April 6 possible, and they cannot be overlooked.

As it was, the Confederates almost canceled their attack, precisely because the conventional wisdom among Johnston's subordinates was that Grant's army *would* be heavily entrenched, alerted by the careless Rebel advance and all the unexpected delays incurred in forming for the attack. Beauregard was not experiencing a failure of nerve on the night of April 5 when he counseled abandoning the assault; he was instead only arguing what should have been the reasonable expectation. Surprise was clearly lost, and no prudent defender would fail to heed those warnings. For this reason, Johnston's determination to "attack them if they were a million" was the next most crucial decision. Had he also bowed to conventional wisdom, there would have been no battle at all—or at least a much less dramatic day of combat.

But against all reason, Grant left his army naked and exposed. Equally against all reason, Johnston attacked. Grant guessed wrong while Johnston guessed right, and the result was a tactical Confederate victory on April 6. It was very nearly a complete triumph.

Johnston's second most influential decision came early in the day, at the Eighteenth Wisconsin's camp, with his determination to begin the army's wheel to the northwest. While Johnston's intuition had proved right in deciding to attack in the first place, it let him down here. The Rebels turned prematurely, entirely missing David Stuart's brigade on the actual Federal left. Then, when his soldiers belatedly discovered the real Federal flank, Johnston compounded his error by reversing course, peeling off brigades to march farther east. These decisions greatly exacerbated the ongoing fragmentation of the Confederate battle line, which was already edging into disarray due to the poorly conceived prebattle deployment. Even veteran commands would have had trouble retaining cohesion in combat. For Johnston's raw troops and equally green commanders, that cohesion proved impossible. As a result, the Confederate army was hardly any more combat effective by the end of the day than were Grant's shattered divisions; the Rebels simply ran out of steam before all the elements of a truly decisive victory could be secured.

While Grant's and Johnston's prebattle decisions certainly determined that Shiloh would occur, subordinate officers' decisions still had a profound influence on events. Col. Everett Peabody's independent decision to send out a substantial reconnaissance before dawn on April 6 saved the Federal army, if only just barely. Peabody's patrol provided just enough warning to just enough Federals for the lurid newspaper accounts of Union soldiers being bayonetted in their tents to remain exaggeration, not reality. At Shiloh, every Federal regiment was able to form up, fall in, and meet the enemy with weapons in hand—though, in some cases, they did so literally amid the tents of their camps.

Equally vital was the joint decision by Sherman and McClernand to counterattack. Their assault at noon on April 6 caught the Rebels off guard, drew the bulk of the Army of the Mississippi's combat units to the Federal right flank, and bought time for two other important events: the solidification of a new Federal line along the Hornets' Nest–Sunken Road–Peach Orchard axis, and time for Grant to organize a final line at the landing later in the day. Both elements were crucial in saving the Federals to fight again on April 7.

While also critical, the decision by Wallace and Prentiss to stand fast in the Hornets' Nest proved more of a mixed bag. While their stubborn resistance inspired Johnston to make a fatal choice of his own—leading the afternoon assault against the Peach Orchard that cost him his life—after about 4:00 p.m. Wallace and Prentiss's unyielding stance turned from an advantage into a liability. With both flanks exposed, these two commands were eventually surrounded and captured, eliminating a substantial portion of Grant's remaining combat power before Buell's or Lew Wallace's men had yet reached the field. Fortunately, this surrender came late enough in the day on the sixth to preclude any further attack against the Pittsburg Landing line. However, the commands' final sacrifice was possibly unnecessary, for had Prentiss and W. H. L. Wallace fallen back alongside Hurlbut's, Sherman's, and McClernand's troops at about 4:00 p.m., they would have added a substantial reinforcement to Grant's final line at a key moment.

Easily the most controversial decision of the entire battle, at least in hindsight, was Beauregard's order to call off the fighting on April 6 before seizing the landing. At the time, few officers argued against the decision. But of course, in time many would claim that stopping short of securing the fruits of victory cost the Confederacy the entire battle, even to the extent of dooming Southern independence. While no such decision can really be completely evaluated—there is no way to fully know the outcome had Beauregard elected to continue the fight—the odds of pressing home a successful attack on the landing that night were slim. Further, many Confederates believed that there would still be an opportunity to finish the battle the next day, mopping up Grant's battered remnants at leisure. That, of course, was not to be.

In the end, while not inevitable, Beauregard's halt order was probably the sensible course. Less understandable is why Beauregard did not use the halt to restore the army's cohesion overnight, or even starting at dawn on the seventh. That failure cost the Rebels dearly the next day.

Conversely, Grant's decision to remain on the field in lieu of retreat and prepare a counterattack is probably his best decision of the battle. Determination in the face of adversity would prove to be Grant's greatest strength as a military commander, and he demonstrated that trait fully at Shiloh. Had he elected to retreat that night, history would record Shiloh as a Confederate triumph, if an incomplete one. Instead, the battle is considered a Federal victory, however slim the margin of that victory proved to be.

In choosing to maneuver, Lew Wallace made the most important decision of April 7. Wallace's movements against the exposed Rebel western flank repeatedly forced the Confederates to retreat, proving far more effective than the Federal frontal assaults delivered by Buell's troops. In part, this result was simply a matter of geography. Wallace had room to maneuver toward the west, while Buell did not. However, Wallace was also reluctant to send troops forward against well-positioned enemy lines, seeking a less costly solution instead. This approach worked, and it ultimately forced Beauregard off the field.

Beauregard's decision to depart was less controversial given the imbalance of forces. It proved to be the smart call. The Rebel army, unlike Grant's men, received no significant reinforcements and had no fresh troops to spearhead the day's combat. Still exhausted and now badly outnumbered, Beauregard's men stood up exceptionally well to Buell's attacks but, as noted, could not find the manpower to extend their flanks against Wallace's efforts. Beauregard understood that eventually one of those flanking efforts would result in disaster and the collapse of his army. Fortunately for the Confederates, he was able to get off the field largely unmolested, withdrawing in stages. The Federals, by and large, were content to let their opponents go.

Less explicable is Grant's decision not to mount an aggressive pursuit. Though he did at least nominally order a pursuit, why choose Sherman and his extremely battered and still-fragile division to lead that effort? Both Lew Wallace and General Buell expected that mission since their troops for all intents and purposes were relatively fresh. Wallace's losses on April 7 were slight, reflecting his preference for flank maneuvers over frontal assaults; and even if losses among Buell's most heavily engaged brigades were significantly higher, they still did not match Sherman's casualties. Further, Buell had completely unbloodied divisions readily at hand. Grant, usually considered among the most aggressive of Civil War leaders, here exercised extreme caution, allowing the larger fruits of victory to slip from his grasp.

Grant's caution almost certainly reflected Halleck's sensibilities more than his own. In this case, Grant read the tea leaves correctly. Halleck had repeatedly warned him about the dangers of bringing on any engagement before the theater commander had assembled the full power of his budding grand army at Shiloh. As was soon borne out, Halleck was quietly furious at Grant for being surprised on April 6. Had Grant rushed forward heedlessly and suffered a sharp reverse, Halleck might well have relieved him on the spot. Halleck's unwillingness to move forward was soon obvious to all. Certainly, he made no effort to capitalize on any Rebel discomfiture when he arrived on April 11, just four days after the battle. Nor would he be ready to move anytime soon. By the time Halleck ordered his army to advance in early May, Beauregard had been granted ample time to construct extensive defensive works encircling Corinth, converting that objective into a bastion of immense strength. Only a siege would have been able to reduce it, and a siege was exactly the stratagem Halleck favored.

Shiloh's place in the larger story of the Civil War serves as a transition: it marks the end of that period of the war—roughly the first twelve months—when both sides believed an early (and relatively bloodless) conclusion of hostilities was still possible. Shiloh emphatically demonstrated that the war would be prolonged, bloody, and destructive.

APPENDIX I

BATTLEFIELD GUIDE TO THE
CRITICAL DECISIONS AT SHILOH

Visiting the location of a military event often provides a perspective not always available through reading or map study alone. The military staff ride uses this concept to help impart lessons that go beyond classroom work. This appendix uses the same approach, taking the reader to the site of as many of the decisions discussed in the preceding chapters as possible. The objectives of this guide are twofold: to give the reader a better sense of that geographical perspective, and to impart a greater sense of immediacy to the discussion of those decisions. These goals adhere to one of the very reasons why the national military parks were created in the first place, as quoted in the enabling legislation of the first national military park, Chickamauga-Chattanooga: "for the purpose of preserving and suitably marking for historical and professional military study the fields of some of the most remarkable maneuvers and most brilliant fighting in the War of the Rebellion."

The stops in this guide are generally organized chronologically, in keeping with the presentation of each decision. Of course, not every decision can be covered in this manner; it is obviously impractical to visit St. Louis, where Halleck decided to concentrate on the Tennessee River, or Murfreesboro, where Johnston settled on Corinth for the site of the Confederate concentration of forces. Further, in some cases, the decisions are presented to minimize excessive travel time, especially regarding the outlying locations in Corinth and Savannah, and along Lew Wallace's march route of April 6.

Most of these sites are within the park boundaries, but some are not. While there are parking areas at or close to most of the tour stops, visiting a couple of these sites will require short walks. Where there is no designated parking area, please pull to the side of the road. Please park legally and respectfully at those sites not on public land, and be careful not to trespass. While driving through the park, please watch for pedestrians.

***

Begin your tour at the National Park Visitor Center at 501 W. Linden Street, Corinth, Mississippi 38834

To the Crossroads Museum

Exit the visitor center, and turn right onto Linden Street. Travel one block, and turn right again at North Fulton Drive. Travel one more block, and turn left onto Waldron Street. Cross the railroad tracks, and in three blocks turn right onto Fillmore Street. In two more blocks, turn left onto Wick Street. Follow the signs to the Crossroads Museum. The rail junction in front of the museum marks the crossing of two wartime railroads: the Memphis & Charleston and the Mobile & Ohio.

Tour Stop 1 (Decision #2): Albert Sidney Johnston Concentrates the Confederates at Corinth

This crossroads made Corinth an obvious concentration point. Beauregard's and Johnston's forces could use the wartime rail net to reach it easily; so, too, could Bragg's forces coming from Mobile, and the troops ordered north from New Orleans. Even Earl Van Dorn's army could use the rails to move quickly, at least once the men reached Memphis. For a time in the spring of 1862, this rail junction was one of the most important objectives of the Civil War for both Halleck, who desired to capture it, and Johnston, who needed to defend it.

Both Beauregard and Johnston laid claim to Corinth as the spot for the grand concentration, though, admittedly, Johnston's partisans had to claim that honor for him posthumously, since Johnston had perished on April 6. As discussed in the text, however, the town was the obvious choice. Corinth perfectly suited Johnston's need for a grand concentration not only because of troops could be assembled there quickly, but also because supplies could be brought up along three different sets of rails, greatly complicating any Union effort to isolate the Rebels gathering there. Though neither Beauregard nor Johnston was physically present when Corinth was selected as the point of concentration, the presence of the crossroads proved vital in reaching that decision.

To Bragg's Headquarters

Take Wick Street back to Fillmore Street, and turn left. Drive four blocks north to Childs Street, and turn left again. In one block, turn right, and pull over in front of 705 Jackson Street.

Tour Stop 2 (Decision #6): Johnston Decides to March on April 2

Today this dwelling, the Curlee House, is a private museum available for tours when open. In 1862, Braxton Bragg made his headquarters here. Johnston and Col. Thomas Jordan hurried to this home from Johnston's own quarters at the Inge residence (also known as Rose Cottage) some three hundred feet away on Fillmore Street, between Bunch and Childs Streets. The two men found Bragg in his nightshirt, but very soon the residence was abuzz with activity. Beauregard arrived next, and after some discussion, Johnston decided to attack. Using a table in Bragg's bedroom, Colonel Jordan sketched out the preliminary orders alerting the army to march at 6:00 a.m. on April 3, with a more detailed march order and battle plan to follow.

To Beauregard's Headquarters

Continue north on Jackson Street to the next block, Bunch Street, and turn right. Travel seven blocks to Kilpatrick Street and turn right again. Stop at the corner of Kilpatrick and Childs Streets. This is the Fishpond House, named for an unusual rooftop rainwater collection system. Beauregard's pre-battle headquarters was located here.

Tour Stop 3 (Decision #8): P. G. T. Beauregard Draws Up the Army's Deployment and Plan of Attack

As discussed, Johnston suggested in a hasty telegram to Davis one plan of attack that proved much different from the formation ultimately adopted. After composing the preliminary movement order, Jordan returned to his own quarters for a few hours. He was called away from an early breakfast to this location, the Duncan House, by Beauregard. Johnston and Beauregard were already present; Beauregard had used the backs of old dispatches and telegrams to explain his plan of attack to Johnston, going so far as to draw a rough sketch map on a tabletop with a pencil. It fell to Jordan to translate these notes and

Beauregard's verbal outline into the final attack orders of April 3, reproduced in the *Official Records*. Those directives were not complete until later in the day, and so were sent out after the army had already begun to march.

After Johnston was killed, arguments arose as to whether Beauregard (and by extension Jordan, following Beauregard's notes) changed Johnston's plans without authorization—arguably, a change that cost the Confederacy a victory on April 6. Given that Johnston was present for the discussion in which Beauregard explained his plans, that charge seemed unfounded. For good or ill, Johnston agreed to Beauregard's plan.

To Johnston's Final Bivouac

From the Fishpond House, take Kilpatrick Street back north to Bunch Street, and turn right. In 0.6 miles, turn left and head north onto Parkway Street. In 0.7 miles, turn right onto E. Shiloh Road. In 0.4 miles, at the intersection with Harper Road, Shiloh Road will branch to the left. Turn left here and stay on Shiloh Road. In 3.1 miles, turn right onto Mississippi Route 2. In 0.9 miles, Route 2 turns left as it intersects with Mississippi Route 350. Turn left and stay on Route 2. In 1.0 mile, you will enter the state of Tennessee, where Mississippi Route 2 changes to Tennessee Highway 22. In another 9.8 miles (10.8 miles from the last turn), look for some Civil War markers on the left side of the road. You have reached the site of Albert Sidney Johnston's last bivouac.

Tour Stop 4 (Decision #8): Johnston Overrides His Generals and Decides to Attack on the Night of April 5

At Beauregard's headquarters, not far from this roadside bivouac and a hair over two miles from the Union army, Johnston and his generals conferred on the night of April 5. The day had been filled with frustration and delay. While the original Confederate plan called for a dawn attack on the fifth, the slow, straggling march up precluded any such assault. Further, skirmishes with the Federals suggested that the enemy was now alert to the Rebels' presence. Beauregard and Bragg were convinced that surprise was now impossible, leaving the army no choice but to abandon the assault and return to Corinth. Polk and Breckinridge still favored attacking. After hearing their combined counsel, Johnston revealed his own determination to continue. "I would attack them if they were a million," he declared.

Here at this site, Johnston remained equally determined on the morning of April 6, when the debate erupted anew before dawn. Overriding Beauregard's continued objections, Johnston insisted that the Confederates must attack. At 5:00 a.m. the first rattle of musketry settled the matter once and for all.

To Pittsburg Landing

Drive north on Tennessee Route 22 for 6.3 miles until you reach Pittsburg Landing Road, which is the main entrance to Shiloh National Military Park. Turn right and drive 0.9 mile until you see the park visitor center, the bookstore, and the National Cemetery. Do not turn into the parking lot. Instead, turn right at Riverside Drive, and then immediately bear to the left onto National Cemetery Road, which takes you down to the Tennessee River. Park here.

Tour Stop 5 (Decision #3): Charles F. Smith Chooses Pittsburg Landing as the Federal Campsite

Take a minute to turn back and look at the height of the bluff on which the National Cemetery sits. Also notice the Tennessee River. In March 1862 the Tennessee was running at flood stage, with the water level high on the bank. Pittsburg Landing was one of the few places where steamboats could unload on dry land, avoiding the swamps and bottomland that surround much of the Shiloh plateau. The landing was usable year round, which made it a regular stopping point for commerce and travelers to or from Corinth.

When William T. Sherman first saw the site, he suggested to Gen. Charles F. Smith (commanding the expedition in Grant's absence) that the landing be garrisoned; and on March 14, after his unsuccessful expedition against the rail bridges, Sherman decamped his whole force there. Discovering that Pittsburg Landing had ample well-drained open ground for campsites, Sherman informed Smith that the landing was perfect, and so the Federal army began to come ashore.

Tour note: The tour route breaks chronological sequence here to begin exploring the Battle of Shiloh. Chronologically, the journey should continue to Savannah from this point, and then back to the battlefield. However, the tour will also require a second trip northward to cover Lew Wallace's approach, which will instead be combined into a single excursion later in the tour.

To Colonel Everett Peabody's Campsite

Drive back up to the visitor center, and continue following Pittsburg Landing Road for 0.3 mile. Turn left onto Confederate Road. Travel 1.0 mile to the Eastern Corinth Road, and turn left again. In 0.6 mile, turn right onto the Hamburg–Purdy Road. In 0.8 mile, turn left onto the Corinth (also called Restricted Confederate) Road, past Shiloh Church. In 0.5 mile, turn left again onto Peabody Road. Drive another 0.5 mile, stop, and park when you see an upright cannon on a central concrete base surrounded by four pyramids of cannonballs. This is Colonel Peabody's mortuary monument.

Tour Stop 6 (Decision #5 and #9): Grant Does Not Order the Army to Entrench, and Colonel Everett Peabody Sends Out a Reconnaissance

Two critical decisions can be discussed from this ground. First, recall the terrain you just drove through, especially the hill you descended after you passed Shiloh Church. The terrain provides some important natural advantages to a defender, and General Sherman's regiments would use them during the first stages of the fighting on April 6.

However, not all parts of the field offered those same benefits. Most of Sherman's men camped around Shiloh Church or to the west (excepting David Stuart's brigade) and could thus take advantage of the ridge you just passed. Only the Fifty-Third Ohio Infantry camped south of the ridge. You passed their camp in Rhea Field just a few seconds before. Here, at Peabody's brigade camp, you are now within the lines of Prentiss's division, and as you can see, the terrain advantage is negligible. You should further note that you are in the very front lines of the Union position; though there is a Federal picket line to the south, no other US units are camped in that direction. Farther to the east are the camps of Col. Madison Miller's brigade and also of Prentiss's headquarters.

Imagine if Prentiss and Sherman had been ordered to construct earthworks along their divisional fronts. General McClernand thought they should have been ordered to do so; even cantankerous Col. Thomas Worthington believed that the army would have benefited from entrenchments. Might the Confederate assaults have foundered running up against stout Union defenses? And even if the Federals did not dig in, what about moving more veteran troops to the front in case of a possible attack? Here again, McClernand thought that the army should be reorganized, with the divisional camps coordinated in some sort of "grand plan" of defense, a suggestion Grant, Smith, and Sherman ignored. The Union Army of the Tennessee's senior leadership displayed a near-fatal overconfidence that spring.

It was also from this spot that a mere Union colonel worried about a Confederate attack disobeyed his superiors and sent out a strong patrol before dawn on April 6. Peabody, at least, was not overconfident. Concerned with Confederate activity on his front over the past two days, Peabody authorized a battalion-sized patrol to reconnoiter in front of both his own and Sherman's lines and his own. The result was the fighting in Fraley Field, which alerted the Federal army to the danger it now faced. While Peabody's reconnaissance was insufficient to counteract weeks of Federal overconfidence, his action did help mitigate some of the surprise. As a result, no Union regiment was attacked before its soldiers were formed up in line, weapons in hand. Of course, in some cases, that formation came within the Federals' own camps. Unquestionably, however, Peabody's action saved the US Army from a much worse disaster. His early death in the fighting of April 6 occurred here, within his camps.

To the Camp of the Eighteenth Wisconsin

Continue east on Peabody Road for 0.4 mile to Eastern Corinth Road. Turn right and drive 0.1 mile. You are now at the southern end of the national park, and you should see Brig. Gen. Gladden's mortuary monument (similar to Peabody's monument) on the east side of the lane. Park here. The rest of this trip to the Eighteenth Wisconsin's camp is on foot, following a park trail. The field you see behind Gladden's monument is Spain's Field. You are in the southwest corner. Walk across the field or around it (if not mowed) to the northeast corner. A park trail enters the woods here, at the northeast corner. Walk the trail to its end, approximately 0.3 mile, until you reach the sign denoting the camp of the Eighteenth Wisconsin Infantry.

Tour Stop 7 (Decisions #10 and #11): Johnston Orders the Army to Pivot in the Eighteenth Wisconsin Camp; Capt. Samuel H. Lockett Reports a Federal "Division" Farther to the Federal Left

Two of the most critical decisions of the battle were made here, both by Johnston, and both within approximately half an hour. The raw troops of the Eighteenth Wisconsin regiment were overrun here, fighting at the edge of their camp, routed by Chalmers's and Jackson's Brigades. As victorious Rebels stopped to plunder their spoils, Johnston chided them, urging them to keep moving. For his share of the pickings, Johnston grabbed a simple tin cup, the same one he would later use to good effect in motivating the attack on the Peach Orchard; and here also he instructed his personal surgeon to stay and help some wounded Yankees.

Perceiving the lack of any resistance farther east, Johnston presumed that he had turned the enemy flank. Here is where he ordered his battle line to begin the pivot to the northwest to drive the Federals away from the landing and back into the flooded Owl Creek bottomlands. The reason Johnston thought he turned the Union left was simple: at the time, there were no other Union troops off to the left (east) for at least three-quarters of a mile. The Union Sixth Division was slated to gain a third brigade in the coming days, but those troops had not yet arrived, and the wooded ground between this point and Larkin Bell's Field (where Col. David Stuart's brigade was camped) was being left open for their campsites. Several of those regiments had, in fact, reached the landing that very morning. Had they arrived even a day sooner, Johnston would have found those men occupying that space, and the Battle of Shiloh would have taken a different course.

Johnston's second important decision came shortly thereafter, when he discovered he was wrong in locating the Union left here. Captain Lockett's report that another enemy "division" still lay eastward reached him here after his orders to pivot had gone out and begun to take hold. Though that "division" was in fact only Stuart's Federal brigade of three regiments, the information was alarming enough that Johnston immediately pulled Jackson's and Chalmers's Confederate brigades out of the movement in order to shift them south and east, with orders to turn the real Union left.

To Barnes Field

Return to your vehicle. Turn around, and head back north on the Eastern Corinth Road. Drive 0.6 mile to the intersection of the Hamburg–Purdy Road, park, and exit the vehicle.

Tour Stop 8 (Decision #12): Braxton Bragg, William J. Hardee, and Leonidas Polk Divide Up Command

The open field to your left is Barnes Field, considerably more open today than it was in 1862. After the collapse of Prentiss's initial line, at least two brigades of Confederate infantry halted in Barnes Field awaiting further orders. Both Brig. Gen. Randall Gibson's mixed Arkansas and Louisiana brigade came to rest here, while Gladden's shot-up Alabamians halted in the woods just east of the road. The latter brigade was now commanded by Col. Daniel W. Adams.

The exact spot where Bragg and Polk decided on the arbitrary geographical assignment of responsibility for the Confederate battle line cannot be known with certainty. It is likely, however, that the fateful discussion happened close to this spot, for soon after—Bragg gave the time as 12 o'clock in a letter home—Bragg selected Gibson's Brigade to assault the Hornets' Nest position just a few hundred yards to the north. The actual meeting probably happened west of here, somewhere along the Hamburg–Purdy Road.

Here Bragg suggested that the Bishop "take care of the center" while he himself "went to the right." Hardee was not present. He had been with Johnston back at the camp of the Eighteenth Wisconsin until the army commander sent him to the far left. Word of that assignment clearly reached Bragg and Polk, for they reported as much after the battle. At the time,

Bragg did not know that Johnston, too, would head for the army's right flank, in keeping with his personal intention of finding the Union flank. The afternoon's combat was thus directed by Johnston on the far right, Bragg in the right-center, Polk in the left-center, and Hardee on the Confederate left.

To Jones Field

Drive north on the Eastern Corinth Road for 0.6 mile until you reach Confederate Road. Turn right here. In 0.4 mile, turn left onto the Hamburg–Savannah Road. In another 0.1 mile, turn left onto Cavalry Road. In 0.8 mile, after Cavalry Road enters Jones Field, the road will curve to the left and become Sherman Road. Stop and park at the south end of Jones Field, where you will see a line of Union markers.

Tour Stop 9 (Decision #14): William T. Sherman and John A. McClernand Decide to Counterattack

For many years, after the park rerouted the auto driving tour, Jones Field was not even a stop on that journey. Fortunately, that lapse has been amended. The decision jointly reached by McClernand and Sherman to launch a noontime counterattack proved extremely important to the outcome of the day's fighting on April 6.

When troops of the two divisions stumbled onto Jones Field after being driven from the crossroads, they rallied and recovered, thanks largely to a pause in the Confederate juggernaut. Those Rebels had been almost as badly disrupted by success as the Federals had by their defeat, and so some sort of pause was probably inevitable. However, it gave both divisional commanders time to gather their wits. McClernand's men attacked on the east side of the road, angling south and then east, while Sherman's troops followed on the west side of the road, trying to protect McClernand's flank. The wooded ravine to the west (visible if you venture southwest a short ways) became the scene of a bloody contest between McArthur's brigade of Sherman and Trabue's Confederates.

This area lends itself to a short walk, if you are so inclined. Follow Sherman Road south as far as Woolf Field, and then turn right into the woods to follow the path that curves around back north. You will pass a Confederate burial trench and then several monuments and markers set in the woods. These markers indicate the fishhook-shaped shank of the Union assault, principally comprising McDowell's brigade of Sherman's division, as well as other units caught up in the counterattack.

To Johnston's Death Site

Once back at your vehicle, travel south on Sherman Road for 0.7 mile to the Hamburg–Purdy Road. Turn left there and drive 1.5 miles. Turn left again onto the Hamburg–Savannah Road, and drive 0.1 mile farther to the first pull off. This is tour stop 15. Park here.

Tour Stop 10 (Decision #15): Johnston Decides to Lead from the Front on the Critical Right Wing

Johnston's decision to lead from the front had enormous consequences. Look across the Hamburg–Savannah Road to the open ground on the west side, Sarah Bell's Cotton Field. It was there that Johnston organized the final assault that at last cleared the Peach Orchard. After watching one attack fail, Johnston rode from the rise to the south into the field and among Brig. Gen. John Bowen's brigade of Trans-Mississippians, mostly Arkansans and Missourians. When Breckinridge feared that the men could not be induced to charge again, Johnston insisted they could, riding along the ranks and tapping their bayonets with the tin cup he had seized earlier. Johnston also instructed several other brigades to move forward. The multibrigade movement he coordinated soon drove Hurlbut's Federals from the Peach Orchard, and eventually exposed the rest of the Sunken Road position.

Johnston's decision to intervene had been a good one, producing success where it was desperately needed. But it came at what turned out to be a staggering cost. As noted, Johnston did not initially understand the nature of his wound, and by the time he was reeling in his saddle, it was too late. His aides dismounted him and carried him to the ravine behind you, where he died at about 2:30 p.m. The most significant cost of his death would come later in the day, as Grant built up his final line and Beauregard eschewed that last assault. Would Johnston's personal presence and charisma then have made the same difference it made here, in Bell's Cotton Field? That question would never be put to the test, for Johnston was no more.

To the Hornets' Nest

Turn left out of the pullout, and head south on the Hamburg–Savannah Road. Drive 0.1 mile to the Hamburg–Purdy Road and turn right. Drive 0.7 mile to the Eastern Corinth Road and turn right again. In 0.3 mile you will come to the Hornets' Nest. Park here.

Tour Stop 11 (Decision #16): W. H. L. Wallace and Benjamin M. Prentiss Hold the Hornets' Nest

The Hornets' Nest has become one of the focal points of the entire battle, thanks in part to the fact that future park historian David W. Reed was engaged here as a private in the Twelfth Iowa Infantry. As a historian, he naturally emphasized the defense of the Hornets' Nest as the decisive element in the first day's fighting. A side effect of this focus, however, was that it de-emphasized the McClernand-Sherman counterattack on the Union right. Up to about 2:30 or 3:00 p.m., that offensive drew more Confederate attention (and more troops) than did the fighting here. It was only after Sherman and McClernand retreated, and after Hurlbut was compelled to fall back, that Confederate forces began to converge on Wallace and Prentiss.

Wallace was engaged here, with Prentiss commanding the segment of the line to Wallace's left, seven hundred yards east toward the Peach Orchard. Grant met both officers here, imparting his instructions to "hold at all costs" and, in turn, motivating Prentiss to do exactly that when Hurlbut began to fall back. Since Wallace was mortally wounded late in the afternoon, then never regained consciousness and perished a few days hence, we have only Prentiss's recounting of that decision. But it is a fact that Wallace did begin to retreat once he realized his right flank was fatally compromised—at perhaps 5:00 p.m. He was shot approximately a half hour later, several hundred yards to the rear.

Nevertheless, the fight here unquestionably bought Grant time, allowing the final line to be assembled and the first of Buell's troops to appear. The Rebel pincer movement that converged behind this position further disrupted Beauregard's formations, which played a role in determining whether the Confederates could launch any last attack against the landing. This strong position proved impervious to several frontal assaults. It had to be taken before any final move toward the landing could be made.

To Grant's Final Line

Drive north along the Eastern Corinth Road for 0.3 mile until you intersect with Confederate Road. Then turn right. Continue for 0.9 mile to Pittsburg Landing Road, and turn right. Drive a further 0.2 mile until you see several unusually large guns of the Union siege artillery on your right. These cannon mark the position of Battery B, Second Illinois Light Artillery. Park here.

Tour Stop 12 (Decision #17): Grant Builds a Final Line

A considerable number of Federal artillery batteries were located around Pittsburg Landing, many of them having come ashore only recently. They included Capt. Relly Madison's Battery B, Second Illinois Light Artillery, which belied their designation: Madison's Battery was equipped with a mix of heavy siege cannon intended to be used in the forthcoming Union siege of Corinth. These guns were among the first Colonel Webster placed when Grant ordered him to begin assembling that final line of defense.

Grant began preparing this line at about 3:00 p.m., anticipating the need for a fallback before nightfall, as well as a place to make a final stand until Lew Wallace and Buell could reinforce him. The line extended to both the left and right. Other heavy Union guns were positioned on a spur to your left, placed where they could shoot down the length of the Dill Branch Ravine, and to the right as far as the intersection of modern Route 22, where the line bent northward to cover the Hamburg–Savannah Road. Most of the artillery, however, was concentrated along this stretch of the line. Except in a couple of instances, there was not time to prepare earthworks, so few of the Federal positions were improved, but the Dill Branch Ravine made the line a natural fortress of sorts.

To Dill Branch Ravine

This stop requires some walking to properly grasp the nature of the ravine. There is a moderate slope, but you will not be descending all the way down into the ravine.

Walk east toward the visitor center until you reach the service road, which will be on your left. Turn right here, opposite the service drive, and walk across the field south of the road until you reach the tree line. Here, a trail heading south takes you to several markers. Pass the campsite marker for Stone's Battery, K, First Missouri Artillery, and keep going until you reach the tablet for Chalmers's Brigade. Beyond Chalmers's tablet, the ground will drop off sharply into the ravine.

Tour Stop 13 (Decision #18): Beauregard Breaks Off the Attack

While this decision point could also be discussed back at the Crossroads area or at Shiloh Church—both headquarters sites for Beauregard on the afternoon and evening of April 6—it is best understood from this location at the edge of the Dill Branch Ravine. The reality confronting the Confederates by 6:00 p.m. is most starkly presented right here. The extreme difficulty of the terrain, combined with Union enfilading fire shooting up the ravine from your left, gives some idea of how difficult coordinating a full-scale Rebel attack on Grant's last line would have been. Even if multiple brigades could be assembled along the south rim of the ravine and sent forward simultaneously, the nature of the ground and Federal fire could quickly disrupt even the freshest, most disciplined of forces. The assault would emerge fragmented, deteriorating into a series of smaller piecemeal attacks. Add in the fast-approaching night, and here was a recipe for failure. It is no wonder that at the time, few Rebel generals argued against Beauregard's decision. It was only after the battle was over and the Confederates were forced back to Corinth that the loudest protests were raised.

To the National Cemetery

This stop can be reached either by driving or walking. Simply return to the Pittsburg Landing Road, and travel east to the National Cemetery. The distance is about a quarter of a mile. If driving, park in the parking lot and enter the cemetery. You should see a distinctive bronze monument of three large black cannon sitting upright to form a pyramid; this marks Grant's headquarters on the night of April 6.

Tour Stop 14 (Decision #19): Grant Decides to Stay and Fight

Grant's decision to not only stay on the field but also vigorously counterattack the next day was a crucial moment in the Battle of Shiloh. With nightfall and the easing of Confederate pressure, a retreat to better ground was now possible. As it was, the Union army was still essentially trapped between Owl Creek and the Tennessee River; should the Confederates successfully renew their attacks in the morning, the narrowly averted disaster of April 6 could still occur.

Grant's decision was made here, at the landing, amid rain and the suffering of so many agonized wounded. Exhausted soldiers and the detritus of war surrounded him. Panicked stragglers thronged the riverbank behind him. The Union army, Grant included, further believed that the Rebels had amassed a huge force to make this attack—upward of one hundred thousand troops. But it was not Grant's nature to retreat, and, despite everything that had happened, the general retained his innate optimism and aggressiveness. Grant would attack.

To the Cherry Mansion, Savannah, Tennessee

The next two destinations will take you out of the park to visit Savannah and Crump's Landing, and follow a bit of Lew Wallace's route to the battlefield.

Return to your car, and head out of the park on Pittsburg Landing Road. Drive 1.0 mile to Tennessee Route 22. Turn right here, and drive 5.0 miles north to US Highway 64 E. Turn right here and drive 4.0 miles. You will cross the Tennessee River and enter the town of Savannah. As you enter the town, turn left onto the first street, Riverside Drive. Proceed one block, and turn left again onto Main Street, which ends here. The Cherry Mansion (privately owned) is to your left front, and a path on the right leads down to an overlook from which you can view the river.

Tour Stop 15 (Decisions #1 and #4): Henry W. Halleck Concentrates His Forces along the Tennessee River; Ulysses S. Grant Establishes His Headquarters at Savannah

Henry Halleck chose Savannah as a concentration point because it was one of the few sizable settlements along this stretch of the Tennessee, because it had good steamboat access, and because it offered a connection with Buell's approaching army. Further, the Cherry Mansion, offered up for Federal use by its Unionist owner, made an ideal headquarters. Large enough to hold senior officers and key staff, the comfortable home provided direct access to the river for steamboat use and was perfect for any commander's needs. Both Charles F. Smith and Sherman used it before Grant arrived. Both C. F. Smith and W. H. L. Wallace died in the house, Smith of his infected leg and Wallace of his mortal head wound. It was here, while at breakfast on April 6, that Grant and his staff first heard the firing upriver that marked the beginning of the Battle of Shiloh.

Grant's decision to remain here even after his growing army was concentrating at the landing could be considered controversial. Certainly, he had better access to both Halleck and Buell from this location, but only marginally so. In addition, Grant's absence from the immediate conflict in the early hours meant he took that much longer to grasp the size and scope of the enemy attack.

To Stoney Lonesome

Head back east on Main Street to Riverside Drive. Turn right, and at the next block, turn right again onto US Route 64. Drive 5.6 miles on US 64 until you reach Blanton Road, and turn left onto Blanton Road. Stop by the side of the road.

Tour Stop 16 (Decision #13): Lew Wallace Marches to the Battle via the Shunpike

You have reached the wartime settlement of Stoney Lonesome, situated about halfway between Crump's Landing, which you drove through after you crossed the Tennessee River, and Adamsville, farther west ahead of you. Lew Wallace had a brigade here, one at Crump's, and one pushed forward as far as Adamsville. When Wallace received Grant's warning to be ready to march to Shiloh, he chose to concentrate his division here, minus the troops left behind to guard Crump's Landing. From here, the Shunpike (which Wallace had worked hard to improve since arriving in March) was the fastest way to connect with the main army's right flank, McDowell's brigade of Sherman's division, camped in Ben Howell Field. Accordingly, when Grant's order to join the army arrived at 11:30, Wallace set out on what he thought was the fastest route to link up with the Army of the Tennessee's right flank: the Shunpike. Since Grant's original order was verbal, and since the hastily scrawled written order was lost, history will never know whether Grant's instructions clearly indicated the River Road, or remained silent on the route.

However, a second part to this decision that merits further exploration: Wallace's course of action once he discovered his mistake.

To the Turnaround

Today, Blanton Road does not follow the route Wallace once used. You will have to travel to Adamsville and then south to approximate that approach.

Turn left back out onto US 64 headed west. Travel 2.5 miles to Tennessee Route 117, and turn left. Travel 4.3 miles until you come to Clear Creek. Stop here.

***

The head of Lew Wallace's column reached this point, Clear Creek, when Capt. William Rowley of Grant's staff arrived bearing word from the army commander. Rowley's news convinced Wallace that he must reverse course and move over to the River Road, lest he be cut off and destroyed by the Rebels. Instead of having everyone about-face, however, Wallace elected to countermarch, trying to keep the head of his column intact—no easy feat on these narrow roads and swampy fields. This choice, of course, cost even more time and kept Wallace from reaching the field before nightfall.

To the River Road

As much as possible, you will be directed along Wallace's countermarch route. Turn around, and head north on Tennessee Route 117. Drive 4.0 miles to Old Shiloh Road in Adamsville, and turn right here. Follow Old Shiloh Road for 2.0 miles, where it will change names to Caney Branch Road. In 2.5 miles, Caney Branch Road will intersect with Snake Creek Loop. Turn left to stay on Caney Branch Road. In 0.3 mile, you will reach Tennessee Route 22.

***

Much of the original route has been lost, swallowed by time and development, but this driving tour takes you on some portions of the original road traces.[1] Thanks to the confusion and his own choice to countermarch, Lew Wallace did not reach the battlefield until 7:00 p.m., after the day's fighting concluded. Grant, disappointed and frustrated, intended for Wallace's men to spearhead his own attacks the next morning.

To Sowell Field—Wallace's Maneuver, Part 1

Turn right onto Tennessee Route 22, and drive southwest. Drive 3.4 miles until you reach the turnoff into the Shiloh National Military Park picnic area. Turn right here and park.

Tour Stop 17 (Decision #20): Lew Wallace Chooses to Maneuver

Wallace began his advance on April 7 from the vicinity of Russian Tenant Field, which is approximately 0.75 mile northeast of your current location and on the east side of Tilghman Branch Ravine. After an artillery duel with Rebel cannon in Jones Field, Wallace pushed forward in a southwestern arc to this spot, where he halted to wait for the rest of Grant's men to catch up. Take note of the War Department tablets here, especially that of Thayer's brigade, for you will be visiting more of their tablets later. Looking south into Crescent Field, Wallace noticed that his own right flank extended past the opposing Confederate left decided on to try and turn the enemy flank.

That turning movement dislodged Beauregard's left, forcing the Rebels into an additional retreat. If you were to walk due south from the picnic area parking lot for 0.75 mile, you would reach the intersection of Sherman, Hamburg–Purdy, and Confederate Roads just north of Shiloh Church, better known as the Crossroads. Wallace, however, directed his movement even farther west, constantly overlapping Beauregard's flank and ultimately compromising the entire Confederate position.

To Ben Howell Field—Wallace's Maneuver, Part 2

Return to your vehicle, exit the picnic area, and turn right onto Tennessee Route 22. Drive 0.9 mile to the Hamburg–Purdy Road (also known as Tennessee Route 142 to the left), and turn left, reentering the park. Drive for 0.1 mile, and park alongside the road. You are now in Ben Howell Field. For the best understanding of the nature of Wallace's movement, you will need to walk another 0.1 mile or so, crossing the road and the field to enter the woods to the north. There is a short trail here that takes you back to the Twenty-Third Indiana Monument and a War Department tablet for the First Nebraska Infantry of Thayer's brigade.

***

By following Thayer's advance, you can grasp how much farther west you have traveled. The Crossroads, focal point of the final Confederate defensive line on the afternoon of April 7, is still 0.4 mile to the east. From their location here, Thayer's men were now threatening Beauregard's line of retreat south along the Corinth Road. Beauregard now faced a serious dilemma.

To the Crossroads

Return to your vehicle, and drive the 0.4 mile to the Crossroads. Park along the road here.

Tour Stop 18 (Decision #21): Beauregard Quits the Field

This was the scene of heavy fighting—perhaps the heaviest fighting of the engagement—on both days of the Battle of Shiloh. At 1:00 p.m. on April 7, Brig. Gen. Sterling A. M. Wood's Confederate brigade surged through this area in the last Rebel counterattack of the day, achieving some success and penetrating to the far end of Woolf Field. But as you have just seen, Lew Wallace's repeated flanking moves ensured that Wood's success could only be fleeting. The farther north any Rebel line drove, the more exposed its flank became.

Beauregard decided he must retreat at about 1:00 p.m., and he did so because of the fighting here. To the east, Buell's and Grant's remaining forces were largely stymied, worn out from a series of unsuccessful frontal attacks that left the Rebel line dented but unbroken. But Beauregard also believed that his own circumstances were fragile, that the army was akin, as Colonel Jordan so aptly described, to "a lump of sugar thoroughly soaked in water, . . . preserving its original shape, [but] ready to dissolve." And that dissolution would be disastrous if Wallace's division attacked and interdicted the Corinth Road.

The Rebels retreated in stages: first to a point near their original start line that afternoon, and then back again to a new position near Michie on April 8. Virtually the entire army was back in Corinth by the ninth. It was a bitter pill to swallow for so many Confederates who would come to believe that victory was within their grasp when the firing stopped on April 6.

To Fallen Timbers

Return to your vehicle, turn around, and drive back out to Tennessee Route 22. Turn left and head south. Travel 1.0 mile, and turn right onto Pratt Lane. Travel 0.7 mile until the road name changes to Joe Dillon Road. You will not need to turn; just continue straight ahead. In another 2.3 miles, you will turn right onto Harrison Road. In a further 0.5 mile, you will see the historical marker for the action at Fallen Timbers. Stop here.

Tour Stop 19 (Decision #22): Grant Fails to Pursue

Grant's decision to send only a small part of the reinforcements to follow the Confederate army signified his close adherence to Halleck's extremely cautious injunction, amplified by his decision to place Sherman in charge of the movement. Having paid the price for his brash overconfidence before the battle, Sherman was not about to provoke any larger fight on April 8. The action here, at what has come to be known as Fallen Timbers, proved just that. Col. Nathan Bedford Forrest's 350 cavalrymen overran a Union skirmish line slowly crossing the open field, inflicting some losses. Sherman promptly halted and deployed his lead infantry brigade. Forrest then retreated, allowing a Rebel field hospital to fall into Union hands, but Sherman only sent a small cavalry patrol beyond this position. The cavalrymen soon brought back word that the Rebel army was headed for Corinth. Faithful to his orders, Sherman then ended his pursuit and returned to the Federal campsites. It would be almost another month before Halleck's combined army moved on Corinth, and yet another month before Beauregard finally abandoned Corinth at the end of May.

Return to Shiloh Park or Corinth

Retrace your route back to Tennessee Route 22. From there, turn left to return to Shiloh National Military Park.

To return to Corinth, turn right on Route 22. When Route 22 crosses the state line into Mississippi, it will become Mississippi State Route 2. When Route 2 turns west after intersecting with State Route 350, turn right and stay on Route 2. Soon you will come to Route 145, and then US Highway 45, both of which will take you into Corinth if you head south (left) as directed.

APPENDIX II

UNION ORDER OF BATTLE

ARMY OF THE TENNESSEE
Maj. Gen. Ulysses S. Grant

FIRST DIVISION
Maj. Gen. John A. McClernand

First Brigade
Col. Abraham Hare (w), Col. Marcellus Crocker
8th Illinois
18th Illinois
11th Iowa
13th Iowa

Second Brigade
Col. C. Carroll Marsh
11th Illinois
20th Illinois
45th Illinois
48th Illinois

Third Brigade
Col. Julius Raith (mw), Lieut. Col. Enos P. Wood
17th Illinois
29th Illinois

43rd Illinois
49th Illinois

ARTILLERY
Battery D, 1st Illinois Light Artillery
Battery D, 2nd Illinois Light Artillery
Battery E, 2nd Illinois Light Artillery
14th Ohio Light Artillery

CAVALRY
1st Battalion, 4th Illinois Cavalry
Carmichael's Company, Illinois Cavalry
Stewart's Company, Illinois Cavalry

SECOND DIVISION
Brig. Gen. William H. L. Wallace (mw), Col. James M. Tuttle

FIRST BRIGADE
Col. James M. Tuttle
2nd Iowa
7th Iowa
12th Iowa
14th Iowa

SECOND BRIGADE
Brig. Gen. John McArthur (w), Col. Thomas Morton
9th Illinois
12th Illinois
13th Missouri
14th Missouri
81st Ohio

THIRD BRIGADE
Col. Thomas Sweeney (w), Col. Silas D. Baldwin
8th Iowa
7th Illinois
50th Illinois
52nd Illinois
57th Illinois
58th Illinois

ARTILLERY
Battery A, 1st Illinois Light Artillery

Cavender's Battalion Missouri Artillery
Battery D, 1st Missouri Light Artillery
Battery H, 1st Missouri Light Artillery
Battery K, 1st Missouri Light Artillery

CAVALRY
Companies A and B, 2nd Illinois Cavalry
Company C, 2nd United States Cavalry
Company I, 4th United States Cavalry

THIRD DIVISION
Maj. Gen. Lew Wallace

FIRST BRIGADE
Col. Morgan L. Smith
11th Indiana
24th Indiana
8th Missouri

SECOND BRIGADE
Col. John M. Thayer
23rd Indiana
1st Nebraska
58th Ohio
68th Ohio

THIRD BRIGADE
Col. Charles Whittlesey
20th Ohio
56th Ohio
76th Ohio
78th Ohio

ARTILLERY
9th Indiana Light Artillery
Battery I, 1st Missouri Light Artillery

CAVALRY
3rd Battalion, 11th Illinois Cavalry
3rd Battalion, 5th Ohio Cavalry

FOURTH DIVISION
Brig. Gen. Stephen A. Hurlbut

FIRST BRIGADE
Col. Nelson G. Williams (w), Col. Isaac C. Pugh
28th Illinois
32nd Illinois
41st Illinois
3rd Iowa

SECOND BRIGADE
Col. James C. Veatch
14th Illinois
15th Illinois
46th Illinois
25th Indiana

THIRD BRIGADE
Brig. Gen. Jacob C. Lauman
31st Indiana
44th Indiana
17th Kentucky
25th Kentucky

ARTILLERY
2nd Michigan Light Artillery
Battery C, 1st Missouri Light Artillery
13th Ohio Light Artillery

CAVALRY
1st Battalion, 5th Ohio Cavalry
2nd Battalion, 5th Ohio Cavalry

FIFTH DIVISION
Brig. Gen. William T. Sherman

FIRST BRIGADE
Col. John A. McDowell
40th Illinois
6th Iowa
46th Ohio

SECOND BRIGADE
Col. David Stuart (w), Col. Kilby Smith
55th Illinois
54th Ohio
71st Ohio

THIRD BRIGADE
Col. Jesse Hildebrand
53rd Ohio
57th Ohio
77th Ohio

FOURTH BRIGADE
Col. Ralph P. Buckland
48th Ohio
70th Ohio
72nd Ohio

ARTILLERY
6th Indiana Light Artillery
Battery B, 1st Illinois Light Artillery
Battery E, 1st Illinois Light Artillery

CAVALRY
1st Battalion, 4th Illinois Cavalry
2nd Battalion, 4th Illinois Cavalry

SIXTH DIVISION
Brig. Gen. Benjamin M. Prentiss

FIRST BRIGADE
Col. Everett Peabody (k), Col. John L. Doran
12th Michigan
21st Missouri
25th Missouri
16th Wisconsin

SECOND BRIGADE
Col. Madison Miller
61st Illinois
18th Missouri
18th Wisconsin

INFANTRY NOT BRIGADED
15th Iowa
16th Iowa
23rd Missouri

ARTILLERY
1st Minnesota Light Artillery

3rd Ohio Light Artillery
5th Ohio Light Artillery

CAVALRY
11th Illinois Cavalry

UNATTACHED ARMY TROOPS

INFANTRY
15th Michigan
14th Wisconsin

ARTILLERY
Battery H, 1st Illinois Light Artillery
Battery I, 1st Illinois Light Artillery
Battery L, 1st Illinois Light Artillery
Battery B, 2nd Illinois Light Artillery
Battery F, 2nd Illinois Light Artillery
8th Ohio Light Artillery

ARMY OF THE OHIO
Maj. Gen. Don Carlos Buell

SECOND DIVISION
Brig. Gen. Alexander McD. McCook

FOURTH BRIGADE
Brig. Gen. Lovell H. Rousseau
6th Indiana
5th Kentucky
1st Ohio
1st Battalion, 15th US Infantry
1st Battalion, 16th US Infantry
1st Battalion, 19th US Infantry

FIFTH BRIGADE
Col. Edward N. Kirk (w)
34th Illinois
29th Indiana
30th Indiana
77th Pennsylvania

SIXTH BRIGADE
Col. William H. Gibson
32nd Indiana
39th Indiana
15th Ohio
49th Ohio

ARTILLERY
Battery H, 5th US Artillery

FOURTH DIVISION
Brig. Gen. William Nelson

TENTH BRIGADE
Col. Jacob Ammen
36th Indiana
6th Ohio
24th Ohio

NINETEENTH BRIGADE
Col. William B. Hazen
9th Indiana
6th Kentucky
41st Ohio

TWENTY-SECOND BRIGADE
Col. Sanders D. Bruce
1st Kentucky
2nd Kentucky
20th Kentucky

CAVALRY
2nd Indiana Cavalry

FIFTH DIVISION
Brig. Gen. Thomas L. Crittenden

ELEVENTH BRIGADE
Brig. Gen. Jeremiah T. Boyle
9th Kentucky
13th Kentucky
19th Ohio
59th Ohio

FOURTEENTH BRIGADE
  Col. William S. Smith
  11th Kentucky
  26th Kentucky
  13th Ohio

ARTILLERY
  Battery G, 1st Ohio Light Artillery
  Batteries H and M, 4th US Artillery

CAVALRY
  3rd Kentucky Cavalry

SIXTH DIVISION
  Brig. Gen. Thomas J. Wood

TWENTIETH BRIGADE
  Brig. Gen. James A. Garfield
  51st Indiana
  13th Michigan
  64th Ohio
  65th Ohio

TWENTY-FIRST BRIGADE
  Col. George D. Wagner
  10th Indiana
  15th Indiana
  57th Indiana
  24th Kentucky

k—killed, c—captured, mw—mortally wounded, w—wounded

APPENDIX III

CONFEDERATE ORDER OF BATTLE

ARMY OF THE MISSISSIPPI
  Gen. Albert Sidney Johnston (k)
  Gen. Pierre G. T. Beauregard

FIRST CORPS
  Maj. Gen. Leonidas Polk

CAVALRY
  1st Mississippi Cavalry
  Brewer's Mississippi and Alabama Battalion

UNATTACHED
  47th Tennessee (arrived April 7)

FIRST DIVISION
  Brig. Gen. Charles Clark (w), Brig. Gen. Alexander P. Stewart

FIRST BRIGADE
  Col. Robert M. Russell
  11th Louisiana
  12th Tennessee
  13th Tennessee

22nd Tennessee
Bankhead's Tennessee Battery

SECOND BRIGADE
Brig. Gen. Alexander P. Stewart
13th Arkansas
4th Tennessee
5th Tennessee
33rd Tennessee
Stanford's Mississippi Battery

SECOND DIVISION
Maj. Gen. Benjamin F. Cheatham (w)

FIRST BRIGADE
Brig. Gen. Bushrod R. Johnson (w), Col. Preston Smith (w)
Blythe's Mississippi Regiment
2nd Tennessee
15th Tennessee
154th Tennessee (senior)
Polk's Tennessee Battery

SECOND BRIGADE
Col. William H. Stephens
Col. George Maney
7th Kentucky
1st Tennessee Battalion
6th Tennessee
9th Tennessee
Smith's Mississippi Battery

SECOND CORPS
Maj. Gen. Braxton Bragg

CAVALRY
Smith's Company, Alabama Cavalry

FIRST DIVISION
Brig. Gen. Daniel Ruggles

FIRST BRIGADE
Col. Randall L. Gibson
1st Arkansas
4th Louisiana
13th Louisiana
19th Louisiana
Bain's Mississippi Battery

SECOND BRIGADE
Brig. Gen. Patton Anderson
1st Florida Battalion
17th Louisiana
20th Louisiana
Confederate Guards Response Battalion
9th Texas
5th Company, Washington (New Orleans) Artillery

THIRD BRIGADE
Col. Preston Pond
16th Louisiana
18th Louisiana
Crescent (Louisiana) Regiment
Orleans Guard Battalion
38th Tennessee
Ketchum's Alabama Battery

CAVALRY
Jenkins's Alabama Battalion

SECOND DIVISION
Brig. Gen. Jones M. Withers

FIRST BRIGADE
Brig. Gen. Adley H. Gladden (mw), Col. Daniel W. Adams
21st Alabama
22nd Alabama
25th Alabama
26th Alabama
1st Louisiana
Robertson's Alabama Battery

SECOND BRIGADE
Brig. Gen. James R. Chalmers

5th Mississippi
7th Mississippi
9th Mississippi
10th Mississippi
52nd Tennessee
Gage's Alabama Battery

THIRD BRIGADE
Brig. Gen. John K. Jackson
17th Alabama
18th Alabama
19th Alabama
2nd Texas
Girardey's Georgia Battery

CAVALRY
Clanton's Alabama Regiment

THIRD CORPS
Maj. Gen. William J. Hardee (w)

FIRST BRIGADE
Brig. Gen. Thomas C. Hindman (w), Col. R. G. Shaver
Hindman commanded his own brigade and the Third Brigade
    as an ad hoc division.
2nd Arkansas
6th Arkansas
7th Arkansas
3rd Confederate
Swett's Mississippi Battery
Miller's Tennessee Battery

SECOND BRIGADE
Brig. Gen. Patrick R. Cleburne
15th Arkansas
6th Mississippi
2nd Tennessee
5th (35th) Tennessee
23rd Tennessee
24th Tennessee

ARTILLERY
Maj. Francis A. Shoup

Trigg's Arkansas Battery
Calvert's Arkansas Battery
Hubbard's Arkansas Battery

THIRD BRIGADE
Brig. Gen. Sterling A. M. Wood (w), Col. William K. Patterson
16th Alabama
8th Arkansas
9th (14th) Arkansas Battalion
3rd Mississippi Battalion
27th Tennessee
44th Tennessee
55th Tennessee
Harper's Mississippi Battery
Avery's Georgia Dragoons

RESERVE CORPS
Brig. Gen. John C. Breckinridge

FIRST BRIGADE
Col. Robert P. Trabue
4th Alabama Battalion
31st Alabama
3rd Kentucky
4th Kentucky
5th Kentucky
6th Kentucky
Crew's Tennessee Battalion
Byrne's Kentucky Battery
Cobb's Kentucky Battery
Morgan's Kentucky Cavalry Squadron

SECOND BRIGADE
Brig. Gen. John S. Bowen (w), Col. John D. Martin
9th Arkansas
10th Arkansas
2nd Confederate
1st Missouri
Hudson's Mississippi Battery

THIRD BRIGADE
Col. Winfield S. Statham

15th Mississippi
22nd Mississippi
19th Tennessee
20th Tennessee
28th Tennessee
45th Tennessee
Rutledge's Tennessee Battery

UNATTACHED ARMY TROOPS

ARTILLERY
Hubbard's Arkansas Battery
McClung's Tennessee Battery

CAVALRY
Forrest's Tennessee Regiment
Clanton's Alabama Regiment
Wharton's Texas Regiment

k—killed, c—captured, mw—mortally wounded, w—wounded

NOTES

Preface

1. William G. Robertson, *The Staff Ride* (Washington, D.C., Center for Military History, 1987). p. 4.

Introduction

1. For an overview of Forts Henry and Donelson, see Russell F. Weigley, *A Great Civil War: A Military and Political History, 1861–1865* (Bloomington: University of Indiana Press, 2000), 108–11. Note that Johnston's full line ran closer to five hundred miles, but the most vulnerable section was that Kentucky-Tennessee portion, extending from Cumberland Gap to the banks of the Mississippi River.

2. US War Department. *The War of the Rebellion: A Compilation of the Official Records of the Union and Confederate Armies*, 128 vols. (Washington, DC: US Government Printing Office, 1880–1901), series 1, volume 7, page 813. Hereafter, this source is cited in the following format: *OR*, ser. 1, vol. 7, p. 813. The abbreviation *pt.* is used in place of *part* as necessary.

3. Charles P. Roland, *Albert Sidney Johnston: Soldier of Three Republics* (1964; repr., Lexington: University Press of Kentucky, 2001), 272–73.

4. John H. Eicher and David J. Eicher, *Civil War High Commands* (Stanford, CA: Stanford University Press, 2001), 830, 840; Ezra J. Warner, *Generals in Blue: Lives of the Union Commanders* (Baton Rouge: Louisiana State University Press, 1964), 51, 195–96.

5. *OR*, vol. 7, p.563.

6. Charles P. Roland, "Albert Sidney Johnston," in *The Confederate General*, ed. William C. Davis (Harrisburg, PA: National Historical Society, 1990), 3:188.

7. John F. Marszalek, *Commander of All Lincoln's Armies: A Life of General Henry W. Halleck* (Cambridge, MA: Harvard University Press, 2004), 41–44; Antoine Henri Jomini, *Life of Napoleon*, trans. H. W. Halleck (New York: D. Van Nostrand, 1864), 1:3.

8. Marszalek, *Commander of All Lincoln's Armies*, 105–8.

9. Brooks D. Simpson, *Ulysses S. Grant: Triumph over Adversity, 1822–1865* (Boston: Houghton Mifflin 2000), 110.

10. See Marszalek, *Commander of All Lincoln's Armies*, 114–17; and Simpson, *Ulysses S. Grant*, 108–10.

11. Marszalek, *Commander of All Lincoln's Armies*, 115.

12. Simpson, *Ulysses S. Grant*, 122–24.

13. Eicher and Eicher, *Civil War High Commands*, 274, 833.

Chapter 1

1. Thomas Lawrence Connolly, *Army of the Heartland: The Army of Tennessee, 1861–1862* (Baton Rouge: Louisiana State University Press, 1967), 131–33.

2. Earl J. Hess, *The Civil War in the West, Victory and Defeat from the Appalachians to the Mississippi* (Chapel Hill: University of North Carolina Press, 2012), 25–26.

3. William L. Shea and Earl J. Hess, *Pea Ridge: Civil War Campaign in the West* (Chapel Hill: University of North Carolina Press, 1992), 3. The Mississippi River flows north to south into the Gulf of Mexico, but the Tennessee, just one hundred miles to the east, and the Cumberland, just an additional twenty miles farther east, both flow south to north into the Ohio River.

4. For the best book on the battle of Pea Ridge, see Shea and Hess, *Pea Ridge*.

5. *OR*, vol. 10, pt. 2, p. 28.

6. Robert C. Black III, *The Railroads of the Confederacy* (Chapel Hill: University of North Carolina Press, 1952), 5. The extension to Colum-

bus was only completed on April 22, 1861, after hostilities had already begun.

7. For an excellent reference guide to the various railroads and gauges in 1860, see John P. Hankey, "The Railroad War," *Trains: The Magazine of Railroading* 71, no. 3 (March 2011): 34–35.

8. *OR*, vol. 7, p. 674; and *OR*, vol. 10, pt. 2, p. 7.

9. *OR*, vol. 10, pt. 2, pp. 12, 24.

10. *OR*, vol. 10, pt. 2, pp. 33, 42.

11. David J. Eicher, *The Longest Night: A Military History of the Civil War* (New York: Simon and Schuster, 2001), 161–63.

12. Roland, *Albert Sidney Johnston*, 297; Timothy B. Smith, *Shiloh: Conquer or Perish* (Lawrence: University Press of Kansas, 2014), 24–25.

13. *OR*, vol. 7, p. 912; *OR*, vol. 6, p. 819.

14. *OR*, vol. 7, pp. 904–5; Connolly, *Army of the Heartland*, 138.

15. *OR*, 7, pp. 905, 908. On February 25, Beauregard reported to Richmond that "heavy reinforcements [had been] received at Cairo and Paducah, detailed from Federal Army of the Potomac." This last piece of information was, of course, not true, but it showed the level of panic and rumor spreading among the Confederates in West Tennessee.

16. *OR*, vol. 7, p. 900.

17. *OR*, vol. 6, pp. 824–29, 832; Grady McWhiney, *Braxton Bragg and Confederate Defeat*, 2 vols. (1969; repr., Tuscaloosa: University of Alabama Press, 1991), 1:202.

18. Roland, *Albert Sidney Johnston*, 306; Alfred Roman, *The Military Operations of General Beauregard in the War between the States, 1861 to 1865: Including a Brief Personal Sketch and a Narrative of His Services in the War with Mexico, 1846–8*, 2 vols. (New York: Harper and Brothers, 1884), 2:506; William Preston Johnston, *The Life of General Albert Sidney Johnston: His Service in the Armies of the United States, the Republic of Texas, and the Confederate States* (New York: D. Appleton, 1879), 501.

19. Johnston, *General Albert Sidney Johnston*, 504.

20. Roland, *Albert Sidney Johnston*, 309; Connolly, *Army of the Heartland*, 136.

21. Robert G. Hartje, *Van Dorn: The Life and Times of a Confederate General* (Nashville, TN: Vanderbilt University Press, 1967), 166–69.

22. William T. Sherman, *Memoirs of Gen. William T. Sherman*, 2 vols. (New York: D. Appleton, 1875), 1:226.

23. James D. Brewer, *Tom Worthington's Civil War: Shiloh, Sherman, and the Search for Vindication* (Jefferson, NC: McFarland, 2001), 68.

24. Sherman, *Memoirs*, 1:226.

25. Allen H. Mesch, *Teacher of Civil War Generals: Major General Charles Ferguson Smith, Soldier and West Point Commandant* (Jefferson, NC: McFarland, 2015), 244, 250.

26. Sherman, *Memoirs*, 1:227.

27. Sherman, *Memoirs*, 1:227.

28. Smith, *Shiloh: Conquer or Perish*, 14; Gail Stephens, *Shadow of Shiloh: Major General Lew Wallace in the Civil War* (Indianapolis: Indiana Historical Society Press, 2010), 64–66.

29. C. F. Smith to John A. Rawlins, March 15, 1862, in John Y. Simon, ed. *The Papers of Ulysses S. Grant*, 31 vols. (Carbondale: Southern Illinois University Press, 1972), 4:487. "*Chetam*" is actually Benjamin F. Cheatham, a Tennessee politician turned Confederate general.]

30. Ulysses S. Grant, *Personal Memoirs of U. S. Grant*, 2 vols. (New York: Charles L. Webster, 1885), 1:327.

31. Grant, *Memoirs*, 1:331–32.

32. Joseph A. Rose, *Grant under Fire: An Exposé of Generalship & Character in the American Civil War* (New York: Alderhanna, 2015), 95; see also US Army, *Revised United States Army Regulations of 1861* (Washington, DC: Government Printing Office, 1861), 82.

33. *OR*, vol. 10, pt. 2, pp. 67, 84.

34. Grant, *Memoirs*, 1:333.

35. William T. Sherman to Ellen Sherman, April 3, 1862, Sherman Family Papers, Hesburgh Library, University of Notre Dame, South Bend, IN; Grant, *Memoirs*, 1:334.

36. Edward Hagerman, *The American Civil War and the Origins of Modern Warfare: Ideas, Organization, and Field Command* (Bloomington: Indiana University Press, 1988), 6–13.

37. Hagerman, *American Civil War*, 14.

38. *OR*, vol. 7, p. 175.

39. Richard L. Kiper, *Major General John Alexander McClernand: Politician in Uniform* (Kent, OH: 1999), 101.

40. Grant, *Personal Memoirs*, 1:299.

41. Richard L. Hamilton, *Shiloh to Durham Station: The 18th Wisconsin In-*

fantry Regiment, with Captain Robert S. McMichael's Civil War Letters (n.p.: Richard L. Hamilton, 2010), 4–5.

42. Timothy B. Smith, *Grant Invades Tennessee: The 1862 Battles for Forts Henry and Donelson* (Lawrence: University of Kansas Press, 2016), 267.

43. Thomas Worthington, *Shiloh: The Only Correct Military History of U. S. Grant and of the Missing Army Records, for Which He Is Alone Responsible, to Conceal His Organized Defeat of the Union Army at Shiloh, April 6, 1862* (Washington, DC: M'Gill and Witherow, 1872), 120. While Worthington was a difficult subordinate, arrogant and certain his talents were underused, his criticisms of Sherman's laxness are not far off the mark.

44. Smith, *Shiloh: Conquer or Perish*, 72, 74–75.

45. As quoted in Roland, *Albert Sidney Johnston*, 313.

46. *OR*, vol. 10, pt. 2, p. 381; John Allan Wyeth, *That Devil Forrest: Life of General Nathan Bedford Forrest* (Baton Rouge: Louisiana State University Press, 1959), 60; Roland, *Albert Sidney Johnston*, 316; Thomas Jordan and J. P. Pryor, *The Campaigns of General Nathan Bedford Forrest and of Forrest's Cavalry* (New Orleans: Blelock, 1868), 101.

47. *OR*, vol. 10, pt. 2, p. 387.

48. David W. Reed, *The Battle of Shiloh and the Organizations Engaged* (Washington, DC, 1902), 110.

49. Roman, *Military Operations of General Beauregard*, 1:271.

50. *OR*, vol. 10, pt. 1, pp. 393–94.

51. Roman, *Military Operations of General Beauregard*, 1:272.

52. Roland, *Albert Sidney Johnston*, 321–23.

53. Roland, *Albert Sidney Johnston*, 321; McWhiney, *Braxton Bragg and Confederate Defeat*, 1:223; Louis Phillipe Albert d'Orleans, Le Compte de Paris; *History of the Civil War in America, 4 vols.* (Philadelphia, 1876), 1:558.

54. *OR*, vol. 10, pt. 1, pp. 392–95; Thomas Jordan, "Notes of a Confederate Staff Officer at Shiloh," in *Battles and Leaders of the Civil War*, ed. Robert U. Johnson and Clarence C. Buel, 4 vols. (New York: Century, 1884), 1:595.

55. Wiley Sword, *Shiloh: Bloody April* (New York: William Morrow, 1974), 113.

56. Nothing makes this point clearer than a good map. See Mark Adkin, *The Waterloo Companion: The Complete Guide to History's Most Famous Land Battle* (Mechanicsburg, PA: Stackpole Books, 2001), 162.

57. Warner, *Generals in Blue*, 429–30.

58. Winfield S. Scott, *Infantry Tactics: In Three Volumes*, 3 vols. (New York: George Dearborn, 1835), 3:2–3.

59. John Bigelow Jr., *The Campaign of Chancellorsville: A Strategic and Tactical Study* (New Haven, CT: Yale University Press, 1910), 291–93.

60. P. G. T. Beauregard, "The Campaign of Shiloh," in *Battles and Leaders of the Civil War*, ed. Robert U. Johnson and Clarence C. Buel, 4 vols. (New York: 1884), 1:586–87

61. Smith, *Shiloh: Conquer or Perish*, 65–68.

62. O. Edward Cunningham, with Gary D. Joiner and Timothy B. Smith, eds., *Shiloh and the Western Campaign of 1862*, (New York: Savas Beatie, 2007), 139–40.

63. Smith, *Shiloh: Conquer or Perish*, 69–70; Johnston, *General Albert Sidney Johnston*, 563.

64. Smith, *Shiloh: Conquer or Perish*, 71.

65. Roman, *Military Operations of General Beauregard*, 1:277–78; McWhiney, *Braxton Bragg and Confederate Defeat*, 1:226; William C. Davis, *Breckinridge: Statesman, Soldier, Symbol* (Baton Rouge: Louisiana State University Press, 1974), 303.

66. Roland, *Albert Sidney Johnston*, 325; Smith, *Shiloh: Conquer or Perish*, 75.

67. It should be noted that Brig. Gen. Benjamin M. Prentiss, commanding the Sixth Division and equally exposed in the Federal front line, was similarly adamant that no attack was forthcoming. He worked as assiduously as Sherman to quash any preparations for or talk of such an event. Prentiss, however, was neither the senior commander nor in charge of the overall Federal camp. Sherman assumed that position and authority, and Prentiss took his cue from Sherman.

68. Ephraim C. Dawes, "My First Day under Fire at Shiloh," in *Sketches of War History, 1861–1865: Papers Prepared for the Ohio Commandery of the Military Order of the Loyal Legion of the United States, 70 vols.* (Cincinnati, OH: Robert Clarke, 1896), 4:4.

69. *OR*, vol. 10, pt. 1, p. 94; *OR*, vol. 2, pt. 2, p. 89.

Chapter 2

1. Smith, *Shiloh: Conquer or Perish*, 82; Thomas Wentworth Higginson, ed. *Harvard Memorial Biographies* (Cambridge, MA: Sever and Francis, 1867), 164.

2. Higginson, *Harvard Memorial Biographies*, 161, 164; Smith, *Shiloh: Conquer or Perish*, 82. As noted, Prentiss, like Sherman, dismissed the idea of a Rebel attack out of hand.

3. Cunningham, *Shiloh*, 144–45; Smith, *Shiloh: Conquer or Perish*, 82–83.

4. Franklin H. Bailey to Dear Parents, April 8, 1862, Franklin H. Bailey Papers, Bentley Historical Library, University of Michigan, Ann Arbor.

5. *OR*, vol. 10, pt. 1, p. 603.

6. Smith, *Shiloh: Conquer or Perish*, 84.

7. Higginson, *Harvard Memorial Biographies*, 164.

8. "The 18th at Shiloh," *Milwaukee (WI) Sunday Telegraph*, June 6, 1886.

9. Horatio Wiley to Josie Wiley, April 11, 1862, Horatio Wiley Letters, Northeast Mississippi Museum Association, Corinth.

10. Horatio Wiley to Josie Wiley, April 11, 1862.

11. Johnston, *Albert Sidney Johnston*, 612.

12. Smith, *Shiloh: Conquer or Perish*, 130.

13. Smith, *Shiloh: Conquer or Perish*, 129.

14. Johnston, *Albert Sidney Johnston*, 597; *OR*, vol. 10, pt. 1, p. 574. Hindman was at the time commanding a demi-division of two brigades within Hardee's Third Corps, which itself was only three brigades strong.

15. Smith, *Shiloh: Conquer or Perish*, 130.

16. *OR*, vol. 10, pt. 1, pp. 203, 548.

17. S. H. Lockett, "Surprise and Withdrawal at Shiloh," in *Battles and Leaders of the Civil War*, ed. Robert U. Johnson and Clarence C. Buel, 4 vols. (New York: Century, 1884), 1:603.

18. *OR*, vol. 10, pt. 1, pp. 532, 548.

19. Smith, *Shiloh: Conquer or Perish*, 134. The Kentucky Orphan Brigade gained its nickname when its home state of Kentucky remained in the Union instead of joining the nascent Confederacy. Even though the Confederate Congress later accepted a pro-Confederate Kentucky government in exile, the bulk of the state remained committed to the Federal cause.

20. Smith, *Shiloh: Conquer or Perish*, 135; *OR*, vol. 10, pt. 1, p. 624.

21. J. Boone Bartholomees Jr., *Buff Facings and Gilt Buttons: Staff and Headquarters Operations in the Army of Northern Virginia, 1861–1865* (Columbia: University of South Carolina Press, 1998), 2–4; Joseph H. Crute

Jr., *Confederate Staff Officers, 1861–1865* (Powhatan, VA: Derwent Books, 1982), 102.

22. Crute, *Confederate Staff Officers, 1861–1865*, 154–55; C. T. Quintard, Arthur Howard Noll, ed., *Doctor Quintard: Chaplain, C.S.A. and Second Bishop of Tennessee, Being His Story of the War (1861–1865)*, ed. Arthur Howard Noll (Sewanee, TN: University Press, 1905), 50; James Arthur Lyon Fremantle, *Three Months in the Southern States, April–June, 1863* (New York: John Bradburn, 1864), 172.

23. *OR*, vol. 10, pt. 1, pp. 403, 408, 465–66, 569.

24. William M. Polk, *Leonidas Polk: Bishop and General*, 2 vols. (New York: Longmans, Green, 1915), 2:105.

25. Bruce Catton, *Grant Moves South* (Boston: Little, Brown, 1960), 222–23. One reason for relocating the headquarters to the landing was that major general's commissions had been received for both John McClernand and Lew Wallace, making them the ranking officers in the army besides Grant and Smith. This meant McClernand would supplant Sherman as the on-site commander.

26. Catton, *Grant Moves South*, 223.

27. Grant, *Personal Memoirs*, 1:336; Stephens, *Shadow of Shiloh*, 82.

28. Stephens, *Shadow of Shiloh*, 84–85.

29. *OR*, vol. 10, pt. 1, pp. 169, 184. For a detailed examination of this dispute, see Stephens, *Shadow of Shiloh*, 84–86.

30. Anonymous, "The March of Lew Wallace's Division to Shiloh," in *Battles and Leaders of the Civil War*, ed. Robert U. Johnson and Clarence C. Buel, 4 vols. (New York: Century, 1884–87), 1:607.

31. Anonymous, "March of Lew Wallace's Division," 1:607; Lew Wallace, *Lew Wallace: An Autobiography* (New York: Harper and Brothers, 1906), 464.

32. Stephens, *Shadow of Shiloh*, 87–89.

33. Wallace, *Autobiography*, 467.

34. Wallace, *Autobiography*, 467.

35. Wallace, *Autobiography*, 469.

36. Stephens, *Shadow of Shiloh*, 87–89. Wallace's Bridge was named for a local, not for either Federal general.

37. Stephens, *Shadow of Shiloh*, 91.

Chapter 3

1. *OR*, vol. 10, pt. 1, p. 116; Cunningham, *Shiloh*, 220.

2. Stacy D. Allen, "Shiloh!," in *Blue & Gray Magazine's Shiloh!—a Visitor's Guide* (Columbus, OH: Blue and Gray Press, 2001), 24; James Lee Mc-Donough, *William Tecumseh Sherman: In the Service of My Country; A Life* (New York: W. W. Norton, 2016), 12.

3. Cunningham, *Shiloh*, 220.

4. *OR*, vol. 10, pt. 1, pp. 160–61, 286–89.

5. Position marker for the Eighth Illinois Infantry, 11:30 a.m. to noon, and monument for the Seventh Illinois Infantry, 9:00 a.m. to 4:00 p.m., Duncan Field, Shiloh National Military Park, Shiloh, TN. Hereafter, Shiloh National Military Park will be abbreviated as SNMP.

6. *OR*, vol. 10, pt. 1, pp. 117, 250.

7. Allen, "Shiloh!," 28; Kiper, *Major General John Alexander McClernand*, 109.

8. Cunningham, *Shiloh*, 249; Cobb's Kentucky Battery tablet, just north of Woolf Field, SNMP.

9. Cunningham, *Shiloh*, 249–50.

10. T. Harry Williams, *P. G. T. Beauregard: Napoleon in Gray* (Baton Rouge, LA: Louisiana State University Press, 1955), 100–101.

11. *OR*, vol. 10, pt. 2, p. 387. As discussed in chapter 1, Johnston, in his April 3 telegram to President Davis announcing the impending attack, indicated an entirely different deployment: "Polk, left; Hardee, center; Bragg, right wing; Breckinridge, reserve."

12. McWhiney, *Braxton Bragg and Confederate Defeat*, 1:223.

13. Hardee did use Thomas C. Hindman, heading up Hardee's First Brigade, as an ad hoc divisional commander to direct both his own brigade and S. A. M. Wood's Third Brigade during the battle.

14. Johnston, *General Albert Sidney Johnston*, 570.

15. Smith, *Shiloh: Conquer or Perish*, 104.

16. Smith, *Shiloh: Conquer or Perish*, 187–88.

17. Cunningham, *Shiloh*, 273–76.

18. Cunningham, *Shiloh*, 277–78.

19. Warner, *Generals in Blue*, 536–37.

20. Iowa Hornet's Nest Brigade Association, *First Reunion of Iowa's Hornet's*

Nest Brigade, 2nd, 7th, 8th, 12th, and 14th Infantry (Oskaloosa, IA: Globe Printing Company, 1888), 12–13.

21. Timothy B. Smith, *Rethinking Shiloh: Myth and Memory* (Knoxville, TN: University of Tennessee Press, 2013), 50–52; Isabel Wallace, *The Life and Letters of General W. H. L. Wallace* (Chicago: R. R. Donnelly and Sons, 1909), 20.

22. *OR*, vol. 10, pt. 1, pp. 278–79.

23. *OR*, vol. 10, pt. 1, p. 279; Tablets for Seventh and Eighth Illinois regiments, Duncan Field, SNMP; Cunningham, *Shiloh*, 277–78, 288–90.

24. *OR*, vol. 10, pt. 1, 279.

25. *OR*, vol. 10, pt. 1, pp. 118, 250.

26. *OR*, vol. 10, pt. 1, p. 118; Pond's Brigade tablet, east of Cavalry Field, SNMP.

27. *OR*, *vol.* 10, pt. 1, p. 250.

28. *OR*, vol. 10, pt. 1, p. 204.

29. Cunningham, *Shiloh*, 298.

30. Lockett, "Surprise and Withdrawal at Shiloh," 1:605.

31. *OR*, vol. 10, pt. 1, p. 149; Wallace, *General W. H. L. Wallace*, 198. Anne Wallace had just arrived at Pittsburg Landing that morning, hoping to surprise her husband, but she was unable to disembark due to the battle. William Wallace was not killed outright, but mortally wounded. He was found on the field the next day and removed to the Cherry Mansion, where his wife tended him until he finally passed on April 10, 1862.

32. Trabue's and Chalmers's War Department tablets, near Cloud Field, SNMP; Smith, *Shiloh: Conquer or Perish*, 215.

33. Smith, Shiloh: Conquer or Perish, 214.

Chapter 4

1. Smith, *Shiloh: Conquer or Perish*, 42–44.

2. For a more detailed examination of the twin Battles of Jena and Auerstedt, October 14, 1806, see David G. Chandler, *The Campaigns of Napoleon* (New York: McMillen, 1966) , 479–504.

3. Edwin C. Bearss, "Artillery Study—Shiloh NMP," Shiloh National Military Park files, Shiloh, TN.

4. Albert D. Richardson, *A Personal History of Ulysses S. Grant* (Hartford, CT: American Publishing Company, 1868), 250.

5. *OR*, vol. 10, pt. 1, p. 110; Smith, *Shiloh: Conquer or Perish*, 220–21.

6. T. J. Lindsley, *Ohio at Shiloh: Report of the Commission* (Cincinnati: Clarke 1903), 53; Board of Commissioners, *Minnesota in the Civil and Indian Wars, 2 vols.* (St. Paul, MN: Pioneer Press1891), 1:643; Smith, *Shiloh: Conquer or Perish*, 221. Munch's Minnesota battery was down one gun, put out of action with a broken trail.

7. The best illustration of the composition of this line is to be found in Larry J. Daniel, *Shiloh: The Battle That Changed the Civil War* (New York: Simon and Schuster, 1997), 247.

8. E. Hannaford, *The Story of a Regiment: A History of the Campaigns, and Associations in the Field, of the Sixth Regiment Ohio Volunteer Infantry* (Cincinnati, OH: Published by the Author, 1868), 256–57.

9. Smith, *Shiloh: Conquer or Perish*, 222–23; Richardson, *Personal History of Ulysses S. Grant*, 251.

10. Roman, *Military Operations of General Beauregard*, 1:299–300.

11. *OR*, vol. 10, pt. 1, p. 466.

12. David B. Flanigan, *The Culminating Point and U.S. Army Tactical Doctrine* (Fort Leavenworth, KS: government Printing Office, 1991), 4.

13. *OR*, vol. 10, pt. 1, pp. 466, 550; Smith, *Shiloh: Conquer or Perish*, 231; Nathaniel Cheairs Hughes, "William Joseph Hardee, C.S.A. 1861–1865" (PhD diss., University of North Carolina, 1959), 128.

14. Daniel, *Shiloh*, 250–51.

15. Roman, *Military Operations of General Beauregard*, 1:529, 531.

16. Smith, *Shiloh: Conquer or Perish*, 227–28; Sixteenth Louisiana, Orleans Guard [Orleans Guard?], Eighteenth Louisiana position marker, east of Cavalry Field, SNMP.

17. *OR*, vol. 10, pt. 1, pp. 410, 467, 569.

18. Roman, *Military Operations of General Beauregard*, 1:535–36.

19. *Woodstock (IL) Sentinel*, April 27, 1911.

20. *OR*, vol. 10, pt. 1, pp. 324, 354. For numbers, see Reed, *Battle of Shiloh*, 102.

21. *OR*, vol. 10, pt. 1, p. 170; Reed, *Battle of Shiloh*, 98.

22. Catton, *Grant Moves South*, 239–40, 242.

23. Grant, "The Battle of Shiloh," in *Battles and Leaders of the Civil War*,

ed. Robert U. Johnson and Clarence C. Buel, 4 vols. (New York: Century, 1884)1:476.]

24. Whitelaw Reid, *Ohio in the War: Her Statesmen, Generals, and Soldiers*, 2 vols. (Columbus, OH: Moore, Wilstach & Baldwin, 1893), 1:375. Catton, *Grant Moves South*, 241. As Catton notes, Reid's anecdote is interesting, for Reid was a newspaper correspondent with the army, and one of Grant's major detractors in the days after the battle. Much of the mythology of Shiloh, especially concerning Federals being surprised and bayonetted in their tents, originated with Reid.

25. *OR*, vol. 10, pt. 1, pp. 324, 355.

26. Wallace, *Autobiography*, 2:542.

Chapter 5

1. *OR*, vol. 10, pt. 1, p. 528.

2. Wallace, *Autobiography*, 2:544–45.

3. Wallace, *Autobiography*, 2:547–49.

4. Wallace, *Autobiography*, 2:549.

5. Wallace, *Autobiography*, 2:550–53.

6. *OR*, vol. 10, pt. 1, p. 293; Smith, *Shiloh: Conquer or Perish*, 262.

7. Thomas Jordan and J. P. Pryor, *The Campaigns of General Nathan Bedford Forrest and of Forrest's Cavalry, with Portraits, Maps, and Illustrations* (New York, 1868), 137.

8. See Cunningham, *Shiloh*, 353–60 for a general description of this action.

9. Smith, *Shiloh: Conquer or Perish*, 354.

10. Smith, *Shiloh: Conquer or Perish*, 362; *OR*, vol. 10, pt. 1, p. 171.

11. *OR*, vol. 10, pt. 1, p. 171.

12. *OR*, vol. 10, pt. 1, pp. 171, 194, 539; Smith, *Shiloh: Conquer or Perish*, 363.

13. *OR*, vol. 10, pt. 1, pp. 171, 418–19.

14. *OR*, vol. 10, pt. 1, p. 419.

15. Smith, *Shiloh: Conquer or Perish*, 363. Smith has made a strong case for Wallace's impact on the battle.

16. *OR*, vol. 10, pt. 1, p. 411; Roman, *Military Operations of General Beauregard*, 1:313.

17. Smith, *Shiloh: Conquer or Perish*, 266–67.

18. *OR*, vol. 10, pt. 1, p. 387; Jordan, "Confederate Staff Officer at Shiloh," 1:603; Lockett, "Surprise and Withdrawal at Shiloh," 1:605.

19. Smith, *Shiloh: Conquer or Perish*, 313.

20. *OR*, vol. 10, pt. 1, p. 504.

21. Smith, *Shiloh: Conquer or Perish*, 389.

22. Jordan, "Confederate Staff Officer at Shiloh," 603.

23. Jordan, "Confederate Staff Officer at Shiloh," 603; *OR*, vol. 10, pt. 1, p. 388.

24. *OR*, vol. 10, pt. 1, p. 388; Smith, *Shiloh: Conquer or Perish*, 383, 390.

25. *OR*, vol. 10, pt. 1, p. 388; Smith, *Shiloh: Conquer or Perish*, 398.

26. *OR*, vol. 10, pt. 1, p. 108; *OR*, vol. 10, pt. 2, pp. 96–97. Monterey, Tennessee, is labeled on some Federal maps as Pea Ridge.

27. *OR*, vol. 10, pt. 1, pp. 336, 380.

28. Wallace, *Autobiography*, 2:568–69.

29. *OR*, vol. 10, pt. 1, p. 295.

30. *OR*, vol. 10, pt. 1, p. 639.

31. *OR*, vol. 10, pt. 1, p. 640.

32. *OR*, vol. 10, pt. 1, p. 640.

33. *OR*, vol. 10, pt. 1, p. 640.

34. Grant, "Battle of Shiloh," 1:478–79.

35. Buell, "Shiloh Reviewed," in *Battles and Leaders of the Civil War*, ed. Robert U. Johnson and Clarence C. Buel, 4 vols. (New York: Century, 1884),1:533–34.

Chapter 6

1. Reed, *Battle of Shiloh*, 110.

2. Curt Anders, *Henry Halleck's War: A Fresh Look at Lincoln's Controversial General-in-Chief* (Carmel, IN: 1999), 102–3.

3. Timothy B. Smith, *Corinth 1862: Siege, Battle, Occupation* (Lawrence, KS: University of Kansas, 2012), 18–19.

4. For Confederate strength, see *OR*, vol. 10, pt. 1, pp. 791–92, and *OR*, vol. 10, pt. 2, pp. 548–49, where on May 26 Beauregard reported 75,492 aggregate present. Of those 75,000 men, the Confederates were burdened

with many sick and wounded, leaving them only 53,000 effectives. See also Smith, *Corinth 1862*, 89–93.

5. Sherman, *Memoirs*, 1:255; Simpson, *Ulysses S. Grant*, 143, 147, 156.

Appendix I

1. Historian Timothy B. Smith has researched and uncovered most of the original route, as documented in his essay on the subject. See Timothy B. Smith, "Rewriting History: Locating Lew Wallace's Route of March to Shiloh," in *Rethinking Shiloh: Myth and Memory* (Knoxville: University of Tennessee Press, 2013), 85–97.

BIBLIOGRAPHY

Primary Sources

Online Sources

Journal of Philip H. Goode, Fifteenth Iowa Infantry
http://iagenweb.org/civilwar/regiment/infantry/15th/journalgoode.htm

William H. Rees Letters, Fifth Kentucky Infantry, CSA, Rees Family
Genealogy Page
http://members.aol.com/SHelveston/reeslets.html (link no longer active,
copies in author's collection)

The Civil War Letters of John E. Richardson, Forty-Eighth Ohio
http://www.48ovi.org/oh48jer2.html (link no longer active, copies in
author's collection)

William Richardson Letters, Twenty-Fifth Indiana Regiment, Indiana in
the Civil War
http://www.indianainthecivilwar.com/letters/25th/WmRichardson.htm

Archival and Repository Sources

Cairo Public Library, Cairo, Illinois
W. D. Harland Diary (Eighteenth Illinois Infantry)

Chickamauga and Chattanooga National Military Park, Fort Oglethorpe,
     Georgia
     John Dwight Beach Letter (Fifty-Fifth Illinois Infantry)
     W. W. Whitney Letter (Ninth Indiana Infantry)

Crawfordville Public Library, Crawfordville, Indiana
     Reminiscences of W. A. Oliphant (Twenty-Fourth Indiana Infantry)
     Lew Wallace, "My Own Account of the First Day at Shiloh" (from
     Appleton's Booklovers' Magazine, no date given, pp. 72–77)

Filson History Museum, Louisville, Kentucky
     Anonymous Letter, Union Soldier
     Don Carlos Buell Collection
     Bernard Hund Letter (Sixth Kentucky, USA)
     Reason M. Nichols Letters (Sixth Kentucky Infantry, USA)
     William Pirtle Memoir (Seventh Kentucky Infantry, CSA)
     Channing Richards Diary (Thirteenth Missouri Infantry, USA)
     Laurens W. Wolcott Letter (Fifty—Second Illinois Infantry)

Geneva History Center, Geneva, Illinois
     Jonathan P. Carlin Diary (Fifty-Second Illinois Infantry)

Indiana State Library, Indianapolis
     Phelix Adair collection (Sixth Indiana Infantry)
     Seely Jayne Letter (Sixth Indiana Infantry)
     Adam Lee Ogg Letters (Third Iowa Infantry)
     Ormsby Letters (Unit Unknown)
     James N. Shepherd (Thirty-First Indiana Infantry)

Jacksonville Public Library, Jacksonville, Illinois
     James William Covington Diary (Fourteenth Illinois Infantry)

Laras College, Center for Dubuque History, Dubuque, Iowa
     Col. Joseph B. Dorr Papers (Twelfth Iowa Infantry)

Lilly Library, Indiana University, Bloomington
     Albion P. Hovey Letters
     William Allen Howard Letters (Thirty-Third Tennessee Infantry)

Lincoln Library, Springfield, Illinois
     George Dodd Carrington Diary (Eleventh Illinois Infantry)
     Adolph Engleman Letters, Engleman-Kercher Papers (Forty-Third
     Illinois Infantry)
     Michael Gapen Letters (Twenty-Eighth Illinois Infantry)
     Balzer Grebe Diary (Fourteenth Illinois Infantry)
     Douglas Hapeman Papers (Eleventh Illinois Infantry)

George Hinman Journal (Fourteenth Illinois Infantry)
Henry F. Hole Letters (Seventeenth Illinois Infantry)
Thomas F. Miller Letter (Twenty-Ninth Illinois Infantry)
McConnell Diary (Fourteenth Illinois Infantry)
William Ross Letters (Fortieth Illinois Infantry)
William R. Rowley Letters (Grant's Staff)
    Lew Wallace Letter
Z. Payson Shumway Letters (Fourteenth Illinois Infantry)
Abram J. Vanauken Diary (Seventeenth Illinois Infantry)
James R. Zearing Letters (Fifty-Seventh Illinois Infantry)

Louisiana State University, Shreveport
    John Harris Letters (Nineteenth Louisiana Infantry)

Michigan State University, East Lansing
    Irenus McGowan Letters (Twenty-Ninth Indiana Infantry)

Millersville College, Millersville, Pennsylvania
    John Obreiter Diary (Seventy-Seventh Pennsylvania Infantry)

Mississippi State University, Starkville
    Horn Papers
        M. S. Hunter Letter (Seventeenth Louisiana Infantry)
    Rice Family Papers
        Maj. John J. Walker Letters (Braxton Bragg's Staff)

Missouri Historical Society. St. Louis
    Bragg Papers
    Henry Cist Papers
        Newspaper Clipping, Edward Jonas, "With Prentiss at Shiloh"
    F. Gore Letters (Second Iowa Infantry)
    Henry Family Papers
        Patrick Ahern Reminiscences (Thirteenth Arkansas Infantry)
    Martin Family Papers (Fourth Illinois Cavalry)
    Madison Miller Diary (Miller's Brigade)
    Elias Perry Letter (Eighteenth Missouri Infantry)
    Hilory Shiflett Letter (First Ohio Infantry)
    Wyckoff Family Papers
        Letter from "Thomas" (Fifty-First Indiana Infantry)

Montana State University, Bozeman
    William H. Storrs Diary (Seventy-Seventh Ohio Infantry)

Newberry Library, Chicago, Illinois
    Ephraim C. Dawes Letters (Fifty-Third Ohio Infantry)
    Oliver Perry Newberry Letters (Thirteenth Missouri Infantry)

Northeast Mississippi Museum Association, Corinth
  Horatio Wiley Letters (Twenty-Second Alabama Infantry)
Ohio Historical Society, Columbus
  A. S. Bloomfield Letters (Battery A, First Ohio Artillery)
  Edwin Witherby Brown Reminiscences (Eighty-First Ohio Infantry)
  Samuel Evans Letters (Seventieth Ohio Infantry)
  William H. Kemper Diary (Seventeenth Indiana)
  George Wansbrough Letters (Fifth Ohio Cavalry)
Ohio University, Athens
  I. N. Alexander Letters, Alexander Family Papers (Forty-Sixth
    Ohio Infantry)
Rutherford B. Hayes Presidential Library, Fremont, Ohio
  Eric Bergland Diary (Fifty-Seventh Illinois Infantry)
  Henry Buckland Letters (Seventy-Second Ohio Infantry)
  William C. Caldwell Letters (Seventy-Second Ohio Infantry)
  Orin England Letters (Seventy-Second Ohio Infantry)
  Jonathan Harrington Letters (Seventy-Second Ohio Infantry)
  Andrew C. Parker Papers (Forty-First Ohio Infantry)
  John B. Rice Letters (Seventy-Second Ohio Infantry)
Shiloh National Military Park, Shiloh, Tennessee
  Ed Bearss, "Artillery Study—Shiloh NMP"
  H. Duncan Recollections (Third Kentucky Infantry, CSA)
  War Department Tablets on Battlefield
Smith Library, Indiana Historical Society, Indianapolis
  Wayne and Lafayette Alford Letters (Sixth Indiana Infantry)
  George W. Baum Diary (Ninth Indiana Infantry)
  Sylvester C. Bishop Letters (Eleventh Indiana Infantry)
  John Day Papers (Thirty-First Indiana Infantry)
  Sylvester Wellington Fairfield (Twenty-Fifth Indiana, Veatch's Staff)
  Forty-Fourth Indiana Regimental Association Collection—Regimental
    Histories Folder
  Thomas Joshua Harrison Letters (Thirty-Ninth Indiana Infantry)
  Frederick A. Huering Journal (Twenty-Fifth Indiana Infantry)
  John Klingaman Diary (Thirty-Ninth Indiana Infantry)
  James M. Little Diary (Thirty-Ninth Indiana Infantry)
  Price-Moore Family Papers, James A. Price Letter (Tenth Indiana
    Infantry)
  Abraham Showmaker (Eleventh Indiana Infantry)
  Jeremiah Warren Letters (Tenth Indiana Infantry)

Tennessee State Library and Archives, Nashville
  William Wallace Fergusson Papers (Second Tennessee Infantry)
  Bradford Nichol Diary and Memoir (Rutledge's Battery)
  James D. Thompson Papers (Thirty-Eighth Tennessee Infantry)

University of Illinois, Illinois Historical Survey, Urbana
  J. A. Carlin Diary Transcript (Fifty-Second Illinois Infantry)
  George S. Durfree (Eighth Illinois Infantry)

University of Michigan, Bentley Historical Library, Ann Arbor
  Franklin H. Bailey Papers (Fifteenth Michigan Infantry)

University of North Carolina, Southern Historical Collection, Chapel Hill
  J. K. Street Papers (Ninth Texas)

University of Notre Dame, Hesbergh Library, South Bend, Indiana
  Sherman Family Papers

University of Tennessee, Knoxville
  William Blake Letter (Third Iowa Infantry)
  T. J. Walker Reminiscences (Ninth Tennessee Infantry)

University of Tennessee at Martin
  Oliver Oglevie Civil War Letters (Union, Unknown Unit)

Virginia Polytechnic Institute and University, Blacksburg
  Miles Washington Coe Letters (Forty-Second Indiana Infantry)
  John H. Myers Memoir (Fifty-Fifth Illinois)

Western Michigan University, Kalamazoo
  Byron E. Churchill Letter, Allan Giddings Collection (Fifteenth
    Michigan Infantry)
  Willard G. Eaton Letters, Lola J. Warrick Collection (Thirteenth
    Michigan Infantry)
  William E. Davis Letters, Barrien County Historical Collection
    (Twelfth Michigan)
  Samuel F. Pike Diary/Memoir, James Brady Collection (Thirty-Sixth
    Indiana Infantry)
  William Tillroe Letters, Homer Arnett Collection (Twelfth Michigan
    Infantry)
  Clement C. Webb Letters, Phyllis Burnham Collection (Thirteenth
    Michigan Infantry)
  Brayton S. Wright Diary, Barbara Henschel Collection (Fifteenth
    Illinois Infantry)

Western Reserve Historical Society, Cleveland, Ohio
  George Hurlbut Diary (Fourteeth Ohio Battery)

John Mason Papers, Jeremiah Mason Letter (Third Ohio Cavalry)
Regimental Papers
    T. N. Lewis Letter (Eleventh Illinois Infantry)
Wisconsin Historical Society, Madison
    William W. Campbell Reminiscences (Eighteenth Wisconsin Infantry)
    L. H. Cowan Papers (Forty-Fifth Illinois Infantry)
    Henry Miller Culbertson Letters (Sixteenth Wisconsin Infantry)
    William Fagg Diary (Fourteenth Wisconsin Infantry)
    William W. Felton Diary (Eighteenth Wisconsin Infantry)
    Edwin Hubbard Letters (Forty-Sixth Illinois Infantry)
    David G. James Letters (Sixteenth Wisconsin Infantry)
    James Dougal McVicar letters (Sixteenth Wisconsin Infantry)
    Levi Minkler Diary (Eighteenth Wisconsin Infantry)
    Samuel F. Thompson Diary (Tenth Indiana Infantry)

Newspapers

(All date from 1862 unless otherwise noted.)
Belleville (IL) Weekly Advocate
Bureau County (IL) Reporter
Carlinville (IL) Free Democrat
Carrollton (IL) Gazette
Chilicothe Ohio Soldier, 1888
Keithsburg (IL) Observer
Milwaukee Sunday Telegraph, 1886
Monmouth (IL) Atlas
Quincy (IL) Daily Whig and Republican
Quincy (IL) Herald
Rock River (IL) Democrat
Rockford (IL) Republican
Woodstock (IL) Sentinel

Government Documents

Reed, David W. *The Battle of Shiloh and the Organizations Engaged.* Washington, DC: US Government Printing Office, 1902.

US Army. *Revised United States Army Regulations of 1861.* Washington, DC: US Government Printing Office, 1861.

US War Department. *The War of the Rebellion: A Compilation of the Official Records of the Union and Confederate Armies*. 128 vols. Washington, DC: US Government Printing Office, 1880–1901.

Dissertation

Hughes, Nathaniel Cheairs. "William Joseph Hardee, C.S.A., 1861–1865." PhD diss., University of North Carolina, 1959.

Articles

Anonymous. "The March of Lew Wallace's Division to Shiloh." In *Battles and Leaders of the Civil War*, edited by Robert U. Johnson and Clarence C. Buel, 1:607–10. New York: Century, 1884.

Baker, H. C. "Comments on the Battle of Shiloh: A Letter by H. C. Baker." *Independence County [AK] Chronicle* 3, no. 3 (April 1962): 30–32. (Eighth Arkansas Infantry)

Buell, Don Carlos. "Shiloh Reviewed." In *Battles and Leaders of the Civil War*, edited by Robert U. Johnson and Clarence C. Buel, 487–536. New York: Century, 1884.

Camm, William. "Diary of Colonel William Camm, 1861–1865." *Journal of the Illinois State Historical Society* 28, no. 4 (January 1926): 793–970. (14th Illinois Infantry)

Clark, Robert T., Jr. "The New Orleans German Colony in the Civil War." *Louisiana Historical Quarterly* 20, no. 4 (October 1937): 5–6. (Twentieth Louisiana Infantry)

Cockerill, John A. "A Boy at Shiloh." *Blue and Gray* 1, no. 1 (January 1893). (Seventieth Ohio Infantry)

Dixon, William Tucker, III. "The Civil War Travels of William A. Brown." *The Rebel Yell: The Jackson Civil War Round Table* 39, no. 3 (November 2002). (Stanford's Mississippi Battery)

Flemming, Robert H. "The Battle of Shiloh as a Private Saw It." In *Sketches of War History, 1861–1865, Papers prepared for the Commandary of the State of Ohio, Military Order of the Loyal Legion of the United States. 70 vols.* Cincinnati: Monfort, 1908. 6:132–46.

Grant, Ulysses S. "The Battle of Shiloh." In *Battles and Leaders of the Civil War*, edited by Robert U. Johnson and Clarence C. Buel, 1:465–86. New York: Century, 1884.

Hankey, John P. "The Railroad War." *Trains: The Magazine of Railroading* 71, no. 3 (March 2011): 34–35.

Jordan, Thomas. "Notes of a Confederate Staff Officer at Shiloh." In *Battles and Leaders of the Civil War*, edited by Robert U. Johnson and Clarence C. Buel, 1:603. New York: Century, 1884.

Lennard, George W. "'Give Yourself No Trouble about Me': The Shiloh Letters of George W. Lennard." Edited by Paul Hubbard and Christine Lewis. *Indiana Magazine of History* 76, no. 1 (March 1980): 21–53.

Lockett, S. H. "Surprise and Withdrawal at Shiloh." In *Battles and Leaders of the Civil War*, edited by Robert U. Johnson and Clarence C. Buel, 1:603–6. New York: Century, 1884.

McBride, George W. "My Recollections of Shiloh." *Blue and Gray* 2, no. 1 (January 1894) 8-12. (Fifteenth Michigan Infantry)

Morton, J. W., Jr. "A Georgia Boy at Shiloh." *Blue and Gray* 1, no. 1 (January 1893) 19-27. (Hardee's Corps)

Roland, Charles P. "Albert Sidney Johnston." In *The Confederate General*, edited by William C. Davis, 3:188–89. Harrisburg, PA: National Historical Society, 1990.

Sword, Wiley. "Shiloh—Before and After." *Blue & Gray* 26, no. 2 (Summer 2009): 28–29. (Sgt. Martin V. Miller, Seventh Illinois Infantry)

Winschel, Terrance J. "We Have Seen the Elephant: The 48th Ohio at Shiloh." *Lincoln Herald* 85, no. 2 (Spring 1985): 55–60.

Regimental Histories and Personal Memoirs

Barbe, Lucius W. *Army Memoirs of Lucius W. Barbe.* Chicago: J. M. W. Jones Stationery, 1894. (Fifteenth Illinois Infantry)

Bell, John T. *Tramps and Triumphs of the Second Iowa Infantry.* Omaha, NE: Gibson, Miller, and Richardson, 1886.

Bering, John A., and Thomas Montgomery. *History of the Forty-Eighth Ohio Vet. Vol. Inf.* Hillsboro, OH: Highland News Office, 1880.

Blanchard, Ira. *I Marched with Sherman: Civil War Memoirs of the 20th Illinois Volunteer Infantry.* San Francisco: J. D. Huff, 1992.

Boyd, Cyrus F. *The Civil War Diary of Cyrus F. Boyd, Fifteenth Iowa Infantry, 1861–1863.* Edited by Mildred Throne. Iowa City: State Historical Society of Iowa, 1953.

Burge, William. *Through the Civil War and Western Adventures.* Lisbon, IA, n.d. (Eleventh Iowa Infantry)

Connelly, T. W. *History of the Seventieth Ohio Regiment from its Organization to Its Mustering Out.* Cincinnati, OH: Peak Brothers, 1902.

Dawes, Ephraim C. "My First Day under Fire at Shiloh." In *Sketches of War History, 1861–1865: Papers Prepared for the Ohio Commandery of the Military Order of the Loyal Legion of the United States.* Cincinnati, OH: Robert Clarke, 1896. 1-22.

Dorr, Joseph B. *Journal of My Prison Life.* Dubuque, IA, 1877. (Twelfth Iowa Infantry)

Downing, Alexander G. *Downing's Civil War Diary.* Edited by Olynthus B. Clark. Des Moines: Historical Department of Iowa, 1916. (Eleventh Iowa Infantry)

Dugan, James. *History of Hurlbut's Fighting Fourth Division.* Cincinnati, OH: E. Morgan, 1863.

Duke, John K. *History of the Fifty-Third Regiment Ohio Volunteer Infantry, during the War of the Rebellion, 1861 to 1865.* Portsmouth, OH: Blade, 1900.

Foster, John W. *War Stories for My Grandchildren.* Washington, DC: Riverside, 1918. (Twenty-Fifth Indiana Infantry)

Fremantle, James Arthur Lyon. *Three Months in the Southern States, April–June, 1863.* New York: John Bradburn, 1864.

Geer, Allen Morgan. *The Civil War Diary of Allen Morgan Geer, Twentieth Regiment Illinois Volunteers.* Edited by Robert C. Appleman. Bloomington, IL: McLean County Historical Society, 1977.

George, Henry. *History of the 3rd, 7th, 8th and 12th Kentucky C.S.A.* Louisville, KY: C. T. Dearing, 1911.

Grant, Ulysses S. *Personal Memoirs of U. S. Grant.* 2 vols. New York: Charles L. Webster, 1885.

Grisamore, Silas T. *The Civil War Reminiscences of Major Silas T. Grisamore, C.S.A.* Edited by Arthur W. Bergeron. Baton Rouge: Louisiana State University Press, 1993.

Hackemer, Kurt H., ed. *To Rescue My Native Land: The Civil War Letters of William T. Shepherd, First Illinois Light Artillery.* Knoxville, TN: University of Tennessee Press, 2005 (Taylor's Battery B, First Illinois Light Artillery)

Hamilton, Richard L. *Shiloh to Durham Station: The 18th Wisconsin Infantry Regiment, with Captain Robert S. McMichael's Civil War Letters.* N.p: Richard L. Hamilton, 2010.

Hannaford, E. *The Story of a Regiment: A History of the Campaigns, and*

Associations in the Field, of the Sixth Regiment Ohio Volunteer Infantry. Cincinnati, OH: Published by the author, 1868.

Hart, E. J. *History of The Fortieth Illinois Inf.* Cincinnati, OH: H. S. Bosworth, 1864.

Hobart, Edwin L. *Semi-history of a Boy Veteran of the Twenty-Eighth Regiment Illinois Infantry Volunteers, in a Black Regiment.* Denver, CO: n. pub. 1905.

Howell, Grady, Jr. *Going to Meet the Yankees.* Jackson, MS: Chickasaw Bayou Press, 1981.

Huffstodt, Jim. *The Story of General W. H. L. Wallace, General T. E. G. Ransom, and Their "Old Eleventh" Illinois Infantry in the American Civil War (1861–1865).* Bowie, MD: Heritage Books, 1991.

Iowa's Hornets Nest Brigade Association. First Reunion of Iowa's Hornet's Nest Brigade. Oskaloosa, IA: Globe, 1888.

Johnston, William Preston. *The Life of General Albert Sidney Johnston: His Service in the Armies of the United States, the Republic of Texas, and the Confederate States.* New York: D. Appleton, 1879.

Jordan, Thomas, and J. P. Pryor. *The Campaigns of General Nathan Bedford Forrest and of Forrest's Cavalry.* New Orleans: Blelock, 1868.

Kiner, F. F. *One Year's Soldiering.* Lancaster, OH: E. H. Thomas, 1863. (Fourteenth Iowa)

Quintard, C. T. *Doctor Quintard: Chaplain, C.S.A. and Second Bishop of Tennessee, Being His Story of the War (1861–1865).* Edited by Arthur Howard Noll. Sewanee, TN: University Press, 1905.

Roman, Alfred. *The Military Operations of General Beauregard in the War between the States, 1861 to 1865: Including a Brief Personal Sketch and a Narrative of His Services in the War with Mexico, 1846–8.* 2 vols. New York: Harper and Brothers, 1884.

Sherman, William T. *Memoirs of Gen. William T. Sherman.* 2 vols. New York: D. Appleton, 1875.

Simon, John Y., ed. *The Papers of Ulysses S. Grant.* 32 vols. Carbondale: Southern Illinois University Press, 1967–2009.

Smith, Henry V., Ed. *Life and Letters of Pvt. Samuel T. Smith, Fifteenth Indiana Reg. Volunteers, Civil War.* Bloomington, IN: Monroe County Historical Society, 1976.

Trowbridge, Silas Thompson. *Autobiography of Silas Thompson Trowbridge, M.D.: Late Surgeon of the 8 Reg. Ill. Vol. Inf., Surgeon in Chief of the 3. Division, 17 Army Corps, President of the Illinois State Medical Society.* Vera Cruz, Mexico: Family of the author, 1872. (Eighth Illinois Infantry)

Vaughn, Alfred J. *Personal Record of The Thirteenth Regiment Tennessee Infantry.* Memphis, TN: S. C. Toof, 1897.

Wallace, Lew. *Lew Wallace: An Autobiography.* New York: Harper and Brothers, 1906.

Worthington, Thomas. *Shiloh, or The Tennessee Campaign of 1862.* Washington, DC: M'Gill and Witherow, 1872. (Forty-Sixth Ohio Infantry)

Worthington, Thomas. *Shiloh: The Only Correct Military History of U. S. Grant and of the Missing Army Records, for Which He Is Alone Responsible, to Conceal His Organized Defeat of the Union Army at Shiloh, April 6, 1862.* Washington, DC: M'Gill and Witherow, 1872. (Forty-Sixth Ohio Infantry)

Wright, Henry. *A History of the Sixth Iowa Infantry.* Iowa City: State Historical Society of Iowa, 1923.

Secondary Sources

Allen, Stacy D. "Shiloh!" In *Blue & Gray Magazine's Shiloh!—a Visitor's Guide.* 4-74. Columbus, OH: Blue and Gray Press, 2001.

Anders, Curt. *Henry Halleck's War: A Fresh Look at Lincoln's Controversial General-in-Chief.* Carmel: Guild Press of Indiana, 1999.

Bartholomees, J. Boone, Jr. *Buff Facings and Gilt Buttons: Staff and Headquarters Operations in the Army of Northern Virginia, 1861–1865.* Columbia: University of South Carolina Press, 1998.

Brewer, James D. *Tom Worthington's Civil War: Shiloh, Sherman, and the Search for Vindication.* Jefferson, NC: McFarland, 2001. (Forty-Sixth Ohio Infantry)

Catton, Bruce. *Grant Moves South.* Boston: Little, Brown, 1960.

Chandler, David G. *The Campaigns of Napoleon.* New York: McMillan, 1966.

Connolly, Thomas Lawrence. *Army of the Heartland: The Army of Tennessee, 1861–1862.* Baton Rouge: Louisiana State University Press, 1967.

Crute, Joseph H., Jr. *Confederate Staff Officers, 1861–1865.* Powhatan, VA: Derwent Books, 1982.

Cunningham, O. Edward. *Shiloh and the Western Campaign of 1862.* Edited by Gary D. Joiner and Timothy B. Smith. New York: Savas Beatie, 2007.

Daniel, Larry J. *Shiloh: The Battle That Changed the Civil War.* New York: Simon and Schuster, 1997.

Davis, William C. *Breckinridge: Statesman, Soldier, Symbol.* Baton Rouge: Louisiana State University Press, 1974.

Eicher, David J. *The Longest Night: A Military History of the Civil War.* New York: Simon and Schuster, 2001.

Eicher, John H., and David J. Eicher. *Civil War High Commands.* Stanford, CA: Stanford University Press, 2001.

Flanigan, David B. *The Culminating Point and U.S. Army Tactical Doctrine.* Fort Leavenworth, KS: Government Printing Office, 1991.

Hagerman, Edward. *The American Civil War and the Origins of Modern Warfare: Ideas, Organization, and Field Command.* Bloomington: Indiana University Press, 1988.

Hartje, Robert G. *Van Dorn: The Life and Times of a Confederate General.* Nashville, TN: Vanderbilt University Press, 1967.

Hess, Earl J. *The Civil War in the West, Victory and Defeat from the Appalachians to the Mississippi.* Chapel Hill: University of North Carolina Press, 2012.

Higginson, Thomas Wentworth. *Thomas Wentworth Higginson, Harvard Memorial Biographies.* Vol. 1. Cambridge, MA: Sever and Francis, 1867.

Jomini, Antoine Henry. *Life of Napoleon.* Translated by H. W. Halleck. 4 vols. New York: D. Van Nostrand, 1864.

Kiper, Richard L. *Major General John Alexander McClernand: Politician in Uniform.* Kent, OH: Kent State University Press, 1999.

Lindsley, T. J. *Ohio at Shiloh: Report of the Commission.* Cincinnati, OH: C. J. Krehbiel, 1903.

Marszalek, John F. *Commander of All Lincoln's Armies: A Life of General Henry W. Halleck.* Cambridge, MA: Harvard University Press, 2004.

McDonough, James Lee. *William Tecumseh Sherman: In the Service of My Country; A Life.* New York: W. W. Norton, 2016.

McWhiney, Grady. *Braxton Bragg and Confederate Defeat* .Vol. 1. 1969. Reprint. Tuscaloosa: University of Alabama Press, 1991.

Minnesota in the Civil and Indian Wars. St. Paul, MN: Pioneer, 1891.

Polk, William M. *Leonidas Polk: Bishop and General.* 2 vols. New York: Longmans, Green, 1915.

Reid, Whitelaw. *Ohio in the War: Her Statesmen, Generals, and Soldiers.* 2 vols. Columbus, OH: Eclectic, 1893.

Richardson, Albert D. *A Personal History of Ulysses S. Grant.* Hartford, CT: American, 1868.

Roland, Charles P. *Albert Sidney Johnston: Soldier of Three Republics.* 1964, repr.; Lexington: University Press of Kentucky, 2001.

Rose, Joseph A. *Grant under Fire: An Exposé of Generalship & Character in the American Civil War.* New York: Alderhanna, 2015.

Shea, William L., and Earl J. Hess. *Pea Ridge: Civil War Campaign in the West.* Chapel Hill: University of North Carolina Press, 1992.

Simpson, Brooks D. *Ulysses S. Grant: Triumph over Adversity, 1822–1865.* Boston: Houghton Mifflin, 2000.

Smith, Timothy B. *Corinth 1862: Siege, Battle, Occupation.* Lawrence: University of Kansas Press, 2012.

Smith, Timothy B. *Rethinking Shiloh: Myth and Memory.* Knoxville: University of Tennessee Press, 2013.

Smith, Timothy B. *Shiloh: Conquer or Perish.* Lawrence: University Press of Kansas, 2014.

Smith, Timothy B. *Grant Invades Tennessee: The 1862 Battles for Forts Henry and Donelson.* Lawrence: University of Kansas Press, 2016.

Stephens, Gail. *Shadow of Shiloh: Major General Lew Wallace in the Civil War.* Indianapolis: Indiana Historical Society Press, 2010.

Wallace, Isabel. *The Life and Letters of General W. H. L. Wallace.* Chicago: R. R. Donnelly and Sons, 1909.

Warner, Ezra J. *Generals in Blue: Lives of the Union Commanders.* Baton Rouge: Louisiana State University Press, 1964.

Weigley, Russell F. *A Great Civil War: A Military and Political History, 1861–1865.* Bloomington: University of Indiana Press, 2000.

Williams, T. Harry. *P. G. T. Beauregard: Napoleon in Gray.* Baton Rouge: Louisiana State University Press, 1955.

Wyeth, John Allan. *That Devil Forrest: Life of General Nathan Bedford Forrest.* Baton Rouge: Louisiana State University Press, 1959.

INDEX

Page numbers in **boldface** refer to illustrations.

Bragg, Maj. Gen. Braxton, 15, 18, **20**, 36; criticized Beauregard, 45, 47, 48, 49, 67, 70, 88, 97, 107, 109, 111, 130, 143; and deployment, 42–43, 44; headquarters, 151

Breckinridge, Brig. Gen. John C., 39; covers retreat, 133–34, 138; deployment 42–43, 48, 49, 64, 91, 130

Buckner, Simon B., 1

Buell, Maj. Gen. Don C., 2, 8; placed under Halleck, 12, 39, 71, 83; reaches the battlefield, 105, 116, 117, 122, 128, 134, 135, 137, 138–39, 146

Burnsville, MS, 23, 39, 48

Chalmers, Brig. Gen. James R., 57, 61, 64, 67, 97, 109, 112

Chancellorsville, battle of, 46–47

Chattanooga, TN, importance of, 11, 13, 16

Cheatham, Brig. Gen. Benjamin F., 26, 39, 47, 129

Cherry Mansion, Grant's headquarters, 29, 161–62

Chickamauga: battle, xi; park, x

Clausewitz, Carl von, xi, 19

Clear Creek turnaround, 163

Cleburne, Brig. Gen. Patrick R., 49

Columbus, KY, 10, 12

Continental, steamboat, 25, 26, 29

Corinth, MS, 10, 12, 18–19, 38, 130–32, 134, 137; advance on, 142, 150

Critical decision, definition, xii

Crittenden, Brig. Gen. Thomas L., 114, 118, 123

Crittenden, Maj. Gen. George B., 13

Crockett, Leroy, 36

Crossroads, at Shiloh, 165

Crossroads Museum, in Corinth, 150

Crump's Landing, 25, 26, 30, 38, 74, 101, 115, 136

Culminating point, definition of, 107

Cumberland River, importance of and limitations of, 11

Cunningham, Edward, historian, 92, 97

Curlee House, 151

Curtis, Maj. Gen. Samuel R., 8

Danville Railroad Bridge, 22

Davis, President Jefferson, 2, 14, 41

Davout, Louis, Marshal of France, 103

Deas, Col. Zachariah, 58, 61, 127

Department Number 2 (Confederate), 2

Department of the Missouri (Union), 2

Department of the Ohio (Union), 2

Deployment. *See* tactics

Dickey, Capt. Cyrus, 97

Dickey, Col. Lyle, 137, 138

Dill Branch Ravine, 96, 103–4, 105, 109, 110–11, 113, 117–18, 122, 129, 160

Duncan House, 151

Dunlop, Col. Isaac, 65

East Tennessee, importance of, 8

Eastport, MS, 25

Elements of Military Art and Science, 3

Entrenchments, 30–36, 142–43

Fallen Timbers, fight at, 138, 142, 166

Farragut, Flag Officer David G., 21

Fishpond House, 151

Forrest, Col. Nathan Bedford, 39, 59, 122, 129, 138

Fort Donelson, 1, 5, 32

Fort Henry, 1, 5, 22, 27

Fraley Field, 154

Frederick the Great of Prussia, 42

Fremantle, Lt. Col. James Arthur Lyon, 68

Gale, Capt. William D., 68

Gardner, Col. Frank, 97

Lincoln, President Abraham, 8, 9
Lockett, Capt. Samuel H., 61, 62, 65, 97, 129
Louisiana troops
—infantry: *Confederate Guards Response Battalion*, 96; *1st*, 57; *16th*, 96; *18th*, 96
Lovell, Maj. Gen. Mansfield, 18, 21

Madison, Capt. Relly, 103
Mahan, Dennis Hart, 3, 32
Manassas, first battle of (Bull Run), 88
Maney, Col. George, 59
Margraf, Capt. Louis, 104
Marsh, Col. C. C., 81
McArthur, Brig. Gen. John, 65, 83
McClellan, Maj. Gen. George B., 5, 9
McClernand, Brig. Gen. John A., 26, 29; and entrenchments, 32, 34, 81, **82**, 83–85, 96, 124, 135, 145
McCook, Brig. Gen. Alexander McD., 114, 122
McDowell, Col. John A., 85–86
McPherson, James B., Lt. Col., 77, 117
Memphis, TN, 17, 20
Memphis & Charleston Railroad, 7, 16, 23
Michie (or Mickey), 47, 48, 166
Michigan troops
—infantry, *12th*, 55
Military Science, defined, ix
Mill Springs, Battle of, 13
Miller, Col. Madison, 57
Minnesota troops
—artillery, *1st Battery*, 104
Mississippi Central Railroad, 10
Mississippi River, importance of, 10
Mississippi troops
—artillery, *Stanford's Battery*, 133

—infantry, *3rd battalion*, 20, 55–56; *10th*, 20
Missouri troops
—infantry (USA): *13th*, 83; *14th*, 77; *21st*, 56; *25th*, 53, 55
Mobile, AL, defenses of, 18
Mobile & Ohio Railroad, 10
Moltke, Helmuth Von, x
Monterey, TN, 47, 136
Moore, Col. David, 56
Munch, Capt. Emil, 104
Munford, Maj. Edward, 45
Muscle Shoals, on Tennessee River, 11

Napoleon I, 45, 102–3
Nashville, TN, 7, 15, 17
Nashville & Chattanooga Railroad, 16
Nashville & Decatur Railroad, 16
Nebraska troops
—infantry: *1st*, 119, 127
Nelson, Brig. Gen. William "Bull," 73, 105, 114, 117, 122, 124
New Madrid, MO, 142
New Market, xi
New Orleans: defenses of, 18, captured, 21
Nott, Dr. J. C., 112–13

Ohio troops, 142
—artillery: *8th Battery*, 104
—infantry: *6th*, 105–6; *20th*, 128; *46th*, 22, 36; *53rd*, 51; *54th*, 105; *72nd*, 36, 49; *77th*, 138; *78th*, 127
Oliphant, Pvt. Alexander, 128
"Orphan" Brigade, 64
Owl Creek, 37, 41, 124

Paducah, KY, 22
Pea Ridge, Battle of, 9, 18, 130

Peabody, Col. Everett, 53, **54**, 55, 56; mortally wounded, 57, 145
Peach Orchard, fighting in, 91, 145, 158
Pemberton, Lt. Gen. John C., 143
Pickens, Dick (Civilian), 77
Pittsburg Landing, 25, 27, 28, 29, 30, 37, 39, 71, 83, 101, 113, 115, 124, 136, 153
Polk, Capt. William M., 71
Polk, Maj. Gen. Leonidas, 1, 14, 39, 42–43, 47, 48, 49, **67**, 70, 107, 112, 129
Pond, Col. Preston, 67, 96, 111, 119, 127
Pope, Brig. Gen. John, 8, 142,
Powell, Maj. James E., 55, 56,
Prentiss, Brig. Gen. Benjamin M., 27, 31, 53; captured, 97, 109, 130, 145; picture of, 93; relationship with Wallace, 94, 95–96; reprimands Peabody, 56, 57, 79
Preston, Capt. William, 68, 70
Pugh, Col. Isaac C., 91

Raith, Col. Julius, 81–82
Rawlins, Capt. John A., 74, 77, 115
Reed, David W., 159
Reed, Whitelaw, 117
Rhea Field, 154
Richmond, Lt. William B., 68
River Road, 74, 75, 76, 77, 83, 101, 164
Rogers, Capt. George C., 114,
Roland, Charles P., historian, 44, 50
Roman, Col. Alfred, 106–7, 112
Rose Cottage, 151
Rowley, Capt. William, 76
Ruggles, Brig. Gen. Daniel, 67
Russell, Col. Robert M., 127
Russian Tenant Field, 164

Savannah, TN, 21, 22, 23, 25, 26, 29, 30, 71, 115, 134, 161

Scott, Maj. Gen. Winfield, 4, 46
Sherman, Brig. Gen. William T., 9, 22, 24, 25, 26, 29, 30; failure to entrench, 31–32, 36, 49, 51, 81, 83–85, 96, 115, 135; leads pursuit, 137, 138, 145, 146
Shiloh: battle of, xii; field described, 99, 124, 138; losses, 141, 147; park, x
Shiloh Church, 34, 37, 81, 101, 109, 113, 127–28, 130, 154
Shiloh National Cemetery, 161
Shunpike, 74, 75, 76, 79
Smith, Maj. Gen. Charles F., 12, 21–22; injured, 24, 25, 26, 28
Smith, Col. Morgan, 122
Smith, Col. Preston, 86
Smith, Dr. Timothy, xi, xiii, 35, 60, 99, 124, 129
Snake Creek, 37, 77, 83, 99, 121
Soult, Jean, Marshal of France, 45
Sowell Field, 164
Spain Field, 155
Staff ride, x
Statham, Col. Winfield S., 64, 91
Stewart, Brig. Gen. Alexander P., 93
Stoney Lonesome, TN, 26, 162
Stuart, Col. David, 31, 34, 60, 65, 83, 137, 144
Sunken Road, 61, 65, 79, 83, 93, 145, 158
Swift, Maj. Eben, x
Sword, Wiley, historian, 45

Tactics: column vs. line, 42, 43; standard deployment, 46
Tennessee River, importance of, 7, 10, 16, 124
Tennessee troops
—infantry: *1st*, 59
Texas troops
—cavalry: *Wharton's Regiment*, 119